Joss Whedon
and Religion

JOSS WHEDON AND RELIGION

Essays on an Angry Atheist's Explorations of the Sacred

Edited by Anthony R. Mills,
John W. Morehead *and*
J. Ryan Parker

Foreword by K. Dale Koontz

McFarland & Company, Inc., Publishers
Jefferson, North Carolina, and London

LIBRARY OF CONGRESS CATALOGUING-IN-PUBLICATION DATA

Joss Whedon and religion : essays on an angry atheist's explorations of the sacred / edited by Anthony R. Mills, John W. Morehead and J. Ryan Parker ; foreword by K. Dale Koontz.
    p.   cm.
Includes bibliographical references and index.

ISBN 978-0-7864-7290-1
softcover : acid free paper ∞

1. Whedon, Joss, 1964– —Criticism and interpretation. 2. Whedon, Joss, 1964– —Religion. I. Mills, Anthony R., 1978– editor of compilation. II. Morehead, John W., 1964– editor of compilation. III. Parker, J. Ryan, 1980– editor of compilation.
PN1992.4.W49J68 2013
792.4502'32092—dc23   2013029188

BRITISH LIBRARY CATALOGUING DATA ARE AVAILABLE

© 2013 Anthony R. Mills, John W. Morehead and J. Ryan Parker. All rights reserved

No part of this book may be reproduced or transmitted in any form or by any means, electronic or mechanical, including photocopying or recording, or by any information storage and retrieval system, without permission in writing from the publisher.

Front cover image Design Pics/Thinkstock

Manufactured in the United States of America

McFarland & Company, Inc., Publishers
  Box 611, Jefferson, North Carolina 28640
    www.mcfarlandpub.com

Table of Contents

Foreword—K. DALE KOONTZ 1
Preface—ANTHONY R. MILLS 5
Introduction—ANTHONY R. MILLS 7

Varieties of Conversion: Spiritual Transformation in the
 Buffyverse—JEREMY R. RICKETTS 11
The Harrowing of Hell: "Anne" and the Greek Paschal
 Tradition in Conversation—HOPE K. BARTEL *and*
 TIMOTHY E. G. BARTEL 28
Mary and Buffy Walk into a Bar: The Virgin Deity and *Buffy
 the Vampire Slayer*—VALERIE MAYHEW 39
"Oh ... My ... Goddess": Witchcraft, Magick and Thealogy in
 Buffy the Vampire Slayer—JASON LAWTON WINSLADE 51
Apocalypse Now and Again: The Apocalyptic Paradigm and
 the Meaning of Life and (Un)Death in *Buffy the Vampire
 Slayer*—ROSLYN WEAVER 67
Who's Afraid of the Big Black Wolf? Racial Identity and the
 Irrationality of Religious Belief in *Firefly* and *Serenity*
 —DESIRÉE DE JESUS 83
"You're welcome on my boat, God ain't": Ethical Foundations
 in the Whedonverse—DEAN A. KOWALSKI 102
Actives, Affectivity and the Soul: Interpreting *Dollhouse*
 through the Phenomenology of Michel Henry
 —J. LEAVITT PEARL 123
Just to Love and Be Loved in Return: Identity and Love in the
 Dollhouse—JULIE CLAWSON 140

"There's no place I can be": Whedon, Augustine and the
  Earthly City—SUSANNE E. FOSTER *and* JAMES B. SOUTH 152

To Assemble or to Shrug? Power, Responsibility and Sacrifice
  in Marvel's *The Avengers*—RUSSELL W. DALTON 165

National Treasures: Joss Whedon's Assembling of Exceptional
  Avengers—JOHN C. MCDOWELL 183

As It Ever Was ... So Shall It Never Be: Penal Substitutionary
  Atonement Theory and Violence in *The Cabin in the Woods*
  —J. RYAN PARKER 196

"I'm sorry I ... ended the world": Eschatology, Nihilism and
  Hope in *The Cabin in the Woods*—W. SCOTT POOLE 213

About the Contributors 227
Index 231

Foreword

K. Dale Koontz

I can tell you exactly where I was when I first encountered *Buffy the Vampire Slayer*—I can even tell you which episode was airing. (If you're curious, I was in Greenville, South Carolina, and it was the early fall of 1998. The episode was "Becoming: Part 2.") I was marked from that moment. Seldom, if ever, has a television show had such an immediate impact on me. I really cared about these characters. I was entranced by the elaborate mythology that had been spun for this world. I adored the sharp dialogue. In short, this show was amazing, yet it wasn't a blockbuster in the ratings. How could that be? Surely I couldn't be the only person who felt this connection—where were the fans of this incredible show?

It turned out that they were all around me. I quickly found a cadre of fans who were passionate about the show and, as legions of Whedonians can attest (or Whedonists ... there's a debate, but I do not anticipate an outright schism), that's a warm and welcoming circle. But I also quickly found myself looking ever deeper into the show. As much as I enjoyed the annual "Big Bad" and the crisp one-liners, I was drawn to the larger themes which ran throughout the show, leaping easily from season to season. These were important themes, too—far more lasting than Buffy's style choices (remember that awful crimped hair? Shudder.). *Buffy* tackled Big Questions—redemption, grace, community, loss, destiny, and free will were only a few of the issues that received attention throughout the run of the show. I've speculated before that one of the reasons *Buffy* was able to explore these issues was that it was a little show on a start-up netlet with a silly title. In this case, flying under the radar had definite advantages.

Whedon's interest with these issues didn't end with *Buffy*. As his body of work developed, he has continued to wrestle with these Big Questions throughout his work. *Angel* and *Firefly* both feature ensemble casts of characters trying to find significant meaning in a society that often seems cold, uncaring, and directionless. *Firefly*'s untimely cancellation led to *Serenity*, which gave Whedon a larger screen on which to play out his concepts of control, choice, and consequences. The 2007–2008 writers' strike led to Whedon exploring webcasting and the result, *Dr. Horrible's Sing-Along Blog*, showed that Whedon's gift for storytelling could exist over the Internet and that his catchy, Sondheim-influenced tunes could grip our hearts. With his return to the small screen in 2009 with *Dollhouse*, Whedon had a new playground for his ideas regarding feminism, power, and identity. He also continued the slayer story with his work on the graphic novel *Fray* and he has continued to work in the comic book field, sometimes with his own creations and sometimes playing in someone else's sandbox — most notably, with his run on Marvel's *Astonishing X-Men*.

Then came 2012, which in retrospect can be termed "the year of Whedon." Several years prior, he had cowritten and produced *The Cabin in the Woods*, but the film had languished in MGM's vaults as the studio struggled to overcome bankruptcy. Ultimately, the film was released by Lionsgate in April of 2012 and proceeded to turn the horror film genre inside out, albeit in a good way. Possibly Whedon's most overt exploration of free will, *Cabin* quickly became a critical darling. A few weeks later, *Marvel's The Avengers* was released. This film was a monumental undertaking, involving as it did a large ensemble cast of characters, four of whom had already had stand-alone films and all needed to be integrated into a cohesive whole. One of Whedon's hallmarks has long been crafting scripts centering on just how a disparate group of individuals manages to set aside their sizable differences and come together to craft a strong community, and this was a major theme in Whedon's script. He knows how to play to his strengths and the box office receipts (currently well in excess of $1.5 billion worldwide) bore that out.

At the beginning, I mentioned that *Buffy* had an immediate impact on me. I should mention that it also had a *lasting* impact on me, as the show was my launch pad into what is known as "Whedon studies." Beginning early in the run of *Buffy*, academics noticed the show and they flocked to the richness of the text. There was something in here for nearly any discipline — gender studies, media studies, sociology, psychology, and philosophy scholars all used the lenses of their own areas of study to view *Buffy* as well as Whedon's other shows, as they came along.

I entered this arena to answer one seemingly simple question: Why would someone who so adamantly professed himself to be an atheist spend so much time grappling with issues that are often associated with faith in the unseen and unknown? After all, you can't watch three hours of Whedon's work without rubbing up against questions of redemption and grace, examining an expansive definition of family, or confronting the perils of blind zealotry. My writings in this area led me to delve more deeply into Whedon's shows and I have been fortunate indeed to present academic papers and publish on Whedon's work for a number of years now. One result of my ongoing interest was *Faith and Choice in the Works of Joss Whedon*, a book that explores the seeming contradiction of an atheist examining these concepts.

As proud as I am of *Faith and Choice* (and I think it would make quite a handsome companion volume to the book you hold in your hands), it didn't answer all of my questions, and Whedon's work since its publication in 2008 has raised additional questions. This is why I'm so pleased that Tony, John, and Ryan have collected the essays you're about to read.

In contemporary American society, the very word *religion* often seems to be used to narrow and exclude, rather than to celebrate and include. I am firmly of the "Big Tent" belief which states that deeper examination generally leads to the discovery of common ground and a greater understanding of other worldviews. This book is a Big Tent book. The authors come at their individual topics from a wide variety of angles, but all are concerned with clarifying their opinions and explaining their viewpoints. You may not agree with all of them, but I feel confident that the essays contained here will spark the fires of your mind and get you to thinking, which is seldom a bad thing.

Whedon's output is extensive and I can only marvel at the sheer mountain of effort this book represents. Trying to be comprehensive when your subject's productions span the multiple media platforms of television, film, webcasts, and comic books is an immense task. I don't envy the editors the task they took on, but I know I'm glad that they shouldered the burden, for the result is a worthy addition to the fields of both religious studies and Whedon studies.

K. Dale Koontz teaches communications and film at Cleveland Community College in western North Carolina. She received a J.D. from Wake Forest University. Among her published works is Faith and Choice in the Works of Joss Whedon *(McFarland, 2008). She has presented widely on Whedon's work.*

Preface
Anthony R. Mills

The pairing of Joss Whedon and religion may strike some as inappropriate or at the very least ironic. While it is widely known that Whedon has referred to himself as an "angry atheist" (hence the slightly provocative subtitle of this book), he has also admitted to being fascinated by the concept and practice of devotion. Even this admission notwithstanding, many of his texts deal explicitly with gods, goddesses, demons, and other supernatural beings and with belief and disbelief therein. Even where these aspects of religion are absent, other issues are explored which tend to be significant for religions and their followers and theologians, such as metaphysics, humanity, identity, ethics, and the end of the world. Moreover, contemporary hermeneutics has, for a number of reasons, moved beyond the traditional priority of authorial intent in the interpretation of texts, films, and other media. The authors in this book take seriously what Whedon says about his own work, but they recognize that there is often more to be said than this, and so should we. For these reasons we are confident that a book on Whedon and religion does not in and of itself suggest undue impositions on his oeuvre. Whether one will read any particular interpretation in such a way, or as simply wrong, is another matter, and the very diversity of the approaches and perspectives we have represented here will hopefully foster debate thereabout.

As for me, I can say that Whedon's shows and films brought life to my Evangelical faith in a way that church never did. My first real exposure was to *Firefly* roughly a year after it had been cancelled. I immediately noticed that although they may have been out in the black, the folks on Serenity had a firm grasp of companionship, compassion, forgiveness, and protection of the weak, all of the things which I was told to value in Christian circles but which were rarely demonstrated and usually outright opposed in actual practice and politics. But when Inara, the prostitute, gives Shepherd Book, the man of God, what is essentially absolution of sin at the end of the pilot, I was baffled into humility and that space became holy ground.

A few years later I gave *Buffy the Vampire Slayer* a shot. Watching it as one untimely born, as it were, I became hooked and bought the complete series because my local video store only had the first two seasons available for rent. The same thing, that moment of rapt awe, happened when I came across "Amends" from season three. Its breathlessness was in its silence and simplicity. Not by might, nor by power, says the Lord, but by snow in southern California.

There have been many other such experiences throughout my years of being a Whedon fan, without which this book would not have come into being. Sure, some other folks may have thought at some point in the future to put an edited volume like this together, but this one you're reading owes its impetus to those tearful, sacred moments had by a young man alone in his apartment. And, although I have said farewell to God, it remains true that what always drew me to Jesus is what I have seen ever embodied in Whedon's texts: grace, mercy, love, redemption, and the hope of a new day. Even if at the end of all things it really is only us out here in the black, aren't these worth fighting for?

Introduction
ANTHONY R. MILLS

The works of Joss Whedon — from his hit (and not so hit) television shows *Buffy the Vampire Slayer*, *Angel*, *Firefly*, and *Dollhouse*, to his popular comic book writing on *Fray* and *X-Men*, to his cult success *Serenity*, critical darling *Cabin in the Woods*, and box-office smash *Avengers*— are among the most influential pop culture phenomena of the last two decades. They are also among the most provocative when it comes to explorations of religion and the important dimensions of the human condition closely associated with it: family, friendship, sex, forgiveness, redemption, faith, hope, love, and death. All of these Big Questions, as Dale Koontz puts it, loom large in Whedon's opera. While several volumes have been written on Whedon from philosophical and cultural studies perspectives, relatively little attention has been given to the religious significance — and implications — of how he portrays these subjects.

The essays in this volume on Joss Whedon and religion address the above topics and other themes pertinent to Whedon's work through a broad lens, reflecting several academic disciplines, methodological approaches, and, of course, religious convictions. Christianity, paganism, and Western esotericism are the most common dialogue partners, but are approached, in different ways, through theology, history, religious studies, cultural studies, and philosophy of religion. This diversity is meant to present the volume as a strong introduction to the many religiously significant themes and aspects of Whedon's work. At the same time, it is not meant to suggest that religion is the *only* hermeneutical approach to the Whedonverse, but rather to augment the insights of Whedon's other intellectual interlocutors. As such, we consider it a companion volume to the other scholarly anthologies of Whedon's works.

The book is organized in a roughly chronological fashion. It begins with five essays on *Buffy the Vampire Slayer* (1997–2003) and *Angel* (1999–2004). Jeremy R. Ricketts sets the stage for us by exploring the changes from human to vampire (and sometimes back again) in the Buffyverse in terms of spiritual transformation. He interprets this phenomenon, including the gaining and losing of souls, through the work of psychologist and philosopher William James and religious studies scholar Mircea Eliade. In their essay, Hope K. Bartel and Timothy E. G. Bartel put the third-season *Buffy* episode "Anne" in conversation with the Greek tradition of Pascha, or Easter. They explore the parallels between this hell-harrowing episode, on the one hand, and the fourth-century Paschal homily of St. John Chrysostom and fourteenth-century *Anastasis* icon, on the other. Good stuff for you history or Greek Orthodox buffs. Valerie Mayhew goes old school on us as well by arguing that feminine power has been negatively linked to sexuality throughout history, including in the stories of pagan goddesses and Christian women mystics. While Buffy starts to be written in this way, she ends up embracing both her femininity and sexuality in emulable ways, similar to the Virgin Mary. Jason Lawton Winslade provides a detailed historical analysis of the background and uses of Wicca and witchcraft in the Buffyverse and argues that this is key to identifying and understanding the feminist theology, or *thealogy*, of the show. Roslyn Weaver goes to the other end of the temporal spectrum and explores the significance of apocalypse in *Buffy*. Whereas the biblical patterns of apocalypse are overseen or controlled by the divine, the end in Whedon's world is a thoroughly human affair, although with supernatural elements of demons and the undead.

Next come two essays on *Firefly* (2002) and *Serenity* (2005). Desirée de Jesus argues that the black male figures of Jubal Early and the Operative, two men with fanatical devotion to their causes, are written in a way that ties their religiosity to negative racial stereotypes, thereby suggesting both the irrationality of religious belief and the danger of strong black masculinity. Dean A. Kowalski looks at ethics in the Whedonverse and argues that both Mal and Angel pursue courses of action which do not depend on God or divine command, but which can rather be read as examples of an Aristotelian–Kantian ethical synthesis in which one does what's good just because it's right.

Moving right along, we also have two essays on *Dollhouse* (2009–2010), each of which takes a different theological and philosophical approach to how the dolls' identities seem to be in some sense maintained given the show's premise of mind-body dualism. J. Leavitt Pearl borrows heavily from phenomenologist Michel Henry to argue for the existence of a soul, understood as an individual's source of consistent identity, memories, and feelings despite repeated imprints with different personalities. On the other hand, Julie Clawson argues that the dolls' persistent behavior and feelings despite multiple mind wipes owes to human beings' essential interrelatedness, which mirrors what some contemporary theologians refer to as the *social Trinity*, the idea that humans find their identities in relation just as the persons of the Trinity do.

Susanne E. Foster and James B. South cap off our discussion of Whedon's television series by considering the power structures presented therein (e.g. the Initiative, the Alliance, Wolfram & Hart, and the Rossum Corporation) in light of Augustine's political theology. While Whedon's views of the polity are not explicitly Christian, there are surprising parallels to be found with Augustine: both recognize that there are better and worse ways to live communally and they often agree on what characterizes those ways of life.

Next we consider the two films released in 2012 which have helped to make Joss Whedon a household name (at least in those households where *Buffy* reruns were not the norm). Our two essays on *Marvel's The Avengers*, written and directed by Whedon, display different attitudes to the themes of power and superheroism found in the film. On the positive side, Russell W. Dalton compares Whedon with both Stan Lee and Ayn Rand and finds that the former two offer an exemplary ethic of self-sacrifice and protection of the weak, whereas the latter, whose thought has found a home of late among many America policymakers, proffers the kind of ethic preferred by many Marvel villains, including Loki: the weak are to be ruled by those superior to them. On the negative side, John C. McDowell expresses concern over the nationalism and exclusivism expressed in the film, critiques which are not new for the superhero genre but which nevertheless stand out because of Whedon's tendency to subvert the moral and political authority of established power structures in his other works.

Finally, we have two essays on the other 2012 film, *The Cabin in the Woods*, cowritten and coproduced by Whedon. Although this film was made well before *Avengers*, it was released only a month before it in the United States. Moreover, since the end of the world is a major theme in it, we thought it a fitting end to the book. J. Ryan Parker attends to the religious and cultural significance of the violent sacrifice of youth by comparing *Cabin* with the Christian theological doctrine of penal substitutionary atonement — in which Jesus's horrific death is understood as necessary in order to get one right with God — and by eschewing both film and doctrine in favor of a less sadistic solution. W. Scott Poole focuses instead on the eschatology of *Cabin* and sees it as an example of Whedon's joyful nihilism as opposed to the more despairing nihilism of H. P. Lovecraft, who has greatly influenced Whedon and *Cabin* especially. Poole engages two twentieth-century Christian theologians, Jürgen Moltmann and Dorothee Soelle, and argues that despite their more sophisticated approach to eschatology their views leave something to be desired.

Before we get to the good stuff I want to make a few comments about style to help guide the reader. For the most part we have formatted the book according to the 16th edition of the *Chicago Manual of Style*. We have broken from it in a few cases where other practices of citation have become conventional, especially in studies of pop culture. All Bible references, Whedon episode locations, and movie directors and dates are referred to in parentheses in the text instead of in endnotes, except for citation of block quotes where a parenthetical reference may be confusing. For example, we would refer to "The Harvest" as "*Buffy* 1.2," meaning that the episode is from *Buffy the Vampire Slayer*, specifically season one, episode two. Since *Firefly* only had one season, we leave off the "1" so that "Objects in Space," for instance, is referred to as "*Firefly* 14."

Also, we have decided to follow Chicago style's preference for lowercase words whenever it seemed feasible to do so, even when this goes against some practices within Whedon studies. For instance, "Slayer," "Potential," and "Watcher" are here put in lowercase because they are generic terms, except when referring to the full title of a character, such as Buffy the Vampire Slayer. Generic terms which are used as names, however, such as "the Master" or "the Operative," are capitalized, along with special terms like "Big Bad."

Finally, we have chosen to put the names of actors in parentheses only after the first mention of a character's name, whether this comes in the text or an endnote, but only for major or recurring characters in an attempt to avoid clutter. For this reason and to avoid any confusion, we have also chosen not to mention actors or episode locations in works other than Whedon's.

Varieties of Conversion
Spiritual Transformation in the Buffyverse
JEREMY R. RICKETTS

At a casual glance, Joss Whedon's *Buffy the Vampire Slayer* and *Angel* seem like shows that obviously deal with religion. There are crosses, after all, as well as a hellmouth and an occasional nun. A closer look will inform the viewer that while surface elements of religion are clearly present, no main recurring character seems to talk about going to church much (or, in the case of Willow Rosenberg [Alyson Hannigan], synagogue), and specific tenets of traditional religious doctrine are rarely mentioned beyond the definitive existence of a soul.[1] A still deeper analysis will show that while the humans in Joss Whedon's world may not express overt religious sentiments, vampires in the Buffyverse form a locus of religious experience through which viewers can examine important tenets of faith, particularly conversion, salvation, redemption, and the difficulty of change and connection. Thus, through an examination of the symbolic conversion of humans into vampires, one can begin to unravel the philosophy of spirituality evinced within the Buffyverse and discover the manifold religious and spiritual connections within the shows.

When humans are converted into vampires in the Buffyverse, the internal transformation is as powerful and immediate as the external one, mirroring intense religious conversion. The newly initiated embrace their incipient power and disdain their former status to the point of often killing their families as their first act as a vampire. They are sure of their place in the world and have a connection with evil and often with each other. Their conversion is neat and simple. Yet when vampires such as Angel (David Boreanaz), Spike (James Marsters), Darla (Julie Benz), and even Harmony (Mercedes McNab) try to become more human, Whedon emphasizes atonement and redemption as well as agonizing existential questions over right and wrong, good and evil, change and stagnation, and connection and isolation. Vampires sans souls do not engage in such spiritual philosophizing, and in direct opposition to those vampires, Whedon's ensouled vampires do grow and change, but not easily.

This essay argues that Whedon's vampires represent convincing symbols of spiritual conversion that have current relevance to the experiences of converts (and deconverts) worldwide. Whedon's depiction of conversion parallels a nuanced philosophy of religion articulated by William James which argues that those who engage with complex notions of good and evil are often miserable, but ultimately experience life in a fuller way than those who are convinced of their place in the world. Whedon emphasizes the struggle to connect with others that so many contemporary people face. His ensouled vampires encounter profound challenges, but also experience profound change.

William James and the Once- and Twice-Born

In 1900–1902, William James gave the prestigious Gifford Lectures at Edinburgh which led to his influential book *The Varieties of Religious Experience*. The word "variety" is key in this essay because James's lens can be employed to examine many different expressions of religion and spirituality, as he himself did in the lectures. I will use James as a starting point to analyze how Joss Whedon and his collaborators created a universe in which vampires represent the easy and sure path to spiritual satisfaction, a state James calls "healthy-minded." James refers to the healthy-minded as "once-born" in that they do not need a spiritual rebirth to be firm in their religious convictions. He argues that the once-born are "fatally forbidden to linger ... over the darker aspects of the universe.... The capacity for even a transient sadness or a momentary humility seems cut off from them."[2] Speaking of Walt Whitman as a representative of the once-born, James argues that Whitman had "infected" admirers into his "cult," telling words that echo the process of conversion from human to vampire in the Buffyverse.[3] Of course, Whedon's vampires are evil and thus represent a mirror image of the condition James describes.[4] Where the once-born see only good in the world, the vampires experience only evil. Yet authorial intent remains the same: James and Whedon both argue that despite the allure of being completely sure of one's place in the universe and thus healthy-minded, such thinking represents an overly simplistic reading of that universe.

In contrast to the healthy-minded, James notes that the "morbid-minded" or "soul-sick" long for a conversion that will begin to reconcile their divided selves; a conversion which makes them "twice-born." According to James, the morbid-minded more clearly recognize the ebb and flow of good and ill in the world; and James, on behalf of the twice-born, critiques the once-born for their overly simplistic view of life, namely their failure to engage with or at least contemplate matters of ultimate concern. For the once-born, the world is a whole and exciting place. For the soul-sick, it can be "remote, strange, sinister, uncanny."[5] And those who come through the other side of the crisis provoked by being morbid-minded, like Spike, maintain a complex and meaningful view of life but without the tendency to melancholy. It is through this lens that Whedon explores the impact of conversion, spirituality, and the unsettling but realistic fact that one must ask difficult questions in order to grow, change, and deeply connect.[6]

Common Vampires: The Once-Born

While vampires in the Buffyverse seem to have no clear belief in a deity per se, their rites parallel religion at many points and they often think of themselves as god-like. In fact, scholars have often noted that vampires in the Buffyverse seem to be the *only* characters that pay much attention to religion at all. Buffy (Sarah Michelle Gellar) and her comrades use a cross, but it is a defensive weapon against vampires more than an instrument of devotion. Even Buffy, who has been to some version of heaven, has doubts about the existence of God.[7]

In contrast, vampires depend and even thrive on the rituals most often associated with religion, and this is key to understanding how the human-to-vampire conversion is symbolically representative of issues involving religious conversion that are presented throughout the series. When humans first become vampires, they all go through a rebirth of sorts that initiates them into the world of the vampire. As scholar of religion Mircea Eliade points out, all such initiations are religious in nature, because "the change of existential status" leads to a completely new identity.[8] In other words, the new initiate has become "another" through a process equivalent to a new "birth."[9] Vampires in the Buffyverse consistently speak of their conversions as births that open up an entire new world to them. The series also symbolically reinforces this idea in several ways. The vampire Drusilla (Juliet Landau) often refers to her maker Angelus as "Daddy" and likens siring to having a baby. The Master (Mark Metcalf) promises Darla that she will be "reborn" ("Darla," *Angel* 2.7). And, of course, most new vampires are symbolically born when they claw their way out of the earth. It is in this sense that vampires are once-born: they are whole and complete upon conversion. From that moment forward, they are able to avoid morbid-mindedness.

Once a new vampire has entered this world, the rites and symbols most often associated with religion continue. The entirety of season one of *Buffy* deals with the ancient vampire known as the Master, who is trapped in a subterranean church beneath Sunnydale spouting off prophecies with religious élan. In the very first episode of the series his vampire henchman Luke offers a ritualistic prayer complete with an "Amen." In the second, Luke feeds off the Master's blood in a clear allusion to the Eucharist. We even learn that vampires have a patron saint. Yet it is appropriately when humans are first converted into vampires that we see the clearest connections to religious conversion. Vampires tend either to want to convert their family members, as with Spike, or, more often, to kill their family in a complete literal and symbolic rejection of their former way of life, as with Angelus and minor vampire characters such as Zachary Kralik.[10] These violent rejections of identity symbolically parallel the experiences many converts face today as the new initiates undergo a concurrent celebration of their new life and a forceful rejection of their old.

Conversion stories are usually portrayed as joyous occasions — indeed, one of the more famous conversions is the one that C. S. Lewis describes in *Surprised by Joy*. This deeply spiritual joy is mirrored in Whedon's vampire world.[11] The experience of conversion in the Buffyverse was set from the very second episode when Sunnydale High student Jesse McNally is turned into a vampire. When Buffy and fellow "Scooby Gang" member Xander (Nicholas Brendon) find out about the conversion, Xander offers his sympathy.[12] Jesse replies, "I feel good Xander. I feel strong. I'm connected to everything." When Xander tries to remind him of their friendship, Jesse says, "You're like a shadow to me now." The break in identity goes so far that some hours later Jesse refers to himself in the third person, abandoning his name in much the same way that Angelus, Spike, and Darla do. Before being staked, he says, "I'm a new man," an apt description of the sudden change in identity felt by many new converts, almost like flipping a switch.

Bookending the series from Jesse in season one to season seven, in "Conversations with Dead People" Buffy meets up with the recently reborn Holden Webster, her former classmate. As they make small talk, Buffy tells him that she is sorry he was converted, and he immediately comments, "No, no, it feels great. Strong. Like I'm connected to a powerful all-consuming evil." This scene encapsulates one of the more ironic themes of the show: vampires are more connected, at least superficially, than many humans. Their complete and utter faith in their identity renders them able to be at peace in a way that those with souls cannot match. As Angel plainly says about being a soulless vampire, "It's an easy way to live" ("Angel," *Buffy* 1.7).

This model of conversion bears out across time as well as seasons in *Buffy*. In the years 1753 and 1880 respectively, Angelus and Spike awake to what they describe as glorious new worlds in deeply symbolic rituals of being born again. After she bites him, Darla lets Angelus drink blood from her bosom and then oversees what she refers to as a "birth" from the grave ("The Prodigal," *Angel* 1.15). This scene is mirrored in the second season of *Angel* in "Reunion" (2.10) when Drusilla is brought in to sire the momentarily human Darla. Drusilla tells people that she is having a baby and places Darla in dirt from which she will be born in white, gratefully throwing off her recent humanity. And as Spike says about his conversion, "Getting killed made me feel alive for the very first time" ("Fool for Love," *Buffy* 5.7). The ambiguity of those with a soul is so profound that in the Buffyverse only once-born vampires possess absolute certainty about anything.

Yet within the philosophy of spirituality that Whedon articulates, this is consistent. In the Buffyverse, as noted, vampires are most closely associated with religious ritual. Such an association allows the famously "angry atheist" Whedon to implicitly critique those who think that adhering to a specific religious creed assures their spiritual salvation. Whedon taps into one of the major trends of the postmodern age by having his nonvampire characters and those vampires with a soul seek out a nondoctrinal spiritual path that may or may not lead to a resolute religious conviction, but ideally leads to some sort of understanding of their place in the world. As sociologist Charles Taylor notes, there is currently among many people a "sense ... that this life is empty, flat, devoid of higher purpose."[13] That vacuum must be replaced by "a personal search" for meaning; one which plays out for several characters in the Buffyverse.[14] The once-born vampires may be healthy-minded in that they are free of doubt, but without doubt, there can be no questions, and without questions, there can be no growth. The Turok-Han, the protean vampires who reside literally in the hellmouth, are the purest expression of the once-born from the side of evil; killing machines with complete conviction about their purpose in the world and without existential anxiety, but also devoid of connection and the sometimes troubling but necessary search for deeper meaning that is the only route to personal and spiritual growth.

Uncommon Vampires: The Road to Twice-Born

William James notes that to the morbid-minded, the healthy-minded "seem unspeakably blind and shallow."[15] It is true that those with sick souls are cognizant of evil and as a result are often led to morbid-mindedness in their contemplation of the world. Yet their way of being encapsulates far more potential than those who are healthy-minded because the twice-born have an opportunity to experience a "deeper kind of conscious being" than the once-born via their more complete worldview.[16] But even those who long for a second birth still experience a more complete and complex understanding of their existence. In the Buffyverse, Harmony, Darla, Angel, and Spike represent the clearest examples of the way Whedon symbolically uses different notions of conversion, questioning, and connection to express a philosophy of spirituality.

The vampire Harmony presents an opportunity for exploration of the symbolic quest for spiritual satisfaction in that she stands at a liminal space between vampire and human and serves as a counterpoint to Spike and Angel. In high school, Harmony was shallow, vain, and a bit of a ditz. As a vampire, it does not appear that she is much different, but there are key moments that show an element of desire for growth fueled by an uncertainty lacking in other vampires. She attempts friendship with humans, particularly Cordelia (Charisma Carpenter) at first, a friend from her human days. Her attempts to bond with coworker Winifred/Fred (Amy Acker) are even more notable, as Fred is a stranger and not someone she knew from her past. Harmony also successfully swears off of human blood for a time. She even possesses, at least to a degree, that all-important quality in the Buffyverse: introspection. She notes, "I don't have a soul so I have to try a lot harder" ("Harm's Way," *Angel* 5.9). Apparently unique among vampires, she tries to control herself without aid of a soul or any other kind of device such as the implant in Spike.

To fully appreciate the spiritual philosophy of the Buffyverse, it is important to consider how and why Harmony seeks to become good. The ironic answer is that she lacks the connection to a higher power that other vampires in the show mention.[17] She is evil upon conversion, to be sure, as all of Whedon's vampires are, but her half-hearted attempts at villainy produce no concrete results, and her vampire partner of choice, Spike, uses her and ultimately rejects her for the vampire slayer. Harmony then tries to connect with humans, with some success. But with the conversion of her new friend Fred into a demon and the failure of a renewed relationship with Spike, she seesaws back to the dark side and betrays Angel.[18] She learns what Spike and Angel already know: it is not as simple as just saying "I'm one of the good guys now," as she does in the *Angel* episode "Disharmony" (2.17).

Yet Angel understands her betrayal and seems to appreciate her struggles. He appears to recognize that while his soul was restored and Spike began his journey to ensoulment with an inhibitor chip in his head, Harmony set out to be good without any aid. But without connections, her attempts are largely futile. As she affirms in "Harm's Way," "Since I got vamped at graduation, I've had trouble connecting with people." Harmony is unwilling or unable to commit to either being fully vampire or fully good, and thus vacillates between being once- and twice-born. She occupies a position in a kind of Acheron, cut off from connections with good or evil, and is left to fend for herself where other vampires find connections up to and including love.

Darla presents another intriguing case study of conversion. A flashback establishes that she was a syphilitic prostitute who was near death in the year 1609 when she was converted ("Darla"). The Master, ever fond of religious ritual, appears to her in priestly garb as her "savior," and she stays by his side for hundreds of years with an interregnum during her time with Angelus. She is dispatched quickly in season one of *Buffy*, staked by Angel in the seventh episode. Yet it is her resurrection by the evil law firm Wolfram & Hart in *Angel* that propels her on a complicated path to salvation. These lawyers bring her back from the dead in a scheme to turn Angel evil. Darla is brought back as a human, and therefore has a soul, but much like Angel, it was forced upon her as opposed to earned, and her guilt is monumental. Her connection to a higher evil is severed and her certainty is quashed. She begs Angel to turn her back into a vampire to escape the searing doubts that come with being morbid-minded, but he refuses. Darla faces a unique identity crisis in that her soul is moving her away from her vampire self, but she has not been human in four centuries. Much like other vampires, Darla completely rejects her former identity, noting that "I'm not like her, whoever she was" ("Darla").[19]

Angel will not assist Darla back into the certainty of the vampire world through conversion, but rather promises to help her atone. In a series of flashbacks we learn about Darla's selfishness as a vampire; she even left her great love Angelus to a mob at one point ("The Trial," *Angel* 2.9). But as a human, she begins to understand the horrors she caused.[20] She has no time to act on this remorse, however, because Wolfram & Hart brought her back exactly as she was as a human — with terminal syphilis.

Angel thus embarks on a series of trials to win Darla's life back so she can begin a process of redemption.[21] Although Angel is successful, when it is discovered that Darla has already been resurrected once, she is left to die. Yet Darla has seen the trials through Angel's eyes and has gained a new perspective. She fully commits to the idea of atonement in the limited time that remains for her. Darla is thus twice-born via Angel's mediation, willing to accept her fate and die on the cusp of a unified human identity. Drusilla and Wolfram & Hart intervene and Darla is converted into a vampire again ("Reunion," *Angel* 2.10).[22] As a newly sired vampire, Darla is once more full of certainty and consumed by evil.

Angel halts Darla in her typical pattern of destruction in an unexpected manner. Angel, near complete nihilistic despair over the evil he sees in the world, has sex with his old lover Darla, risking a moment of true happiness and the loss of his soul. But not only does he not lose his soul, he returns from the nihilistic precipice and recommits to his own journey of atonement ("Reprise," *Angel* 2.15). Darla's confidence is sorely shaken by her failure to convert Angel, but it is shattered when she discovers that he has impregnated her.

This impossible and unprecedented occurrence in the Buffyverse leads to profound consequences for Darla. She is given a second chance at redemption. Similar to her brief second stint as a human, she at first tries to reject a chance at atonement by aborting the fetus, but the child is under some form of magical protection. She soon begins to feel empathy for her former victims and love for her unborn child, ostensibly because she shares a soul with him. As her pregnancy continues and her love grows, she embraces her feelings but fears that they will disappear after the birth when she no longer shares a soul. In other words, as a twice-born individual, she is deeply aware of evil in the world and even in herself. In an act that consciously reenacts Angelus's birth in an alley, Darla stakes herself and turns to dust, leaving the healthy baby crying, but safe, on the ground ("Lullaby," *Angel* 3.9). This scene forms a counterpoint to one several episodes earlier when Darla tells Angel that she did him a favor by making him a vampire. Angel replies, "You damned me" ("Darla"). In one alley, she took a life. In another, she gave her own life for another's. Through this action her atonement is complete, and her redemption is confirmed in a later episode when she returns as an angelic emissary of sorts ("Inside Out," *Angel* 4.17).

While Harmony and Darla are important examples of conversion to consider, any essay that deals with ensouled vampires must attempt to make sense of Angel and Spike. They are both (eventually) vampires with a soul, but one is morose where one is light, one is Irish where the other is English, and most significantly, one had his soul forced upon him where the other earned his soul through trial. While there is a suggestion that Angel's much longer trials will end in the reward of his becoming human, his soul is not yet at ease. Angel had his soul restored by gypsies, or Romani, who wanted to punish him for killing one of their own. Angel would thus be tormented for eternity with guilt over all he had killed. The Romani also put in a mystical clause that if Angel were to ever have one moment of true happiness, he would lose his soul. This proviso puts him in a much more precarious position than Spike, who earned his soul free and clear. In fact, Angelus does return in season two of *Buffy* and season four of *Angel*. It also takes Angel many decades after his ensoulment to fully commit to redemption. He even links back up with Darla after the restoration of his soul to try and continue their swath of destruction, but his new morbid-minded status prevents him from doing so.

The encounter with Darla during the Boxer Rebellion is significant in that it draws a clear line between healthy- and morbid-mindedness. Angel tries to go back to his vampire family, but as James notes, "To the healthy-minded ... the sick soul seems unmanly and diseased."[23] Darla is disgusted with Angel's doubt and uncertainty and mocks him as a pretend savior to a band of missionaries she killed, whom he was trying to protect ("Darla").

Over the course of the series she frequently castigates his soul as something "filthy" and "disgusting" that "sickens" her. But it is in that moment of Darla's initial rejection that he recognizes his morbid-mindedness; he quickly spins into a decades-long turmoil, completely disconnected from life. Angel thus falls into the deeper part of James's framework of the morbid-minded, in that when atoning for "misdeeds" those who are soul-sick realize that a "mere apology" will never be enough, but that "every pound of flesh exacted is soaked with all its blood."[24] At their most acute, the soul-sick are prone to "ignore that of all good."[25] Angel does not kill anyone, but he does not intervene in life either. He subsists off of rats and makes no connections with anyone.[26] It takes intervention from the demon Whistler, who helps balance good and evil, to get Angel onto the path to redemption and connection. And Buffy, of course. Angel sees Buffy and wants to help her. But when they fall in love, he realizes again how precarious his position is. After they make love and Angelus takes over due to that moment of true happiness, he repeats the old patterns: killing those closest to him; or, as Giles (Anthony Stewart Head) says, those who most remind him of his humanity ("Innocence," *Buffy* 2.14). As Angelus says in that same episode, "[Buffy] made me feel like a human being. That's not the kind of thing you just forgive."

To save the world, Buffy is forced to kill Angel just as his soul is magically restored ("Becoming: Part 2," *Buffy* 2.22).[27] Buffy's action sends Angel into a hell dimension where he suffers one hundred years of agony and torture. Twice Angel had his soul restored by magic. The first time he spent one hundred years on earth in torment, the second time in hell. But in season three of *Buffy*, he comes back from *above* in a white shaft of light ("Faith, Hope, and Trick"). He has earned a measure of redemption through suffering and should be able to feel more at peace with himself. Only by literally going through hell can he regain a firmer hold on his soul through what Eliade notes is a common motif in many cultures: the "initiatory ordeal *par excellence*" of the hero descending into hell.[28] And there is a strong suggestion that Angel will face a smoother road to redemption; a key intervention by some higher power underscores this when in a fit of intense guilt (and spurred on by a primeval force of evil) he tries to kill himself ("Amends," *Buffy* 3.10). He waits for the sun to come up and consume him in flames, but a once-in-a-lifetime snowstorm hits Sunnydale and he is spared.

He is sorely tested later in *Angel* to be sure, but he does not lose his soul after having sex with Darla, and as the series ends he is beginning to explore a relationship with Nina, a werewolf.[29] When Angelus does return in season four of *Angel*, it is a calculated move that could help save the world. The curse is not negated, but he need not withdraw from those to whom he is connected. Angel still faces a road of misery because, as the show establishes, connections are what keep people from too much existential angst and Angel has to be careful that his connections do not make him too happy. On the other hand, he cannot disavow connections because that leads to a deep disaffectedness at best and near-soulless behavior at worst.[30] Ultimately, Angel is mostly able to thread that existential needle through the intervention of friends such as Doyle (Glenn Quinn), Cordelia, and even Spike to a degree. Angel is usually connected to the complex world around him, and as he tells Nina, "If you separate yourself from the ones you love, the monster wins" ("Unleashed," *Angel* 5.3).

Yet the vagaries of his connections remain the reason that Angel cannot move into a full expression of twice-born status and a complete unification of his conflicted soul. As Darla says in an early episode of *Buffy*, "You're not one of them." Angel replies, "No. But I'm not exactly one of you either" ("Angel"). Many scholars argue that Buffy is a savior for both Angel and Spike, and there are certainly overtones of that, but really it is simple human connection that time and again saves them both (and allows Darla to save her son).[31]

Indeed, Spike quests for his soul because of burgeoning connections with others. When considering Spike, it is important to note that his ability to seek reclamation of his soul was arguably aided by the chip which the Initiative placed in his head. The chip essentially negated his ability to harm humans in any way by causing blinding pain in his head if he attempted such harm, but he can fight demons and vampires, and does so with gusto. This puts him in close contact with the slayer, and he forms a connection with her that probably would not have existed otherwise. Yet despite the chip, there has always been something different about Spike. Contrary to most vampires, he converts his mother into a vampire instead of killing her.[32] He does not have the same taste for ritual that other vampires have, as shown in the *Buffy* episode "School Hard" when he kills the Anointed One (whom he calls the "annoying one") and calls for a "little less ritual and a little more fun."[33] He works with the Scooby Gang in season two, *prior* to being defanged, in order to stop Angelus from destroying the world, a place he quite likes. He genuinely mourns the loss of Drusilla as well. More than most vampires, he does not take connections for granted, and is vigilant to maintain them.

Yet his lack of a soul does often frustrate his connections in a manner similar to what Harmony experiences. For example, in *Buffy*'s "Fool for Love," Spike professes his love for Buffy only to be told that he is "beneath" her, a comment echoed by a love interest when he was human. This insult resonates with him even more strongly as a harmless vampire in that it relates to his liminal status between monster and man. He has no soul and is not a man, but he cannot (easily) kill humans either, so he is not a monster. In this state of identity crisis he retrieves a gun to kill Buffy (as noted, the chip causes extreme debilitating pain, but he could conceivably kill), but when he sees her crying he relents and consoles her. She allows him to comfort her, moving him back in the direction of being a man. Indeed, in the final episode of season five, Spike tells Buffy, "I know I'm a monster, but you treat me like a man." Such experiences serve as a dress rehearsal of sorts that allow him to see a glimmer of what a complicated but genuine connection could be like, as opposed to his often ephemeral vampire connections. This idea is underscored by his relationship with Drusilla. As unthinking killing machines, they experienced love and a connection, but arguably not a profound one. When Spike evinced the first hint of change, Drusilla was gone. It took Spike some time to get over her, but when he did, he realized that their connection was a shadow of what it could be as a twice-born individual.

With this history in mind, it is easier to understand *Buffy* episodes like "Crush" (5.14). Spike sees Buffy sitting alone and, recognizing the critical power of connection, tries to talk to her as a friend, or at least a colleague. He is rebuffed, and this lack of connection tilts him back toward evil as he kidnaps Buffy and offers to kill his former lover Drusilla for her. Spike insists he has changed, but Buffy says he is just inhibited by the chip, like "a serial killer in prison." She is partially right, as evidenced by Spike's attack on a woman he thinks is Buffy in "Smashed," his amoral and potentially destructive deal with a demon in "As You Were," and his sexual assault of Buffy in "Seeing Red." Yet while Drusilla thinks Spike is simply being conditioned in the same way that an electric fence conditions a dog, he is growing and changing to the extent that he quests for his soul — an intervention Harmony never experienced. In essence, as a morbid-minded person he longs for a twice-born conversion and actively seeks it, and thus is the purest expression in the Buffyverse of the kind of individual discussed by James.

Spike's growth is reflected in actions like his kindness to Buffy's mother and in the tasks he performs for Buffy for which he will not get credit. More significantly, he does not betray Buffy's sister Dawn (Michelle Trachtenberg) when he has every chance to do so under torture by the evil goddess Glory (another classic once-born character, played by Clare Kramer), a fact Buffy may never have known ("Intervention," *Buffy* 5.18).[34] These acts are done not for calculated reasons, like tricking Buffy into loving him, but for selfless reasons brought on by the connections he is starting to feel. In fact, after Buffy's death at the end of season five, Spike continues to help the Scooby Gang and watch over Dawn. Buffy tells Spike that he cannot love because he has no soul, while Drusilla claims that vampires can experience devotion. But vampire love is for the most part shallow. Angel says that Darla, his lover of 150 years, "never" made him happy because he "didn't have a soul" ("Dear Boy," *Angel*

2.5). Human love based on a more intimate connection is much harder, but broadens life's perspective so much that in the Buffyverse it has spiritual overtones not found among common vampires.

Spike's quest for his soul is even more revealing. He goes to a cave in a village on the other side of the world to participate in a demon trial that will result in the restoration of his soul if successful, which echoes Eliade's discussions of initiation rites ("Villains," *Buffy* 6.20). This poses an interesting ontological question for the series in that vampires in the Buffyverse have the memories and characteristics of the human they inhabit, but a demonic soul.[35] So why does Spike's demonic self voluntarily seek a soul that will suppress it, as we know from Angel's experience? I contend that it is through the experience of longing for twice-born status that was brought on by his connections. He succeeds where Harmony fails.

Despite occasional conflicting descriptions of the nature of a vampire, Giles argues that there are two types of monsters: ones beyond redemption; and ones that not only can be redeemed, but *want* to be redeemed ("Beauty and the Beasts," *Buffy* 3.4). The chip in his head allows Spike, already different from other vampires, to begin the difficult process towards redemption. Giles is also right in seeing a higher purpose in Spike's inability to fight humans ("The I in Team," *Buffy* 4.13). That inhibition led to his soul and arguably his salvation.

Spike's sacrifice during his trials thus allows him to come through the experience of morbid-mindedness into a full expression of being twice-born and what William James describes as "a loss of all worry [with] a willingness to be, even though the outer conditions should remain the same," a condition markedly different from Angel.[36] Spike is far too interesting to be a complete saint in the sense that James describes, but he does unquestionably value the fight for "abstract moral ideals."[37] As the one character that is able to largely unify his disparate halves of monster and man, Spike's symbolic role as savior is even more dramatic. In the *Buffy* episode "Beneath You" (7.2.) he drapes himself over a cross in a church in a classic savior pose. Just like his soul, the cross burns, but his soul allows him to grow throughout season seven and in the last episode to save the world. To solidify the message, Spike *literally* feels his soul as he sacrifices himself for everyone else—like Darla, the ultimate form of atonement. The message is that those that are twice-born such as Spike are exemplars; human enough to continue growing and changing, but internally unified enough to foster connections and avoid chronic depression.

To be sure, Spike does have some redemptive issues to work through in the basement of Sunnydale High during season seven of *Buffy*, but his transition to feeling at relative peace was much smoother than Angel's. Angel himself recognizes this and resents Spike for making it seem so easy. Spike even claims in the *Angel* episode "Just Rewards" (5.2) not to care much about atonement at all, but in "Damage" (5.11) when one of the newly activated slayers mistakes him for the killer of her parents and tortures him, he is forced to once again face his own deeds. He refers to himself and Angel as monsters, and he has changed so much that he is also able to recognize that while he and Angel were both innocent victims as well before they were converted, it does not excuse their subsequent crimes.

Fittingly, just before Spike earns his soul at the end of season six of *Buffy*, the background music is that of Sarah MacLachlan singing the prayer of Saint Francis, which ends with the words "it is in dying that we are born to eternal life." Spike successfully kills his demon self and negates his vampire birth in favor of his rebirth as a twice-born ensouled being. As Buffy herself tells him, "You're alive because I saw you change. Because I saw your penance" ("Never Leave Me," *Buffy* 7.9). He, more than any other character, moves from once-born into a full expression of a twice-born individual to emerge as a complex *and* largely confident character. Usually in the Buffyverse complex characters are not very confident, and confident characters are none too complex. Spike represents the one character that reconciles his twice-born personality, and that makes him unique in the Buffyverse.

Conclusion: The Spiritual Philosophy of the Buffyverse

In the *Buffy* episode "Lie to Me" (2.7), a group of soul-sick humans try to convince a pack of vampires to convert them. Speaking in directly spiritual terms, one young woman asks, "Do you really think [the vampires] will bless us?" For her and her friends, who refer to one another as "true believers," the opportunity to convert represents a chance to "ascend to a new level of consciousness" with a "chance for immortality." But more than anything, the idea of conversion represents the chance to be freed of doubt and loneliness. Angel notes that such desires are far from unique. Buffy of course tries to stop them and is cast as an unbeliever who taints the group. Even the title of the episode evokes a distinction between the once-born and those who crave a second birth. Buffy asks Giles to "lie to me" about whether or not life is easy. Giles replies, "Yes, it's terribly simple. The good guys are always stalwart and true, the bad guys are easily distinguished by their pointy horns or black hats, and we always defeat them and save the day. No one ever dies and everybody lives happily ever after." A classic soul-sick character, Buffy simply replies, "Liar."[38] Similar encounters take place throughout the Buffyverse and help to illustrate Whedon's philosophy of spirituality, a philosophy clearly seen in the vampire characters of *Buffy* and *Angel*.

William James's notion of the once-born and twice-born are clearly reflected in *Buffy* and *Angel*, and conversions in the series symbolically represent a coherent spiritual philosophy. The significance lies in the fact that "healthy-mindedness is inadequate as a philosophical doctrine, because the evil facts which it refuses positively to account for are a genuine portion of reality, and they may after all be the best key to life's significance, and possibly the only openers of our eyes to the deepest levels of truth."[39] Vampires are a mirror image of this position, failing to recognize any good with extremely rare exception, thus forming "a formally less complete" system.[40] They seem to experience deep connections, but they only *feel* deep because of the vampire's lack of an evolved consciousness. Perhaps it is fitting that the atheist Whedon has his vampires perform baroque but empty religious rituals where other characters explore deeper but more abstract notions of spirituality. Whedon effectively mirrors so much of modern life with his emphasis on spirituality over strict religious observance and practice. Those who follow rites and rituals such as the vampires are coded as empty inside. Other characters, the morbid-minded, are nowhere near as satisfied with life, but they are able to touch something of the divine in those moments in which they connect. Whedon thus symbolically emphasizes that although the trials of contemporary life often lead us to feel like the world is ending, if we can only connect, then our friends will be there to fight the demons we all face, at least until the next apocalypse.

Notes

1. Of course, in later seasons Willow becomes a Wiccan and often invokes higher powers. The characters in *Angel* also interact with the mysterious god-like "Powers That Be."
2. William James, *Varieties of Religious Experience* (1902; repr., Charleston: BiblioBazaar, 2007), 85.
3. Ibid., 87. Despite that passage, James admired Whitman in many ways. See John Tessitore, "The 'Sky-Blue' Variety: William James, Walt Whitman, and the Limits of Healthy-Mindedness," *Nineteenth-Century Literature* 62, no. 4 (March 2008): 493–526.
4. K. Dale Koontz correctly notes that in the *Angel* episode "Unleashed" (5.3) Angel says that vampires "can control themselves if they want to." However, Angel was talking about himself and trying to calm down a person who had recently been turned into a werewolf. See Koontz, *Faith and Choice in the Works of Joss Whedon* (Jefferson, NC: McFarland, 2008), 43.
5. James, *Varieties*, 142.
6. Indeed, in the episodes featuring Jasmine (Gina Torres) where a goddess of sorts converts much of humanity to the equivalent of once-born (season four of *Angel*), Angel initially expresses relief that the "constant questioning" is over. But since by nature he is morbid-minded, he eventually turns to those questions once more.
7. In "Conversations with Dead People" (*Buffy* 7.7), Buffy's response when directly queried about whether there is proof of God is, "Nothing solid."
8. Mircea Eliade, *Rites and Symbols of Initiation: The Mysteries of Birth and Rebirth* (1958; repr., New York: Harper & Row, 1965), 1.

9. Mircea Eliade, *Myths, Rites, Symbols: A Mircea Eliade Reader* (New York: Harper & Row, 1975), 164, 174. *Buffy* scholars often rightly note the show's reliance on Joseph Campbell's delineation of monomyth with its attendant concerns of initiation, yet Eliade's emphasis on the religious nature of initiation better explains in this instance the ways in which vampires use it. For a Campbellian perspective, see, for example, Rhonda Wilcox, *Why Buffy Matters: The Art of "Buffy the Vampire Slayer"* (London: I. B. Tauris, 2005), particularly chapter two; and David Fritts, "Buffy's Seven-Season Initiation," in *"Buffy" Meets the Academy: Essays on the Episodes and Scripts as Text*, ed. Kevin K. Durand (Jefferson, NC: McFarland, 2009), 32–44. See also chapter two of Joseph Campbell, *The Hero with a Thousand Faces* (1949; repr., Princeton: Princeton University Press, 1973).

10. Kralik is featured in the *Buffy* episode "Helpless" (3.12). He talks about killing and eating his mother and plans to convert Buffy to a vampire and get her to do the same to her own mother, Joyce (Kristine Sutherland). The rebirth motif is emphasized here as well, as Kralik tells Joyce that Buffy will wake as a vampire and that her face will be the first thing she "eats," as opposed to "sees." Another example is the vampire convert Penn from "Somnambulist" (*Angel* 1.11), who derives such satisfaction from killing his family that he reenacts the murders for two hundred years. Vampires also consider their fellow converts as their new family. The Master and Drusilla in particular are fond of using familial language to describe the vampires they have relations with. In another nod to the rejection of human identity, the further away a vampire gets from his or her human existence, the less human they look. The Master has "grown past the curse of human features" ("Darla"), and the ancient vampire Kakistos has cloven hands and feet and is similarly unable to look human ("Faith, Hope, and Trick," *Buffy* 3.3).

11. Many of the conversion stories that James relates are indistinguishable from the conversions experienced by Whedon's vampires. Since Whedon is so adept with symbols, this is not entirely unexpected, and, as James says, in conversion "a complete division is established in the twinkling of an eye between the old life and the new" (James, 199). One particular convert James refers to recounts, "I did not know where I was: I did not know whether I was Alphonse or another. I only felt myself changed and believed myself another me; I looked for myself in myself and did not find myself. In the bottom of my soul I felt an explosion of the most ardent joy" (206). Such is the experience of Whedon's vampires, minus the soul. Examples such as this can be found throughout a great deal of religious literature, further underscoring the symbolic connection of vampire conversion to religious conversion. In *Expectations and Experience: Explaining Religious Conversion*, Eugene V. Gallagher writes that the religious hymn "Amazing Grace" "implies a strong devaluation of the individual's previous status and an exaltation of the current status. Noteworthy also is the dependence on an outside agent. The transformation so briefly but forcefully recounted is not the result of any individual effort, of earnest reading or the diligent practice of self-help exercises; it was the result of grace — grace so sweet and sudden as to appear 'amazing'" (1). Vampires in the Buffyverse describe their conversions in much the same way.

12. Buffy and her friends often refer to themselves as the "Scooby Gang."

13. Charles Taylor, *A Secular Age* (Cambridge: Belknap Press, 2007), 506.

14. Ibid., 507.

15. James, *Varieties*, 151.

16. Ibid., 147.

17. *Buffy* fans are passionate and articulate and often speculate about such issues. One fan theory is that there is a correlation between how much blood is drained during the siring process and that converted vampire's later human qualities. See, for example, the *Buffy* FAQ page on imdb.com.

18. While beyond the scope of this essay, the struggles that Illyria (Amy Acker) faces (the demon that Fred transforms into) would make an interesting topic of study in terms of conversion narratives within the Buffyverse. Anya (Emma Caulfield) represents another potential topic of study as she converts from vengeance demon to human to vengeance demon to human. Anya in particular stands in counterpoint to vampires, as she is initiated into the world of humans by experiencing hardships such as the death of a loved one and heartbreak in a relationship. Both Illyria and Anya experience deep identity crises; Anya's resolves only through her sacrificial

death to help save the world in the last episode of *Buffy*. Illyria's redemption continues in the canonical *Angel* comic series. On the other side, those converted by Jasmine are clearly onceborn, and it is telling that Whedon has his characters actually reject that world. Finally, other examples of conversion such as in "Halloween" (*Buffy* 2.6), where characters actually transform into the costumes they are wearing, also underscore how Whedon develops a coherent spiritual philosophy by portraying the tantalizing but ultimately unsatisfying status of being once-born.

19. It should be noted that Darla actually is a human at the time of her rejection of her former self, but she is speaking of her 1600s human self. The resurrected Darla more closely identifies with her vampire days, as they were so much longer. In fact, that is much of her problem; she has no human identity to fall back on.

20. In a moment infused with Lacanian overtones, Darla breaks a mirror to avoid her own reflection ("Darla"). Of course, Whedon plays with our preconceived notions as much as he plays with genre, and instead of seeing an ideal "I" in the mirror, Darla sees an "I" she hates — one capable of guilt and remorse. This scene is mirrored, so to speak, in the *Buffy* episode "Who Are You?" (4.16) when Buffy and morally questionable vampire slayer Faith (Eliza Dushku) switch bodies, and Faith-as-Buffy pummels her own self, calling herself "disgusting."

21. Angel's quest in many ways foreshadows Spike's later trials to win his soul.

22. In another nod to the persistent motif in the series of vampire conversion as a birth, Darla feeds on blood from Drusilla's bosom during the transformation.

23. James, *Varieties*, 151–152.

24. Ibid., 131.

25. Ibid., 137. Much of Angel's early existence post–Angelus falls under this paradigm, and season two of *Angel* explores this side to him as well, particularly when he discovers in "Reprise" that Los Angeles, his home base (and indeed the entire planet), is headquarters for a primal form of evil because evil thrives on the harm that humans do to one another. He becomes so prey to what James calls "pathological melancholy" that in the episode "Reunion" he lets Darla and Drusilla murder a home full of lawyers and their spouses.

26. Angel's subsistence on rats further marks a symbolic link to the morbid-minded, as James figuratively discusses such people "grubbing in rat-holes" (152).

27. In a common motif of the series that reflects some religious rituals, blood is the only thing that can close a universe-ending portal, and in this case, it is the blood of Angel.

28. Mircea Eliade, *The Quest: History and Meaning in Religion* (Chicago: University of Chicago Press, 1969), 123.

29. Angel does lose his soul in "Awakening" (*Angel* 4.10) when a shaman creates a fantasy world for him wherein he has sex with Cordelia, but the world is an impossibly saccharine confection that bears little resemblance to his real life.

30. This line between isolation and community is established in, among other episodes, "To Shanshu in L.A." (*Angel* 1.22), where Angel is so disconnected that he does not seem to care about a prophecy about his ultimate fate. When he reestablishes his connections, he reflects on the prophecy, which has been translated to say that he might become human one day, and simply but sincerely states, "That'd be nice."

31. In counterpoint, it is lack of connection that prevents Harmony from becoming twiceborn.

32. Although, of course, Spike's experiment does not work and he has to kill his vampire mother in "Lies My Parents Told Me" (*Buffy* 7.17).

33. The one exception is when Spike finds a way to heal Drusilla and stages an elaborate ritual; significantly, inside of a church ("What's My Line: Part 2," *Buffy* 2.10).

34. It must be noted that Glory's time on the earthly plane was moving her to a more morbid-minded viewpoint.

35. As established by Giles's hypothesis in "Angel," and confirmed by Angel in "Doppelgangland" (*Buffy* 3.16) as well as by Darla in "The Prodigal." While scholars have pointed out that the show is not quite consistent on the issue in precise terms of how much of the old person actually remains, for the purposes of this essay, the fact that there is no human soul present in vampires is key.

36. James, *Varieties*, 224.
37. Ibid., 245.
38. Even as a morbid-minded individual, Buffy can and does experience some happiness and often evinces a peppy personality. But her main worldview is best described by her speech to Dawn in "The Gift" (*Buffy* 5.22): "The hardest thing in this world is to live in it."
39. James, *Varieties*, 152.
40. Ibid., 153.

BIBLIOGRAPHY

Campbell, Joseph. *The Hero with a Thousand Faces*. 1949. Reprint, Princeton: Princeton University Press, 1973.
Eliade, Mircea. *Myths, Rites, Symbols: A Mircea Eliade Reader*. New York: Harper & Row, 1975.
_____. *The Quest: History and Meaning in Religion*. Chicago: University of Chicago Press, 1969.
_____. *Rites and Symbols of Initiation: The Mysteries of Birth and Rebirth*. 1958. Reprint, New York: Harper & Row, 1965.
Fritts, David. "Buffy's Seven-Season Initiation." In *Buffy Meets the Academy: Essays on the Episodes and Scripts as Text*, edited by Kevin K. Durand, 32–44. Jefferson, NC: McFarland, 2009.
Gallagher, Eugene V. *Expectation and Experience: Explaining Religious Conversion*. Atlanta: Scholars Press, 1990.
James, William. *Varieties of Religious Experience*. 1920. Reprint, Charleston: BiblioBazaar, 2007.
Taylor, Charles. *A Secular Age*. Cambridge: Belknap Press, 2007.
Tessitore, John. "The 'Sky-Blue' Variety: William James, Walt Whitman, and the Limits of Healthy-Mindedness." *Nineteenth-Century Literature* 62, no. 4 (March 2008): 493–526.
Wilcox, Rhonda. *Why Buffy Matters: The Art of "Buffy the Vampire Slayer."* London: I. B. Tauris, 2005.

The Harrowing of Hell
"Anne" and the Greek Paschal Tradition in Conversation
Hope K. Bartel *and* Timothy E. G. Bartel

While most of the characters in Joss Whedon's *Buffy the Vampire Slayer* are agnostic at best about the existence of God, they are confident about the existence of hell — they live and study above the mouth of hell, they mention hell on an almost daily basis, and some of them, like Angel and Spike, are in some sense *from* hell. Despite the show's hellish focus from the beginning, it is not until the first episode of season three, "Anne" (one of only twenty-one episodes in the series both written and directed by Whedon), that Buffy herself actually goes to hell. This essay will explore Buffy's first — and, arguably, only[1] — trip to hell. We will place the events of Whedon's "Anne" in conversation with two key artworks from the traditional Greek celebration of Pascha[2] — known in the West as Easter — and will show how Buffy's trip to hell in "Anne" can be read as a Whedonian reworking of the ancient story of Christ's harrowing of hell.[3] By exploring the similarities and differences between "Anne" and the Greek Paschal tradition, we hope to contribute to the conversation about the structures and themes of the Buffyverse, a universe that at its core is concerned with spiritual and physical enfranchisement and the discovery and formation of feminine identity. When Buffy goes to hell, we will argue, she not only acts as a Christ-like savior who defeats evil and frees captives, but also realizes her own true identity and enlightens and empowers those around her to embrace their identities with new conviction, knowledge, and purpose.

"Anne"

"Anne" begins with Buffy no longer in her hometown of Sunnydale, but in Los Angeles. Other changes have occurred as well: she is no longer slaying vampires or going to school, but is working at a diner and goes by the name Anne instead of Buffy. Three major events in the climax of season two have led to these changes: she was expelled from High School, was effectively kicked out the house by her mother, and, most devastating, killed Angel to save the world. Homeless, schoolless, grieving, and aimless, Buffy is now trying to live alone and unknown in Los Angeles. But soon Buffy meets Rickie and Lily (Julia Lee), two street kids with matching tattoos. Careful watchers of the show recognize Lily from the season two episode "Lie to Me" (also scripted and helmed by Whedon). Back then Lily went by the name Chanterelle and was in a cult that worshipped vampires before being saved by Buffy.

Lily recognizes Buffy and calls her by her real name. She reminds Buffy of their earlier connection and explains that she's had three names of late: first Sister Sunshine, then Chanterelle, and now Lily. Buffy tells her that a chanterelle is a type of mushroom, which Lily didn't know. She ends the conversation by warning Lily not to tell anyone who she is, and that she wants to be left alone.

This establishing dialogue about names and identity is immediately juxtaposed with a short scene back in Sunnydale in which Joyce reveals to Giles that she blames him for Buffy running away, not herself. Giles defends himself, "I didn't make Buffy who she is."

"And who exactly is she?" Joyce asks.

Back in Los Angeles Lily again finds Buffy and, distressed, tells her that Rickie is missing. "That's who you are ... you help people and stuff, right?" Lily asks. "Not anymore," says Buffy. Nevertheless, Buffy acquiesces. In her begrudging search for Rickie, Buffy finds an old man, dead, with a tattoo that matches Rickie's. When Buffy tells Lily that Rickie is dead, Lily will not believe her and flees into the street, where she meets Ken, a seemingly mild-mannered man who invites her to a local family home where, he assures her, Rickie is waiting. But Ken proves not so harmless, for he leads Lily to a pool of black liquid and tells her to climb into it. Buffy, having got wise to Ken's mischief, enters the room and accuses Ken of murdering Rickie. Lily is pulled into the black pool by some unseen force, and Buffy and Ken, grappling, fall in after her.

Buffy and Lily are now in a fire- and smoke-filled, dungeon-like realm populated by demon guards and enslaved humans. Ken peels back his human face to reveal that he, too, is a demon, then knocks Buffy unconscious. Buffy awakens in a prison cell where Lily, beside her, laments: "I always knew I would end up here sooner or later. I knew I belonged here."

"Where?" Buffy asks.

"Hell."

"This isn't hell," Buffy says.

"Isn't it?" comes a voice from beyond the bars. It is Ken. He explains, "What is hell but the total absence of hope? The substance, the tactile proof of despair? You're right, Lily, this is where you've been heading all your life. Just like Rickie."

"Rickie?" Lily asks.

"He forgot you. Took him a long time. He remembered your name years after he'd forgotten his own. But in the end."

"So," Buffy asks, "you just work us till we're too old and spit us back out?"

"That's the plan," says Ken. He explains that he singles out homeless young people to enslave.

"You didn't choose me," Buffy says.

"No," Ken sneers, "But I know you, Anne. So afraid, so pathetically determined to run away from whatever it is you used to be — to disappear. Congratulations, you got your wish."

Lily and Buffy are now escorted to a group of new human slaves. A demon guard barks at them: "Whatever you thought, whatever you were, does not matter. You are nothing." He looks at the first of the new slaves and asks, "Who are you?"

"Aaron," the young man responds.[4] The demon strikes him to the ground with a mace, turns to Lily and again asks, "Who are you?"

"No one," Lily responds, terrified. The guard moves to the next slave and asks again, getting another frightened response of "No one." Now he approaches Buffy.

"Who are you?"

Buffy looks up at him and says with glee in her voice, "I'm Buffy. The vampire slayer. And you are?" Buffy kills the now angered guard with ease; turning to the frightened humans, she says, "Anyone who's not having fun here, follow me."

The scene now becomes a chaotic battle, as Buffy knocks down and kills many demon guards, drawing attention away from the escaping humans, who are led by Lily. "You can handle this," Buffy assures the frightened Lily, "because I say so." Ken, however, catches the fleeing Lily on a balcony and holds a knife to her throat, halting Buffy's battle down below.

"Humans don't fight back! That's how this works.... One of you fights, you all die!" He now points his knife at Buffy. "That was not permitted!"

"Yeah," Buffy jeers, "but it was fun." As Ken begins to rage at her again, Lily pushes him off the balcony. Buffy ascends and joins Lily and the others, raising the gate of hell as the slaves duck under it to freedom. But a now bloodied Ken is not defeated yet, and tackles the escaping Buffy; his legs, however, are skewered and pinned beneath hell's falling, spiked gate, and Buffy stands above his prostrate body.

"You ruined ... you..." Ken stammers.

"Hey Ken, you want to see my impression of Gandhi?" Buffy asks, wryly. She raises Ken's mace and brings it down on his head, then joins Lily and the others as they climb out of hell.

In the end, Buffy gives her apartment and her job to Lily, as well as her alias "Anne" after Lily notices Buffy's nametag from the diner. In the last scene, Buffy returns home to her mother in Sunnydale and they embrace.

We have focused most in this summary on the events of the episode that take place in hell because these events have much in common with the Greek Paschal tradition and its celebration of the harrowing of hell by Jesus Christ. We will next look at the celebration of this story as it is found in two central Greek artworks: the fourth-century Catechetical Homily of St. John Chrysostom, and the fourteenth-century *Anastasis* icon in the monastery at Chora in Istanbul.

The Harrowing of Hell in the Greek Paschal Tradition

The story of Jesus Christ found in the New Testament gospels — his birth, ministry, death, resurrection, and ascension — is a familiar one in Western society and is central to nearly all denominations and sects of the Christian religion. The doctrine of Christ's harrowing of hell, however, is more controversial: some Christian traditions reject it, others hold it but do not highlight it, and still others celebrate it as one of the most central and dear doctrines of their faith.[5] The Greek Orthodox Church belongs to this last group. Each year, just before midnight on Holy Saturday, the Orthodox faithful gather for an Easter worship service called the Paschal Liturgy of St. John Chrysostom, which consists of prayers, hymns, and scripture readings focusing not only on the resurrection of Christ, but also on his descent into and harrowing of hell. The sermon preached every year at the Paschal Liturgy is the Catechetical Homily of St. John Chrysostom, a short speech full of the rhetorical flare of its author, the late-fourth-century Greek preacher John Chrysostom. Also central to the Paschal feast is an icon, a religious painting which depicts in vivid color the central event that is being celebrated in the feast. The icon for the great feast of Pascha is the *Anastasis* icon, the most famous of which was painted in the fourteenth century on the walls of the Chora monastery in Istanbul. Though *anastasis* means resurrection, the icon does not depict Christ's emergence from the tomb on Easter morning. Instead, it depicts Christ's triumph in hell on Holy Saturday.

First, let us briefly examine the harrowing of hell as it is recounted in the Catechetical Homily of John Chrysostom. The homily is a short one, consisting of an extended call for all people to celebrate the feast of Pascha. Chrysostom then transitions into a more narrative explanation of the salvation and the defeat of death that is being celebrated: "No one need lament poverty, for the kingdom is seen as universal. No one need grieve over sins; forgiveness has dawned from the tomb. No one need fear death; the Savior's death has freed us from it."[6] According to Chrysostom, poverty, sin, and death have all been done away with by the Savior, Christ. He then explains that this has been accomplished by Christ's descent into and harrowing of hell:

> While its captive He stifled it. He despoiled Hades as He descended into it; it was angered when it tasted His flesh. Foreseeing this, Isaiah proclaimed: "Hades," he said, "was angered when he met You below." It was angered because it was abolished. It was angered because it was mocked. It was angered because it was slain. It was angered because it was shackled. It received a body and encountered God. It took earth and came face to face with heaven. It took what it saw and fell by what it could not see. Death, where is your sting? Hades, where is your victory?[7]

Christ, Chrysostom explains, descended into hell and was made its captive; hell even "tasted his flesh." But instead of being pleased, hell was "angered." Through repetition of grammatical structure in the fourth through seventh sentences, Chrysostom gives four reasons why hell was angered: Christ abolished it, mocked it, slew it, and shackled it. In the next three sentences, Chrysostom creates a new repeating structure, stating first what hell thought it took when it took Christ, then what it actually received. It took a body, but got God; it took earth, but got heaven; it took what was seen, but got what was unseen. He then quotes the well-known New Testament dictum from 1 Corinthians 15:55: "O Death, where is your sting? O Hades, where is your victory?"

Chrysostom, however, is not quite finished. He now turns to the resurrection of Christ and explains in more detail what has happened to hell now that Christ has risen: "Christ is risen and demons have fallen. Christ is risen and angels rejoice. Christ is risen and life rules. Christ is risen and not one dead remains in the tomb. For Christ, having risen from the dead, has become the firstfruits of those that slept. To Him be the glory and the dominion forever. Amen."[8] The focus is no longer hell itself, but the angelic powers and humans involved in its harrowing. First, the evil angelic powers, the demons, are "fallen." The righteous angelic powers, the angels, "rejoice." The humans, those who had been "dead," no longer "remain in the tomb," but are now risen with Christ, for death no longer has dominion over them, but instead "life rules." Further, the risen Christ is the "firstfruits of those that slept," meaning that all who die can now expect to be resurrected as Christ was before them.

To summarize, Chrysostom presents a powerful piece of rhetoric in this homily, depicting Christ as one who descends into hell, angers hell through tricking it, mocking it, abolishing it, and slaying its demons, and, finally, rises from hell, leading its captive dead back up to life along with him. This is Chrysostom's account of the harrowing of hell, a sermon familiar to and beloved by Orthodox Christians around the world, preached yearly at the Church's most holy festival.[9]

Prominently displayed in every church during the Paschal feast is the *Anastasis* icon.[10] As each worshipper enters the Church, she venerates this icon by bowing, making the sign of the cross over herself, and kissing it. The setting depicted in the icon is hell. Two rocky crags jut up in the background on each side of the icon. Beyond the crags is inky blackness. In the foreground, framed by the crags, are three groups of people. The groups on the left and right look toward the central group of three figures—Christ, Adam, and Eve. In the middle of this central group is Christ, wearing white robes, surrounded by a star-spangled blue and white mandorla of heavenly glory, and standing above the fallen gates of hell. In each hand, Christ grasps the wrist of a sinner, raising them up from their respective graves. The bearded sinner on the left is Adam, the first man, and his counterpart on the right is Eve, the first woman. Christ's raising up of Adam and Eve signifies that Christ, in his harrowing of hell, is not just saving a few particular people, but the entire human race descended from Adam and Eve.

As mentioned above, two groups of hell-dwelling humans look on as Christ raises Adam and Eve from their tombs. By their halos, we can tell that the people on the left are saints. Despite their holiness, however, they too are bound by death and can only be freed by Christ. One more figure, somewhat obscured by time, is important in the icon. That figure lies below Christ, alongside the fallen gates of hell. The figure is surrounded by broken locks and chains, and his hands and legs are bound. This figure is Satan, or Death, or both. He is clearly the loser in the painting, pinned and shackled below the triumphant Christ and the newly freed humans over whom he previously ruled.

Though this icon depicts different images than what Chrysostom describes in his homily, they share three major details central to the Orthodox doctrine of Christ's harrowing of hell. First, Christ triumphantly reveals his divine self once he has descended into hell. In both the homily and the icon, Christ is no mere human, no mere suffering servant; he is the triumphant God, his heavenly nature clearly discernible to all.[11] Second, both hell and its demonic inhabitants are frustrated and defeated. In Chrysostom, hell and its demons are not only angered and mocked, but slain and abolished; in the icon this is depicted by the fallen, bound figure below Christ. Third, the dead in hell are raised up to life by Christ. This is described at the end of Chrysostom's homily, and is memorably depicted in the three central figures of the icon.

"Anne" and the Greek Paschal Tradition in Conversation

Now that we have summarized both the work of Whedon and the worship of the Greek Church, we can hold them up to one another and note both similarities and differences. The first and most obvious similarity between "Anne," Chrysostom's homily, and the *Anastasis* icon is that they depict the same basic activities. All three depict a triumphant hero in hell, defeated demonic powers fallen to the ground, and the hero's liberation of hell's human captives.

More similarities stand out when we compare "Anne" with only Chrysostom's homily. Hell is angered in both, and in each this is due to the hero's activities of mocking, slaying, and abolishing it. In Chrysostom, Christ mocks, slays, and abolishes hell itself, and causes the fall of hell's demons. In "Anne," Buffy mocks both her demon guards and Ken, the Satanic ruler of hell. In response to Ken's anger at her defiance, she says, "It was fun, though," and wryly references the peace-loving Gandhi before crushing Ken's head.[12] Instead of answering "No one" to the demon guard's question "Who are you?" Buffy cheerily tells him her name and asks him for his, which enrages the guard.

Just as Christ angers hell by "slaying" it in Chrysostom's homily, so Buffy does her own share of slaying. She not only slays all of the demon guards who attack her, but also ends her adventure by slaying Ken himself, first dropping the gate on him, then crushing his skull. Lily even joins in this slaying by pushing the angry Ken off the balcony. This is also the most explicit parallel of Chrysostom's words "the demons have fallen" in the episode. Finally, just as Christ has abolished hell through his work, Ken's final words to Buffy are that she has ruined something. He does not get a chance to say what exactly she has ruined due to being bludgeoned to death, but Buffy has clearly ruined his whole hellish realm; she has slain him and his demons, and has freed his prisoners. Hell has been abolished.

Next, let us compare "Anne" to the *Anastasis* icon, for there we find an even closer iconic similarity. In the icon, Satan/death lies among the fallen gates of hell, with the triumphant Christ standing above him. In the final scene in hell in "Anne," Ken, the Satanic ruler, lies beneath the fallen gate of hell, shackled not by fetters but by the gate itself. Buffy, like Christ, stands above him, triumphant over her foe, leading hell's captives back up to life.

For all these parallels of action and imagery, however, we have not yet touched on the key thematic union between Whedon's episode and the Greek Paschal tradition. This is the theme of the tricking of hell through first the hidden, then revealed, identity of the harrowing hero. According to Chrysostom, Christ angers hell not just by defeating its demons and freeing its captives, but by *tricking* it. When Christ dies on the cross and descends into hell,

hell tastes Christ's flesh, expecting him to be three things: a physical body, an earthly being, and a merely visible being. In technical theological terms, we might say that, according to Chrysostom, hell only sees Christ's *human nature*. He appears to be just another dead human. But then, with the great power and glory displayed in the *Anastasis* icon, Christ reveals himself to be God, to be heavenly, and to have also an invisible *divine nature*. Hell has been tricked, and its overwhelming reaction to Christ's revelation of his true, divine identity is anger. Conversely, this trickery could be implied to have the opposite effect upon both human and heavenly onlookers. As Christ dies and descends into hell, it seems to those who love him that all has been lost, that his fate is that of all ordinary humans: death and hell. But, as Chrysostom describes, once Christ's true identity is revealed, the "angels rejoice," and those who were in the tomb are raised to life and given a new identity; no longer damned souls, they are now living Christians.

The same tricking of hell is seen in "Anne." We see in the conversation between Ken and Buffy in the prison cell hell's delight at having caught her. Ken gloats that she is in hell, a place where all hope is gone and only despair and namelessness remain. He explains to her who he thinks she is: "I know you, Anne. So afraid, so pathetically determined to run away from whatever it is you used to be — to disappear." In Ken's eyes, Buffy is Anne: afraid, pathetic, and determined to reject her old identity. But in the next scene, Buffy does not call herself "No one" and does not even call herself "Anne," but instead her true name and title: "Buffy the Vampire Slayer." We see that Ken was wrong. She is not afraid, but brave; not pathetic, but inspiring; and, far from rejecting her old identity, she embraces it with deadly results. And this revelation of identity in the depths of hell can be seen as an emotional and thematic center of not only the scene or the episode, but even of the show as a whole.

Feminine Identity in Buffy

For all of the images, events, and themes that "Anne" shares with the Greek Paschal tradition, there are some major differences. First, Buffy is very different from Christ. She is neither God nor a man.[13] Further, there is a real sense in which Buffy is in danger of defeat and despair throughout the episode. Buffy goes to Los Angeles not out of the pure and self-sacrificial love for humankind that Christ brings to Israel, but out of grief. Her motives, even as she helps Lily, are mixed, and she is full of hesitation and anger. Finally, Buffy does not get to hell by dying, but by falling through a dimensional portal. For, as we learn throughout the series, there are many hell dimensions full of suffering and death. Thus, Buffy's harrowing of hell and freeing of the captives only defeats some demons and frees some people; she is far from acting as a universal savior.

Still, our placing of "Anne" in conversation with the Greek Paschal tradition has led us to the theme of identity as central to both. If we look at the character arcs of both Buffy and Lily, we will see the question of identity as paramount in each. Buffy, on coming to Los Angeles, hides her identity by both changing her name and reverting to a normal, human job: she was Buffy the Vampire Slayer, but she becomes Anne the waitress. Further, when Lily recognizes her as Buffy, Buffy rejects her former identity. No longer is she a slayer. In our glimpse of Joyce and Giles back in Sunnydale, Joyce asks the blunt question about Buffy: "Who exactly is she?" Lily, too, has been going through an identity crisis. In season two she was Chanterelle, lover of vampires, until Buffy saved her. Chanterelle was not only mistaken about vampires being venerable, but also about the meaning of her name. In their first one-on-one conversation it is not only Lily who recognizes the true identity of Anne, but also Buffy who recognizes the true meaning of *Chanterelle*.

When Ken tells Buffy in hell that she is running away from what she used to be, he is partially right.[14] And hell, we realize, is the place where identity is lost forever. "I'm no one" is what hell teaches its captives to say. But Buffy can neither call herself "No one" nor let Lily be stripped of whatever identity she has; when she reveals and reclaims her true identity, Buffy empowers Lily. Lily can escape and help others, Buffy tells her, because *she*, Buffy the Vampire Slayer, says she can. And finally, Buffy not only passes on her apartment and job to Lily, but also the name Anne. Thus, when Buffy finds her own identity, those around her are enabled and empowered to discover their identities, too. We learn in season two of *Angel* that Lily, now Anne, does quite well for herself after her adventure with Buffy. She has not only kept a job and an identity, but has also opened up a shelter for homeless kids and from time to time helps Angel Investigations fight evil in Los Angeles. Lily's identity arc in the Buffyverse, then, moves from Chanterelle, who does not even know the meaning of her name; to Lily, who recognizes Buffy as the slayer, but cannot escape hell on her own; to Anne, who cares for and rescues others, mirroring in her capacity as a normal human what Buffy performs in her capacity as a slayer.[15]

A Christian Universe?

Given the many parallels of action, image, and theme between Christ's story and Buffy's, we are led to a provocative question: can the universe of Whedon's "Anne"— and by extension, of *Buffy* as a whole — be called a *Chris-*

tian universe? Though such a reading is tempting, it is wishful and flawed, not only because of Whedon's clearly stated atheism but also because of the nature of the universe he has created. Buffy's world has no known god in it, no fall of man, and, most important, no second person of a triune deity who becomes incarnate to save fallen humanity from death and hell.

The universe in "Anne" does, however, resemble a Christian universe in two major ways. First, hell, a demonic realm of despair where humans are made captive, exists. And second, the heroic response to hell is to descend into it, reveal one's true nature, slay the demons, and free the captives.[16] The harrowing of hell is a distinctly Christ-like *activity*, whether it takes place in a Christian universe or not. In closing, then, we might see Buffy's adventure in "Anne" as a sort of agnostic, feminist version of the Christian narrative of the harrowing of hell: Buffy, the prodigal daughter, slays hell, frees its captives, empowers her female follower, and returns to her mother's house more her true, strong self than ever before. Though she asks Ken if he wants to see her impression of Gandhi, it is Buffy's impression of Christ that lingers long in our minds, and that may — if Whedon has succeeded — empower and uncover in us our own, true selves.

Notes

1. If we do not count Buffy's brief dips into the hellmouth in seasons four and seven, "Anne" is, in fact, the only time in the whole of *Buffy the Vampire Slayer* that Buffy literally descends into hell. There is a major difference between Buffy's descent into hell in this episode and her descents below the hellmouth in "Doomed" (4.11) and "Chosen" (7.22). In "Anne," Buffy descends into another *dimension*, a hell dimension where time passes differently than in the world above. In "Doomed" and "Chosen" Buffy does not enter another dimension when she enters the hellmouth, but finds herself in a cavern that appears to be contiguous with both the geography and the temporality of the environment above the hellmouth.

2. The word *pascha* is a Hellenization of the Hebrew word for *passover*. Further, the Latin word *paschalis* and the English word *passion* come from the Greek *pascha*. Each spring the Jewish festival of the Passover generally coincides with the Roman Catholic celebration of Easter and the Greek celebration of Pascha. This is due, of course, to the fact that Christ's passion, death, and resurrection took place during the Jewish feast of the Passover, thus connecting historically the Jewish feast of Passover and the Christian celebration of Holy Week and Pascha.

3. The term *harrowing* traditionally refers to Christ's frustration and overthrow of the powers of hell along with his emptying hell of its human prisoners.

4. It is worth noting that the only other human named in hell besides Buffy is Aaron. In the Old Testament book of Exodus, Aaron is the right hand and mouth of Moses, who leads the captive Israelites out of Egypt. The exodus from Egypt is the Old Testament narrative on which the Greek Paschal tradition draws most heavily, as can be seen in the Paschal poem of Melito of Sardis. For more on the Paschal appropriation of Exodus and Melito's poem, see Melito of Sardis, *On Pascha*, trans. Alistair Stewart-Sykes (Crestwood, NY: St. Vladimir's Seminary Press, 2001).

5. For a good overview of the development and controversy surrounding this doctrine, see J. A. MacCulloch, *The Harrowing of Hell: A Comparative Study of an Early Christian Doctrine* (Edinburgh: T&T Clark, 1930).

6. Greek Orthodox Archdiocese of America, *Let us be Radiant*, accessed February 2, 2013, http://www.goarch.org/archdiocese/departments/outreach/greatlent/resurrectionhandout.
7. Ibid.
8. Ibid.
9. Traditionally, the congregation takes part in the preaching of the sermon, chanting "It was angered!" and "Christ is risen!" every time the priest reads each phrase.
10. A good, high quality image of this icon can be found at http://en.wikipedia.org/wiki/File:Chora_Anastasis1.jpg.
11. As Alyssa Lyra Pitstick explains, "Christ's clothing, activity, and mandorla in this icon are in unmistakable contrast to the naked, limp, and apparently merely human Christ in icons of the crucifixion. On the cross, he suffers; in hades, he acts with power." Alyssa Lyra Pitstick, *Light in Darkness: Hans Urs von Balthasar and the Catholic Doctrine of Christ's Descent into Hell* (Grand Rapids: Eerdmans, 2007), 78.
12. This reference to Gandhi curiously reinforces the Christ-like activities of the slayer. Gandhi is famed for his resistance to oppression through nonviolence. Though Christ is very active once he is in hell, it is his nonviolent submission to torture and death that enables and leads to the harrowing of hell. Thus, for all the irony of Buffy's Gandhi reference, it serves as a reminder of the submissive, nonviolent subversion involved in the victorious work of both Christ and Gandhi.
13. This is not to say that Buffy is not human, only that she is not male. In that both Christ and Buffy possess a human nature, they are indeed similar at a fundamental level, a similarity that enables Christ, according to Christian theology, to truly save all of fallen humanity. In contemporary discussions of gender and Christology, theologians like Elisabeth Behr-Sigel have helpfully stressed Christ's representation and redemption, in his humanity, of both genders, and his free offer of salvation to woman no less than man. See Elisabeth Behr-Sigel, "Woman Too is in The Image of God," *Mid-Stream* 21, no 3 (July 1982), 369–375.
14. Indeed, one of Whedon's common tropes is to have words of truth come from the mouth of the villain, often at the chagrin of the protagonists.
15. Fruitful research could be done reading Lily's identity arc as parallel to that of the disciples in the New Testament. For the disciples, too, begin in ignorance (1 Peter 1:14), even worshipping demons; then encounter Jesus and recognize him as savior (Matthew 16:15–16); are saved by Christ from death and hell (Romans 8:2); and finally are given a new name and identity in Christ, sent into the world to love and save others (John 1:40–42; Matthew 28:18–20).
16. Such a response is not that of the classical Greco-Roman hero, who, as exemplified by Odysseus and Aeneas, enters hell to gain some knowledge from its inhabitants. This classical hero never angers hell, slays its rulers, or — with the exception of Orpheus — frees its captives. The pagan hero, for the most part, leaves hell as it is. See Homer, *The Odyssey*, book 11; Virgil, *The Aeneid*, book 6; and Ovid, *Metamorphoses*, book 10.

BIBLIOGRAPHY

Behr-Sigel, Elisabeth. "Woman Too Is in the Image of God." *Mid-Stream* 21, no. 3 (July 1982): 369–375.
Greek Orthodox Archdiocese of America. *Let Us Be Radiant*. Accessed February 2, 2013. http://www.goarch.org/archdiocese/departments/outreach/greatlent/resurrectionhandout.
MacCulloch, J. A. *The Harrowing of Hell: A Comparative Study of an Early Christian Doctrine*. Edinburgh: T&T Clark, 1930.
Melito of Sardis. *On Pascha*. Translated by Alistair Stewart-Sykes. Crestwood, NY: St. Vladimir's Seminary Press, 2001.
Pitstick, Alyssa Lyra. *Light in Darkness: Hans Urs von Balthasar and the Catholic Doctrine of Christ's Descent into Hell*. Grand Rapids: Eerdmans, 2007.

Mary and Buffy Walk into a Bar
The Virgin Deity and Buffy the Vampire Slayer

VALERIE MAYHEW

> *The virgin slayer stalks her prey by night, the dim moonlight leaving her sharpened wooden weapon obscured by dark shadows. With super human strength and unnatural speed she works tirelessly to keep her companions safe. She is ... Artemis, the maiden goddess of the hunt and the moon, protectress of women.*

Television writing is messy business. Excruciatingly short deadlines, impossible budgets that never stretch far enough, frantic studio and network management needing to be pleased (not to mention young development executives who are convinced they know more about writing than the writers). It often seems that it is a miracle that anything at all — let alone anything worthwhile — makes it onto the small screen. But every so often the stars align and something not just worthwhile but downright wonderful is born. Such is the case with Joss Whedon's *Buffy the Vampire Slayer*.

Much has been made both in formal papers and informal internet posts about Buffy's feminist hero persona, her groundbreaking gender-bending role, her message of female empowerment. In fact, a June 2012 article in *Slate* magazine counted over two hundred academic papers, essays, and books on *Buffy* with most of those focusing on one of the above themes.[1] But a question arises: was Mr. Whedon's creation — first seen in the 1992 movie and then resurrected in the 1997–2003 series — as groundbreaking as it first seems? Did the arrival of Buffy mark a turning point in male-created female characters, or did it actually hearken back to a figure or figures from long ago? In fact, is there something profoundly archetypal in Buffy Summers, vampire slayer? Something beyond mere heroine that touches upon the divine?

Conceivably one might even posit that the evolution of Buffy the character, especially in the first television seasons, mimics the evolution of female deities through time. And if that is so, perhaps there is a modern theological message to be heard and something new to discover in yet one more exploration of *Buffy the Vampire Slayer*.

Buffy Inherits the Mantle of Kick-Ass Virgin

In the beginning, there was wholeness for female deities. In the Neolithic period of history, as humans moved from a nomadic existence to a sedentary life based on agriculture instead of foraging, it has been hypothesized that a power shift occurred. While men hunted, women became experts in raising a steady food supply. They learned to clothe their families with abundant, pliable woven plant fibers instead of bulky and scarce animal skins. They preserved the fruits of the harvest ensuring supply for future consumption. They enabled the community to grow, instead of having to maintain a scattered sparse population that followed the migrating prey animals. Thus the role of women became central to the survival and success of the tribe.[2] And with the empowerment of women there arrived an age of matriarchy in society and religion. Fertility rites became central to a successful crop. The mother goddess arose in the Mediterranean.[3]

One such mother goddess, Mami, is described in the Old Babylonian epic *Atrahasis*, dated to at least 1700 B.C.E., as the actual creator of mankind, having mixed clay with blood and formed humans to ease the labor of the gods.[4] Another mother goddess is the Sumerian Ianna (often associated with the Assyrian Ishtar), who features prominently as a powerful force in the *Epic of Gilgamesh*.[5] Ianna/Ishtar is a formidable goddess, with jurisdiction over fertility, war, love, and sex.

But by the classical period of Greece the power of the female deities began to wane, reflecting the decreasing stature of women in Greek society. Around 700 B.C.E. the poet Hesiod wrote his *Theogony*, which became the dominant narrative of the evolution of the gods.[6]

At that point, the early Grecian mother goddess Ge (also spelled "Gaia"), one of the natural, earthy emotional deities, is suddenly and rightfully, in Hesiod's opinion, supplanted by the rational male-dominated Olympians.[7] Over time the female deities were reduced, shattered into smaller more manageable pieces. Power and sexuality are forever separated. The six chief Olympian goddesses — Athena, Artemis, Hera, Hestia, Demeter, and Aphrodite — had much more clearly delineated and specialized roles, especially in regard to their relationships with men (immortal and mortal alike).[8]

The two most physically powerful goddesses, Athena and Artemis, are eternal virgins (as is Hestia, ironically the goddess of hearth and home). It is worth noting that in Athena's immaculate birth from Zeus's head, even the significance of women being the sole bearers of progeny is clearly diminished, affirming for Greek society that the father was the true parent of any child.[9] Athena is the goddess of war and of science, wearing armor and often depicted as androgynous in appearance. She is counselor to many powerful men but eschews marriage, thereby never assuming the traditional female role which would, socially speaking, diminish her power.[10]

Artemis avoids men altogether, hunting by moonlight in the company of girls. She is an example of the unchained female; still physically independent, strong, swift, and agile. She controls her own body; a right that for a mortal woman of her time would have become her husband's if she married.

The two goddesses who retain their sexuality are Hera, wife of Zeus, and Aphrodite, goddesses of love and beauty, both now drawn as petty, jealous, and vain. They are known as complainers, troublemakers, and schemers. Hera is particularly hard on any women who dare to defy her as goddess of marriage. She is said to have cursed the daughters of Proetos, who were beautiful but refused to marry, with a foul stench and loss of their hair.[11] She torments her husband Zeus's many lovers with stinging insects.[12] One of the most beautiful objects associated with Hera is the peacock,[13] but even that supposedly comes from the many eyes of her servant Argus — he with the hundred eyes — whom Hera sent to watch over one of her husband's lovers, Io.[14] This misogynistic view of a woman's sexuality is hard to miss, and so ingrained is it in the mythological retellings that it is always the jealousy of Hera that is mocked, not the continued unfaithfulness of her husband, even in modern books for the student.[15]

Besides having a birth that again bypasses a mother by being born of Uranus's castrated testicles flung into the sea[16] — thereby once again illustrating the overriding importance of the semen in reproduction — the overt sexuality of Aphrodite is always a source of trouble. She begins the Trojan War by promising the beautiful but already married Helen to the warrior Paris in exchange for the hero awarding her the golden apple for being "the most beautiful."[17] Note again that it is the vanity of Aphrodite that is blamed for the bloodshed and not the lust and aggression of the Trojan prince Paris.

In the world of the Hebrew scriptures, too, virginity became fetishized. Among the most commonly quoted instances are Genesis 24:16 regarding Rebecca ("The girl was very beautiful and a virgin guiltless of intercourse with any man"); Exodus 22:16–17 about the prohibited seduction of virgins; Deuteronomy 22:13–21 about the importance of proof of virginity; and of course the well-known passage from Isaiah 7:14 ("Behold, a virgin shall conceive, and bear a son"). Virginity became inextricably interlinked with a woman's worth and, thus, her power.

By Roman times, the Olympian goddess Hestia had become known as Vesta and her elaborate temple in Rome was kept by six Vestal virgins whose job was to maintain the sacred fire that kept the darkness out of the temple.[18] Only the untainted, unbroken vessel can be pure enough to keep the holy flame.

This tradition continued into the Common Era. Catherine Benincasa was born in 1347 and took a vow of perpetual virginity at the age of seven.[19] She became one of the most powerful women of her time, instrumental in moving the papacy from Avignon back to Rome. Today she is known as Saint Catherine of Siena.

After her flirtations with a neighbor almost led to her brothers and father having to take up arms to defend her honor, Teresa de Ahumada y Cepeda, born in 1515, decided to remain a virgin and enter a convent at age twenty, freeing herself from what she perceived as the subjection of marriage.[20] Eventually she would become known as St. Teresa of Avila.

Finally, arguably one of the most powerful of the early church virgin mystics, Hildegard of Bingen was born in 1098 and actually given to the church as a tithe offering when she was a small child.[21] She went on to compose the first known opera; write volumes on medicine, natural science, cooking, nutrition, and poetry; become an influential abbess who protected the property rights of her female postulates; experience mystical communion with God; gain renown as an inspired preacher; and displayed little patience with foolish men, whether it be her confessor St. Bernard of Clairvaux or any pope.[22]

Now, into this murky multimillennia soup of Western theological views on virginity, female power, and the divine, enters Buffy Summers. She accepts the great burden of her gifts, first in the film and then (reluctantly) again in the first episode of the series, "Welcome to the Hellmouth." As Giles reminds both her and the audience in that episode, written by Whedon, "Because you are the slayer. Into each generation a slayer is born. One girl in all the world, a chosen one. One born with the strength and skill to hunt the vampires.

There is no question about the echo of the theological in Whedon's words "chosen one." Buffy's role is preordained from above before her birth. Her destiny is set by forces beyond her control; she is the only one blessed with the ability to kill the dark enemy.

In the beginning of the series, the featured enemy is the vampire (demons and other supernatural beings eventually join the adversarial ranks). Vampires in most mythologies, including that of both Whedon and the father of the modern vampire, Bram Stoker, are sensual creatures, often with perverted sexuality and always with a raw carnality that comes with depending on spilling the blood of others for their own survival.

Contrast this crimson-stained debauched world of the vampire with the first glimpse of Buffy from the aforementioned pilot: the camera sweeps into her room to find her chastely asleep in an all-white bed. She has yet to be awakened, literally and metaphorically. In classical terms, therein lies her power. She is the Vestal virgin charged with keeping the sacred flame burning. She is the untouched virgin whose light and purity are the only defense against the defilement and darkness of the encroaching vampires. It is Buffy's living body — clean, chosen, strong, and agile — that stands against the putridity of those who live on in death. It is easy to forget that she is only a teenage girl.

Buffy Awakens to Be Shattered

From the very first episode of the series, the tall dark man makes his presence known. He watches over Buffy. He brings her information. He guides her. And it is no coincidence that his name is Angel.

In the Bible, angels are God's warriors, messengers, and emissaries. They can look upon the very face of God and not be scorched into ash.[23] They wield flaming swords (Genesis 3:24); they make grown men tremble (Daniel 10:5–11); they do God's will (Psalms 102:20–21). Angels are far from the benign winged creatures that clutter up sentimental greeting cards.

As Angel's story is revealed for the first time ("Angel"), it becomes known that he was once a powerful vampire called Angelus, who was cursed by a gypsy to retain his soul although his body was transformed. Formerly a sadistic killer, Angel now eschews the company of other vampires as well as preying on humans. He is caught in a tormented world, neither human nor monster.

For the teenage girl who just happens to be a slayer, he is the perfect bad boy: dangerous, handsome, sexy, misunderstood, willing to fight for her and by her side. For the first season and a half, Angel is there for her. Their relationship grows and their feelings intensify until they make love on Buffy's seventeenth birthday. And then all hell breaks loose.

For Buffy and Angel, the pleasure of eating the "forbidden fruit" leads to their expulsion from their veritable Garden of Eden. Angel — in that one moment of true bliss wherein he doesn't regret the retention of his soul, when his conscience is no longer a burden — breaks the gypsy's curse and so, ironically, his soul is suddenly lost to him. He reverts to the killer vampire Angelus. In that moment of carnality, their innocence is gone, replaced by knowledge. The purity that protected Buffy is washed away by her sexual congress.

There is more to this chapter of the story than the obvious and very clever high school metaphor of the beloved boy who charms his way into the bed of his girlfriend and then turns into a jerk once the deed is done. And while many a teenage girl can claim her boyfriend became a postcoital demon, perhaps Buffy is the only character for whom this is literally true.

There is profound theological resonance in this aspect of the Buffy saga. The price for the loss of virginity is great: Buffy is plunged into emotional turmoil and profound darkness.

Writing on the works of the virgin saint Teresa of Avila, scholar Beverly Lanzetta posits a "night of the feminine" as a stage on a soul's spiritual journey: "When I say it is a feminine night, I mean the soul suffers the afflictions of its most receptive and intimate nature, in terms of ... the negative wounding sustained from the violence of the world."[24] The harshness of the real world's violence has literally torn into Buffy as symbolized by intercourse with the supernatural Angel. She has, in essence, been demoted from her beatific perch in the divine canon of the pure to the brokenness of mere mortality. Her world is turned upside down — her heart broken, her loyalties lost, and her lover becoming the most treacherous of enemies.

There is another parallel in the world of theology here and that is to look at Buffy's transcendent sexual encounter and subsequent negative consequences in light of the experiences of the women religious mystics. The ecstatic, erotic intimacy of the Christian female mystic's experience is clear from the writings of many; from Julian of Norwich in the fourteenth century ("This is the revelation of love which, Jesus Christ, our endless bliss made in sixteen showings")[25] to Saint Therese of Lisieux in the nineteenth century ("Lord, you know it, I have no other treasures than the souls it has pleased You to unite to mine").[26] Again, Lanzetta: "Defined as a caring, closeness, or affection between subjects that is inmost to them, intimacy is a central feature of women's mystical texts.... At the highest states of mystical consciousness, intimacy — as the collapsing, fusing, or annihilating of boundaries between self and Other — is interpretation."[27]

But there are consequences for this uniquely female way of experiencing a divine union as opposed to the church-approved apophatic mystical experience of God as exemplified by male mystics, such as St. John of the Cross in his seminal work *Dark Night of the Soul*. For the male-dominated clergy, God can only be defined by what he is not; the "proper" mystical experience is one of negation and loss of self, rather than the "hysterical," sexualized cataphatic rapture of the female mystic. As Lanzetta goes on to explain, "It is precisely these deeper expressions of divine intimacy that subject the women mystics to scrutiny, accusations of heresy, and, in some cases, death."[28]

Scrutiny, accusations of heresy to her cause, the threat of death — Buffy suffers all these and more because she fell in love and had sex with a vampire, the very creature she has sworn to destroy. She has truly fallen from grace and finds herself confused and full of self-doubt, her mission as the Chosen One in jeopardy.

Buffy Reborn

But Mr. Whedon doesn't leave his character trapped forever there: in despair, regretting her loss of virginity and ignoring her newfound sexuality. No, the viewer is challenged to continue past the easy high school girl parallels as Buffy moves into true womanhood.

There is, of course, one virgin holy figure — a teenager herself, no less — yet to be discussed, and it is along her theological path that Buffy finds the reintegration of her shattered self mirrored: the Virgin Mary.

It is beyond the scope of this paper to delve into the heated debate on the value and historicity of the Virgin Birth. Suffice it to say that Mariology and the doctrine of the virgin birth are among the hottest topics in feminist theology.[29] From complete dismissal of the narrative as patriarchal stereotyping "of the feminine which is variously identified with mothers, affectivity, darkness, or virginity"[30] to denouncing the image of Mary entirely as "symbolically dangerous for women, perpetuating sexual submission and even legitimatizing rape,"[31] the discussions surrounding the impact of Mary and the birth of Jesus are numerous and varied.

However, it can be argued that what informs Buffy's reclaiming of her own power, even with her broken heart, is a sort of divinely sanctioned wholeness through which we can also interpret Mary's story.

In contrast to the classical virgin deities and early Christian saints whose virginity marked them as separate from the mainstream world of men, the story of Mary is one of heavenly affirmation and acceptance. Without social validity through marriage and without religious access through submission to a husband, Mary was deemed good enough, righteous enough, just as she was. Mary was of age to be betrothed so it can be known that the menses was upon her and that her community would have seen her as unclean by religious law; but her God did not see her so. In the virgin birth narratives, her body is more than a way for her husband's seed to carry on a patriarchal name. In fact, her body was good enough to be the vessel for the enfleshing of God — just as she was. Without the ritual cleansing of the *mikvah* prescribed by religious elders, without the betrothed husband decided for her by family contract and village politics, without the patriarchal protection of a tribal name, she was enough for God. Mary was whole just as she was. Here in Mary is the reintegration of the ruptured female deity, the regeneration of the earth mother and all her parts.

Hildegard of Bingen fought against the medieval church's dictate of second-class theological status for women — a church doctrine that went so far as to bar physicians from treating menstrual cramps and childbirth pain because they were the deserved punishment for Eve's temptation at the Fall.[32] She argued against this misogyny, stating that Mary's part in the incarnation has counteracted any special curse the woman may carry from Eve. This is powerfully expressed in her poetry, especially *O virga ac diadema*:

> Then the heavenly organs resounded together
> And the whole earth was amazed,
> O Mary worthy of praise,
> Because God loved you very much.
> O how there must be wailing and mourning
> Because sorrow has flowed into a woman in guilt
> Through the advice of the serpent.
> For that very woman whom God put as the mother of all
> Plucked out her own heart with the wounds of ignorance
> And brought forth full grief to her own race.
> But O Dawn, from your belly
> A new sun has come forth
> Who has erased all the guilts of Eve
> And has brought forth a greater blessing through you
> Than the harm Eve did to mankind.
> So, O Lady Savior, who has brought forth a new light to the human race
> Gather up the limbs of your Son
> To Heavenly Harmony.[33]

Here Hildegard goes so far as to call Mary the "Savior Maiden," attributing a divine role to the mortal virgin. It is also of interest to note that Hildegard attributes to Eve the "wounds of ignorance" in contrast to the sin of gaining knowledge. I think this has particular resonance in the Buffy story, wherein Buffy does not set out to disobey any holy commandment or bring disarray to the sacred order by her encounter with Angel. The "fall" from her graced virgin state has lasting consequences that she could not have foreseen, just as Hildegard suggests with Eve.

In another of her writings, *Liber divinorum operum* (Book of Divine Works), Hildegard again relates the brokenness of the fallen Eve with the healing of Mary's motherhood: "Eve was not created from the seed of man but from his flesh, since God created her with the same power by which He sent His Son into the Virgin. And thereafter none were found to be like Eve, the virgin and mother, nor Mary, the mother and virgin."[34] The belief in the priority of the seed/semen in defining lineage from the classical Greek period well into the early Christian era is openly challenged here, and the schism between sexuality and power in the sacred feminine begins to heal.

So, too, Buffy Summers must come to realize her own strength, her own success without the help and guidance of her male protector Angel. She no longer has the archetypal otherworldly protection of virginity and purity against the dark forces, but she comes to realize she has something just as strong, just as forceful in her new integrated self, if not more so.

There is a further echo of Mary in the Buffy story: they both had to say "yes." In the annunciation narrative told in the first chapter of the book of Luke, the angel Gabriel is sent by God to Mary. The heavenly messenger announces, "'Greetings, most favored one! The Lord is with you.' But she was deeply troubled by what he said and wondered what this greeting could mean" (Luke 1:28–29). Gabriel must explain in detail what God is asking her to do — to bear a son without benefit of husband for the good of all. It is a hard choice, but clearly a choice. Gabriel does not depart from Mary until she has given her answer: "'I am the Lord's servant,' said Mary; 'may it be as you have said.' Then the angel left her" (Luke 1:38).

For Buffy, her initiation begins in the film, where Merrick (Donald Sutherland), sent by the Watchers Council, finds her in her high school gym and explains who he is and what she is, the slayer. Buffy (Kristy Swanson) is troubled, to say the least, although eventually both circumstances and Merrick's knowledge of her recurring dreams convince her and she finally agrees to take on her responsibilities for the greater good. For Buffy in the series, starting at a new school in a new town, vampires are the last thing on her mind and she at first turns away from the new watcher, Giles. Eventually, however, she reaffirms her commitment to the role which fate has dealt her.

The choice for both may seem like an easy one for a modern audience. Who wouldn't want to be special, to be chosen, to have a hand in the salvation of humanity one way or another? That's what heroines do, right?

But credit must be given to Mr. Whedon, for he has fully developed the truth of his universe where the consequences for the teenage Buffy accepting her destiny are indeed serious since he has given a very human face to a supernatural problem. For Buffy, in saying "yes" to her calling, risks popularity, normalcy, dating, and permanently destroying her already fragile relationship with her mother, not to mention life and death.

For Mary, the choice could have been life or death as well. Joseph, her betrothed, could easily have had her stoned to death for adultery when he found her pregnant. This time it is Matthew 1:19 which explains, "Being a man of principle, and at the same time wanting to save her from exposure, Joseph made up his mind to have the marriage contract quietly set aside." But, as it was for Buffy, it is a dream that convinces Joseph to continue his engagement to Mary, to help her fulfill her divine role: "He had resolved on this, when an angel of the Lord appeared to him in a dream and said, 'Joseph, son of David, do not be afraid to take Mary home with you to be your wife. It is through the Holy Spirit that she has conceived" (Matthew 1:20).

Buffy and Mary said "yes." That yes, such a simple and easily spoken word, sends each teenage girl on a difficult, painful journey that ultimately results in the salvation of a broken world.

Conclusion

If there is a modern theological message for women today to take away from the Buffy saga, it surely must be *keep going*. The road ahead is long and often torturous and there may be danger around every corner, but ultimately there is a place of strength, a redemption of the integrated self, a sanctuary full of the power of the sacred feminine in which to rest. It is too easy to get lost and confused and to fill our spirits with a self-doubt that can weary even the staunchest of faithful souls. But if we resist the need for immediate gratification and remember that we stand on the shoulders of thousands of foremothers, we just might find the strength to journey on into the wondrous mystery of the unknown.

Women have wrestled with their place in God's story for thousands of years. Buffy Summers reminds us that sometimes that place is front and center, fighting the good fight, acting fearless in the face of fear, and kicking some demon ass.

Amen, sister.

NOTES

1. Daniel Lametti, Aisha Harris, Natasha Geiling, and Natalie Matthews-Ramo, "Which Pop Culture Property Do Academics Study the Most?" *Slate*, June 11, 2012, http://www.slate.com/blogs/browbeat/2012/06/11/pop_culture_studies_why_do_academics_study_buffy_the_vampire_slayer_more_than_the_wire_the_matrix_alien_and_the_simpsons_.html.
2. Eva Cantarella, *Pandora's Daughters: The Role and Status of Women in Greek and Roman Antiquity*, trans. Maureen B. Fant (Baltimore: Johns Hopkins University Press, 1987), 12.
3. Ibid., 12–13.
4. Stephanie Dalley, trans., *Myths from Mesopotamia: Creation, the Flood, Gilgamesh, and Others* (Oxford: Oxford University Press, 1989), 4.
5. Ibid., 44.
6. Sarah B. Pomeroy, *Goddesses, Whores, Wives, and Slaves: Women in Classical Antiquity* (New York: Random House, 1995), 1.
7. Ibid., 2.
8. Ibid., 4.
9. Ibid., 5.
10. Cantarella, *Pandora's Daughters*, 28.

11. Ibid., 18.
12. Ingri D'Aulaire and Edgar Pain D'Aulaire, *Book of Greek Myths* (New York: Delacorte Press, 1962), 27.
13. *Bulfinch's Mythology*, ed. Richard Martin (New York: HarperCollins, 1991), 8.
14. D'Aulaire, *Greek Myths*, 27.
15. Ibid., 28.
16. Marilyn B. Skinner, *Sexuality in Greek and Roman Culture* (Malden: Blackwell, 2005), 23.
17. D'Aulaire, *Greek Myths*, 180.
18. *Bulfinch's Mythology*, 725.
19. Carol Lee Flinders, *Enduring Grace: Living Portraits of Seven Women Mystics* (San Francisco: HarperSanFrancisco, 1993), 107.
20. Ibid., 162–163.
21. *Hildegard of Bingen: Selected Writings*, trans. Mark Atherton (New York: Penguin Books, 2001), xiii.
22. Shawn Madigan, ed., *Mystics, Visionaries, and Prophets: A Historical Anthology of Women's Spiritual Writings* (Minneapolis: Fortress, 1998), 94.
23. See Origen, *De Principiis,* chapter viii (written c. 230); and Thomas Aquinas, *Summa Theologiae*, part one (written 1265–1274), among many others.
24. Beverly J. Lanzetta, *Radical Wisdom: A Feminist Mystical Theology* (Minneapolis: Fortress, 2004), 125.
25. *Julian of Norwich: Showings*, trans. Edmund Colledge and James Walsh (New York: Paulist Press, 1978), 175.
26. Flinders, *Enduring Grace*, 218.
27. Lanzetta, *Radical Wisdom*, 58–59.
28. Ibid., 59.
29. See Ute Ranke-Heinemann, *Putting Away Childish Things* (San Francisco: HarperSanFrancisco, 1995); Jane Schaberg, *The Illegitimacy of Jesus: A Feminist Theological Interpretation of the Infancy Narratives*, 20th anniversary ed. (Sheffield: Sheffield Phoenix Press, 2006); and Marcella Althaus-Reid and Lisa Isherwood, *Controversies in Feminist Theology* (London: SCM Canterbury Press, 2007).
30. Nicola Slee, "The Holy Spirit and Spirituality," in *The Cambridge Companion to Feminist Theology*, ed. Susan Frank Parsons (Cambridge: Cambridge University Press, 2002), 183.
31. Mary Daly, *Gyn/Ecology: The Metaethics of Radical Feminism* (Boston: Beacon Press, 1990), 75.
32. Barbara Newman, *Sister of Wisdom: St. Hildegard's Theology of the Feminine* (Berkeley: University of California Press, 1987).
33. Translation courtesy Leigh Hansen and James Asturga.
34. Sabina Flanagan, trans., *Secrets of God: Writings of Hildegard of Bingen* (Boston: Shambhala, 1996), 79.

Bibliography

Althaus-Reid, Marcella, and Lisa Isherwood. *Controversies in Feminist Theology*. London: SCM Canterbury Press, 2007.
Bulfinch, Thomas. *Bulfinch's Mythology*. Edited by Richard Martin. New York: HarperCollins, 1991.
Canterella, Eva. *Pandora's Daughters: The Role and Status of Women in Greek and Roman Antiquity*. Translated by Maureen B. Fant. Baltimore: Johns Hopkins University Press, 1987.
Dalley, Stephanie, trans. *Myths from Mesopotamia: Creation, the Flood, Gilgamesh, and Others*. Oxford: Oxford University Press, 1989.
Daly, Mary. *Gyn/Ecology: The Metaethics of Radical Feminism*. Boston: Beacon Press, 1990.

D'Aulaire, Ingri, and Edgar Pain D'Aulaire. *Book of Greek Myths*. New York: Delacorte Press, 1962.
Flanagan, Sabina, trans. *Secrets of God: Writings of Hildegard of Bingen*. Boston: Shambhala, 1996.
Flinders, Carol Lee. *Enduring Grace: Living Portraits of Seven Women Mystics*. San Francisco: HarperSanFrancisco, 1993.
Hildegard of Bingen. *Hildegard of Bingen: Selected Writings*. Translated by Mark Atherton. New York: Penguin Books, 2001.
Julian of Norwich. *Julian of Norwich: Showings*. Translated by Edmund Colledge and James Walsh. New York: Paulist Press, 1978.
Lametti, Daniel, Aisha Harris, Natasha Geiling, and Natalie Matthews-Ramo. "Which Pop Culture Property Do Academics Study the Most?" *Slate*, June 11, 2012. http://www.slate.com/blogs/browbeat/2012/06/11/pop_culture_studies_why_do_academics_study_buffy_the_vampire_slayer_more_than_the_wire_the_matrix_alien_and_the_simpsons_.html.
Lanzetta, Beverly J. *Radical Wisdom: A Feminist Mystical Theology*. Minneapolis: Fortress, 2004.
Madigan, Shawn, ed. *Mystics, Visionaries and Prophets: A Historical Anthology of Women's Spiritual Writings*. Minneapolis: Fortress, 1998.
Newman, Barbara. *Sister of Wisdom: St. Hildegard's Theology of the Feminine*. Berkeley: University of California Press, 1987.
Pomeroy, Sarah B. *Goddesses, Whores, Wives, and Slaves: Women in Classical Antiquity*. New York: Random House, 1995.
Ranke-Heinemann, Ute. *Putting Away Childish Things*. San Francisco: HarperSanFrancisco, 1995.
Schaberg, Jane. *The Illegitimacy of Jesus: A Feminist Theological Interpretation of the Infancy Narratives*. 20th anniversary ed. Sheffield: Sheffield Phoenix Press, 2006.
Skinner, Marilyn B. *Sexuality in Greed and Roman Culture*. Malden: Blackwell, 2005.
Slee, Nicola. "The Holy Spirit and Spirituality." In *The Cambridge Companion to Feminist Theology*, ed. Susan Frank Parsons, 171–189. Cambridge: Cambridge University Press, 2002.

"Oh ... My ... Goddess"
Witchcraft, Magick and Thealogy in Buffy the Vampire Slayer
Jason Lawton Winslade

In 2004, while conducting fieldwork that became a crucial element of my dissertation, I participated in a ritual created by a small group of ceremonial magicians and Pagan practitioners. This ritual was primarily significant because the group had decided to end the form in which it had existed for over twenty years. This group's ritual cycle generally consisted of a heteronormative couple taking on the roles of priest/priestess and god/goddess for a year, ostensibly representing for the group the duotheistic energy associated with the belief system of various Pagan traditions, particularly Wicca. However, this year, because of internal tensions and dissatisfaction with the group leadership, the majority of the members decided to disband the group but carry on the practice and community in a different way. What was most notable about this ritual, though, was the liturgy. At one point, the priestess spoke of the energetic charge carried by the couple chosen for that year. She asked the ritual participants, "What if you could have that power? Now. All of you. I say we change the rules. I say my power should be our power." As a longtime fan of the show, I immediately recognized this speech from the climactic scene of the final episode of *Buffy the Vampire Slayer*, recapitulating the fundamental rebellion against patriarchy that lies at the heart of the show. I was struck by how remarkably transferable Buffy's speech to the potential slayers was to this situation in which a community wished to change the rules by which they functioned as spiritual practitioners.

It was this ritual that brought to life for me an understanding of Joss Whedon's classic genre television program as a narrative functioning within a kind of theological framework. Of course, the surface associations between the show and the practice of witchcraft had been evident from the beginning, the program's fantastical characterization of Wicca notwithstanding. Here, I wish to unpack this association further, revisiting a perennial critique of the uneasy relationship between nature religions, most prominently Paganism and witchcraft, and popular culture, particularly genre television.[1] More importantly, despite Joss Whedon's oft-noted claims to be an "angry atheist,"[2] I want to demonstrate that the primary action of the show's climax, the charging of the potential slayers that undoes centuries of patriarchal tradition, is not only a magical act, brought on by an evocation of "the Goddess," but one that enacts the basic concerns of feminist theology.

In order to contextualize the connections witchcraft and magic have with feminist theology, we must consider not only the explosion of occultism and witchcraft in popular culture that occurred at the turn of millennium when the program was airing, but also the vibrant relationship between goddess spirituality and feminism occurring while Joss Whedon was being raised by his divorced mother as a "radical feminist."[3] Further, we must identify the ways in which *Buffy the Vampire Slayer* frames the main witch character of the series, Willow, and her magical practice as a religion or spirituality, specifically with regards to identity formation and community-building. While several scholars, including me, have focused primarily on how Willow's practice of magic and witchcraft are crucial factors in her identity formation (particularly her sexual identity), viewing that practice out of context with the feminist agenda of the show's overall narrative provides only a limited interpretation.[4] Therefore, I would like to revisit the deployment of witchcraft tropes in the series within the context of feminist and Pagan theology, a nascent field of study that absorbs some of the lessons of feminist theology, such as the role of consensus in community, nonpatriarchal iconography, and the relationship between the individual and deity. This evolving sense of Pagan theology focuses these lessons more directly on their application to nature religions, such as Wicca, but encompasses a broad range of Pagan beliefs and practices. While one could hardly call the presence of Wicca on *Buffy* in any way accurate or realistic, aspects of these theologies do appear throughout the series. Further, I would argue that the resolution of the show's narrative can only be properly contextualized within the discourse of feminist theology.

On the program, Willow and other characters use the terms *Wicca* and *witch* interchangeably.[5] This elision is worth unpacking, especially due to the tendency of practitioners to make clear distinctions between the two. One might make a surface distinction between Wicca as a form of religion and witchcraft as a practice or methodology, as many practitioners I have interviewed over the years have. However, this variance is certainly not universal. A more specific distinction could be made between witchcraft as a broad category of folk practice that encompasses an immense diversity of cultures, including African and European, while Wicca refers specifically to traditions that coalesced in the 1950s with Gerald Gardner, the first publicly self-proclaimed witch to appear on the British scene after the final repeal of England's Witchcraft and Vagrancy Acts. Gardner was a British civil servant who created his "Gardnerian Wicca" by borrowing generously from Freemasonry (even the nickname "The Craft") and European ceremonial magic and initiatory systems, as practiced by the Hermetic Order of the Golden Dawn and the notorious Aleister Crowley, who wrote treatises on magic (spelled "magick") and the magickal lifestyle.[6] Despite the problematic paternalism and essentialism in his practice, Gardner desired to create more active roles and iconography for women, replacing the monotheism of earlier occult and fraternal traditions with a duotheism that worshipped a general god and goddess, embodied by the functional role of priest and priestess.[7] But like these earlier traditions, Gardnerian Wicca was primarily an initiatory path, in which candidates would swear to secrecy and take oaths similar in structure and form to Masonic rites. Ritual tools, like the athame (a blade for symbolic cutting and directing power) and the pentacle, were also borrowed from these older traditions. Inspired by Aleister Crowley's recommended practice of keeping a "magical journal," Gardner further encouraged practitioners to create their own "Book of Shadows" by culling together herbal recipes, spells, rituals, and their own recorded experiences to create a more interactive version of a medieval grimoire.[8]

After Gardner, various followers and competitors emerged with their own versions of Wicca, such as Alex Sanders who created "Alexandrian Wicca." In the late 1960s and early 1970s, a small occult explosion resulted in a number of new "traditions," those who claimed kinship with Gardner's practices, using *Wicca* as a label, while others preferred to identify with the term *witchcraft*. Still others wished to create broader categories of contemporary Paganism, with traditions that built on Wicca while deemphasizing the initiatory aspect. In these early years of modern witchcraft, dispute over terms and who had the right to use them were common, with some practitioners using *Wicca* and *witchcraft* interchangeably while others vehemently maintaining distinctions.[9] A significant development occurred in the movement once it had migrated from the UK to the USA, with Zuzanna Budapest's Dianic witchcraft, an all-female tradition that emphasized ritual practice that valued women's power.[10] Along similar lines, activist Miriam Simos, better known as Starhawk, became a prominent writer, activist, and representative of the Reclaiming Tradition. Reclaiming Tradition also emphasized women's roles but worked with women and men, as well as the broader communities in the San Francisco Bay area. Starhawk's writing, particularly her groundbreaking *The Spiral Dance: A Rebirth of the Ancient Religion of the Great Goddess* (1979), has defined Paganism and goddess worship for a few generations of practitioners.

Though a major influence of the development of contemporary goddess religions, the feminist theology movement operated in its own spheres, building on anthropological trends and feminist critiques of monotheism, particularly Christianity and Judaism. Among a wide variety of authors and scholars exploring feminist theology in the late 1970s, prominent figures like Mary Daly, Carol P. Christ, and Merlin Stone published influential works that proposed significant questions about the inadequacy of traditional monotheism in addressing women's metaphysical needs and inner life. Though these authors did not self-identify as witches, they tended to offer witchcraft as a model for how women might break free from the patriarchy of mainstream religion. Their work in turn influenced feminist witches like Starhawk, who borrowed many of their ideas to encourage the growth of goddess culture. Jone Salomonsen, in her study of Reclaiming Tradition, asserts that these witches have contributed significantly to feminist theology, particularly in terms of magic and ritual practice that tends to "integrate epistemological as well as ontological notions of reality."[11]

Of course feminist theology, like feminism itself, is not a monolithic discourse, and these early authors represent a significant, but by no means universal, viewpoint. Since then, some feminist theologians have opted to rehabilitate their Christian traditions rather than abandon them altogether. But the link between feminist theology and witchcraft so popular in the 1970s very well could have influenced Lee Stearns when she was instilling feminist ideals into her teenage son, Joss Whedon.[12] This link is best demonstrated in a seminal 1979 text, Naomi R. Goldenberg's *Changing of the Gods: Feminism and the End of Traditional Religions*. In this slim volume, Goldenberg introduces the term *thealogy* to describe "goddess talk" that offers women an alternative to patriarchal theology, in which their only recourse is to male deities who denigrate their identities as women.[13] Goldenberg builds on basic critiques of patriarchal religion, mainly that it discounts women's experiences and bodies, as well as on Freudian and Jungian psychoanalysis, to make her case for the establishment of "new gods." Her thealogy consists of a few main points. First, that the gods a culture worships should reflect that culture's range of experiences and that new religious forms should emphasize self-awareness, indicating that these new gods and goddesses should be understood as "inner psychic forces."[14] Goldenberg defends the latter assertion against charges of atheism, asking, "Why should locating myths and religious beliefs within a mental or psychic milieu diminish those beliefs to any great extent?"[15] In other words, Goldenberg reflects a trend in late twentieth-century humanist and feminist thought that maintains the significance and power of religious and mythic belief whether or not they have any external referents, thus conveying more value to an individual's inner spiritual life.

Goldenberg further rails against the creation and continued use of Jungian archetypes to represent actual women, reminding her readers that "one image or one feminine principle can exist only if all females agree about the significance of the chosen symbol or if all those who do not agree are considered deficient in regard to their femininity."[16] She warns feminists against creating any one image of the feminine, as that will close down female potential and fail to recognize the rich diversity of actual women. Significantly, for our purposes, Goldenberg then goes on to praise the new religion of feminist witchcraft as being a model for the creation of a new thealogy. She joyously describes what she has witnessed at witchcraft rituals: "Goddess is acknowledged as an internal presence in the women who are worshiping her, they name each other goddess ... they practice a religion that places divinity or supernatural power within the person."[17] Further celebrating witchcraft, Goldenberg briefly explores the work of Z. Budapest, who uses images of strong ancient goddesses within ritual to inspire women in their mundane lives. Here, the personal is not only political, the spiritual is as well. According to Goldenberg, these feminist witches "feel that a woman will be a more effective feminist if her deep imaginal life has a feminist tone as well as her everyday political life."[18] Thus for Goldenberg, feminist witchcraft, still emerging in the late 1970s, was a crucial step forward in women reclaiming their own spirituality and power.

As witchcraft and Paganism have evolved over the last forty years, many women and men still see the possibilities that Goldenberg predicted, but the sheer diversity of Pagan practices and beliefs, as well as conflicts within various Pagan traditions, has made defining an overarching Pagan theology difficult. Recently, Christine Hoff Kraemer has attempted to characterize "emergent patterns of behavior and belief ... commonalities that cut across lines of group and tradition."[19] These patterns are relevant to our discussion of witchcraft on *Buffy the Vampire Slayer*. According to Kraemer, these commonalities are (1) the experience of divinity in the natural world, manifesting as pantheism, panentheism or animism; (2) reverence towards multiple gods and goddess; (3) respect of nature and the human body; (4) the use of pre–Christian mythologies and/or indigenous traditions as source material; (5) ritual practice, such as the celebration of rites of passage; (6) reliance on personal gnosis (experience as a source of divine knowledge); (7) acknowledgment of the principles of magick (as Willow puts it, "the wacky notion of spells") in which a practitioner applies her will to create changes in consciousness and ultimately in reality; (8) "virtue ethics," described by Kraemer as an individual's relationship "to the self, one's community, and the earth while avoiding harm to others;" (9) and pluralism, in which Pagans acknowledge the diversity and legitimacy of possible spiritual paths.[20]

These principles, while only rarely explored in any direct manner on *Buffy*, still haunt the margins of the series, particularly as Willow develops her magical ability and identity. On the surface, very little if any connection between "TV Wicca" and actual practice seems evident on the show, which chooses instead to focus on fantasy elements like floating pencils, glowing magical lights, electric bursts of power, and pleas to the netherworld. While one of many television programs since the 1960s to portray Hollywood's idea of witchcraft, including prominent examples *Bewitched* and *Sabrina the Teenage Witch*, *Buffy* was part of a brief late 1990s trend to actually use the term *Wicca* to refer to witchcraft. This perhaps started in 1996, only a year before *Buffy*'s premiere, with the release of the teen film, *The Craft* (dir. Andrew Fleming) which introduced young viewers to a fictional kind of witchcraft that nonetheless incorporated actual sections of the Gardnerian initiation and used symbols and tools from Wicca.[21] That same year, the *X-Files* episode "Sanguinarium" featured a Wiccan character suspected of evil-doing who actually turns out to be the protagonist of the story. *Buffy*'s contemporary on the WB network, *Charmed*, also used the term *Wicca*, even using it to pun on episode titles, as in the premiere episode "Something Wicca This Way Comes." Around this time, nonfantasy procedurals like *JAG* and *Judging Amy* featured Wiccan characters in guest roles, a trend that has continued in more recent shows like *The Mentalist* and *Psych*.[22] In rare cases, these "realistic" procedurals portray Wiccan characters as practitioners of a religion, though the *Mentalist* episode "Red Rum" portrayed their Wiccan character as delusional, unethical, potentially dangerous, and socially awkward, with one of the main detective characters referring to Wiccans as "geeks in capes." However, *Buffy* and *Charmed* are some of the only examples of fantasy shows that draw, even if only nominally, from actual magical practice, eliding witchcraft and Wicca.

Another factor in these depictions of witchcraft and magic is the kind of magic being performed. Typically, these programs go for the classics, in terms of tales of medieval witchcraft, with shapeshifting abilities like "glamours" or typical spells based on notions of sympathetic magic and contagious magic, popularized by James Frazer's classic *The Golden Bough* (1890).[23] *The Vampire Diaries*, currently running on the CW network, has created its own mythology, in which the first witch is an African servant, perhaps inspired by Tituba, the seventeenth-century slave at the heart of the Salem witch trials. Thus, almost every witch character on the show is played by a person of color, and the magic itself seems to be a combination of voodoo and hoodoo, with a little Latin thrown in for good measure. On the short-lived *Secret Circle*, which aired on the CW network from 2011 to 2012, the witches gain powers from being magically "bound" in a circle. In a salient social metaphor, the teens lose their individual powers when on their own, but are able to achieve significant power when joined together.[24] On *Buffy*, witchcraft and magic seem to be quite a mélange of European ceremonial magic, medieval grimoires, ancient cultures, liberal use of exotic languages from Latin to Sanskrit, evocations of chthonic gods and demons, and rhyming couplets typical of modern depictions of witchcraft. Since Gardnerian Wicca originally drew from many of these sources, perhaps Willow's identity as Wiccan is more accurate than one might think, at least in terms of actual magical practice. Similarly, the show seems to follow Aleister Crowley's classic definition of magic as "the science and art of causing change to occur in conformity with will."[25] Willow (sometimes nicknamed "Will") trains in her Wiccan studies; she constantly attempts to work her will, even attempting a vague spell for this very purpose in "Something Blue" (4.9).[26] The problem often occurs when she doesn't realize that her will is working, and unknowingly causes havoc by speaking desires that magically manifest in literal form, making her language performative. Unlike many shows that depict magic, Willow is not automatically an expert. She has to learn and fail.

In contrast, a typical Hollywood witchcraft trope often determines that witches gain their magical powers as a result of heredity and genealogy. The Halliwell sisters of *Charmed* are prominent examples of this. Recent and current shows, including *Eastwick* (2009), *Secret Circle*, and *The Vampire Diaries* still utilize this convention, which was popularized by *Bewitched*, even though this kind of hereditary witchcraft is fairly uncommon among actual practitioners. *Buffy the Vampire Slayer* does offer hints of hereditary witchcraft with the characters of Amy (Elizabeth Anne Allen) and Tara (Amber Benson). But it may be unique among these programs in that it features, in Willow, a main character who does not seem to have any magical ancestry but who is nonetheless able to train herself to become an extremely powerful witch. Considering that Buffy herself receives her slayer powers as part of a mystical lineage, Willow may in fact be the most self-actualized character on the show. But for Willow, it is a difficult journey. Through Willow's development, we begin to see some of Kraemer's "emergent patterns" associated with Pagan and feminist theologies, such as ethics, identity politics, tensions between community and the individual, as well as the individual's connection to nature and the cosmos.

Clearly, the show demonstrates reliance on pre–Christian and indigenous traditions, polytheism of a kind, as well as a belief in the principles of magick. Featuring its first nonvampire "monster of the week," as it were, *Buffy*'s first foray into witchcraft was as early as its third episode, "witch." Again, borrowing liberally from *The Craft*, the episode tells a tale of bitter high school rivalries and hex magic. Of course, in Whedon's show, the twist is that the witch Amy has actually been forced to switch bodies with her mother, the true power in the family, because the mother wants to relive her high school glory days as a cheerleader. Thus, we have the first instance in which magic, like other supernatural elements in the show, is used as a metaphor for an adolescent issue, this one being the weight of parental expectations. In this episode, the evil witch mother calls on "the dark gods" to do her bidding. Unlike many instances of spellcraft in which the show's writers simply make up names of higher (or lower) entities, the second season episode "Bewitched, Bothered and Bewildered" (2.16) features chants with recognizable goddesses, as both Diana and Hecate are evoked. Popular classical goddesses in mythology and literature, both have been characters in Shakespeare's works, the latter known as the "goddess of witches." In the episode, Amy, who has become a witch in her own right, evokes Diana, goddess of the hunt, for a love spell. She later evokes Hecate to transform Buffy into a rat, a spell she will later use on herself in "Gingerbread" (3.11).[27] Hecate is also evoked by Willow in the seventh season episode "Him" (7.6) when Willow, under the spell of a cursed varsity jacket, attempts to change the male jacket wearer's gender. When interrupted, she complains, "I've gotta start all over. Hecate hates that."

In a throwaway scene at the beginning of "The I in Team," Willow evokes a fictional goddess of fortune by the name of Neisa to help with her poker hand. When Xander suggests that using magic might be considered cheating, Willow protests that she's praying, not spellcasting, acknowledging a rare distinction in the show. In "Tough Love" (5.19), we see the first glimpse of Dark Willow, floating and with black eyes, when she calls on Hera and Kali, as well as an assortment of fictional gods, to exact vengeance on Glory for debilitating Tara. Willow also calls on the Egyptian god Osiris when dealing with aspects of resurrection, particularly when bringing Buffy back to life in "Bargaining" (6.1) and in her failed attempt to resurrect her lover Tara in "Villains," which directly leads to her full transformation into "Dark Willow" at the climax of the sixth season.[28] All of these instances suggest a rich pantheon of gods, goddesses, and chthonic entities. We even see hints of practices that may be more than just spellcasting, but we certainly do not ever get the sense that these gods are worshipped or that any kind of religion is based around them. In fact, on both *Buffy* and *Angel*, individuals who worship anything are generally presented as evil at worst, delusional at best. This is certainly in keeping with the overall atheism of the Buffyverse that looks critically at anything smacking of mainstream religion. But if, as Goldenberg claims, thealogy consists of acknowledging the divine within, perhaps self-development is the best form of worship.

On *Buffy*, Willow's journey runs afoul of Kraemer's category of "value ethics." While the prewitchcraft Willow seems to always want to do the "right thing," once she is able to act from a position of power, she begins to feel somewhat free of this burden. The results of her magic eventually become more direct, intentional, and potentially dangerous. In their continuing advice to her, both Giles and Tara attempt to make her aware of the consequences of her magic. We begin to see some of the potential ethical differences between Tara and Willow when a grieving Dawn approaches them for a resurrection spell to raise her recently deceased mother in the fifth season episode, "Forever" (5.17). Tara claims, "We don't mess with life and death." Willow adds, "I'm not even sure it's possible," but Tara quickly corrects her: "That's not the point ... witches can't be allowed to alter the fabric of life for selfish reasons. Wiccans took an oath a long time ago to honor that." However, Dawn wisely observes that "they wouldn't have taken an oath if they didn't know they could do it."

Perhaps what Tara refers to is Gardner's supposedly ancient Wiccan rede that instructs witches, "'An it harm none, do what thou wilt." Here, Gardner intentionally uses archaic language, in which '*an* means *if*, though many people, even experienced practitioners, misquote it as *and*. But Gardner's rede is simply a more morally specific version of Aleister Crowley's infamous rule, "Do what thou wilt shall be the whole of the law," often misinterpreted as a call to wanton hedonism. Yet, Crowley himself was paraphrasing St. Augustine by way of Rabelais, who emphasized the notion of true will, a purified state in which selfish desires and lusts are subsumed.[29] Gardner took Crowley's statement and added the "harm none" caveat, and thus the rede has become one of the most repeated aspects of Wicca.[30] Most basic introductions to Wicca emphasize the rede, along with the vaguely karmic rule known as the Threefold Law, that what you do in magic returns to you three times.[31] More recently, these principles have been called into question as adequate guidelines for ethical activity in witchcraft. Wiccan author and activist Phyllis Curott argues that the Threefold Law is still based on a patriarchal theory of punishment. In other words, "it's the weak cousin of morality because it's conduct based purely on deterrence." Furthermore, Curott claims that "the real reason that Witches do not and should not harm, do baneful magic, or use magic to have power over others, is because they experience immanent divinity ... you would simply never do harm, or manipulate someone else because you recognize that they are an embodiment of the divine."[32] Tara, then, seems to adhere to this sense of immanence-based ethics, not necessarily because she focuses on divinity but because she believes in following the "natural order."

Willow, however, ignores this, covertly offering Dawn a book of resurrection spells to bring her mother back, an operation that Dawn wisely abandons at the last moment. Of course, Willow does eventually cross that ethical line when she performs a resurrection spell for Buffy with the help of blood from a sacrificed baby deer. In response, when Giles returns to Sunnydale he vehemently castigates Willow and her naïve arrogance, telling her, "You were the one I trusted most to respect the forces of nature" ("Flooded," 6.4). Leading to her dark turn, Willow continues to selfishly use magic as a shortcut throughout the sixth season, such as her spell to make Tara forget their fight about that very subject ("Once More, with Feeling," 6.7). When Tara discovers this deception, she rightly sees it as a violation and decides to leave her. In a storyline that equates using magic with drug addiction, Willow goes "cold turkey" long enough to rekindle her relationship with Tara. After Tara's accidental murder and Willow's revenge killing of Warren (Adam Busch), all bets are off.

With her torture and murder of Warren, Willow finally becomes a dark witch, marked by her black hair and outfit. Giles returns to Sunnydale once again to stop her, but this time he carries power loaned to him from an English witch coven ("Grave," 6.22). In a last ditch effort, Giles anticipates Willow's hunger for power and lets Willow drain the energy he carries. The results are fascinating. Willow becomes incredibly high on the power. She exclaims, "No mortal person has ever had this much power. Ever. It's like I'm connected to everything. I can feel ... everyone." Yet, at that point Willow's euphoria fades to horror, when the feeling of being connected through power changes to being connected through emotion. She suddenly feels the pain of the world and all of its inhabitants. Ironically, it is this ultimate empathy that leads to her actions to destroy the world. Willow filters the experience through her deep grief and pain over Tara's death, and as she wishes to end her own pain, she transfers this desire to ending the world's pain. Willow's power in this instance is what Starhawk calls "power over," a patriarchal method of control, as opposed to "power within," a way of transforming the self through personal will. In other words, magic. She associates the former with a sense of estrangement, that one is somehow separate from the world, an attitude, she claims, responsible for war and environmental destruction. Power within is based on what she calls the psychology of immanence, and "when we practice magic we are always making connections, moving energy, identifying with other forms of being."[33] When Willow slips, she very obviously follows the former, exerting power over Buffy, Tara, and all the Scoobies, as well as innocents. When she absorbs Giles's power, she is experiencing the ultimate power from within, but because of her dark state of consciousness, mistakenly transforms that power into a destructive force. Not until her spell to call the slayers at the show's finale does she experience that connection as a positive experience.

The coven that provides this sense of connection for Willow, and rehabilitates her offscreen at the beginning of season seven, is quite an anomaly on the show. This never-seen coven is the only example of a functioning magical group on the show whose source of power is not demonic.[34] The only other practicing Wiccans we see on the show are the UC–Sunnydale campus group, whom Whedon presents humorously and Willow mocks as poseurs ("Hush"). These young women use the buzzwords of second wave feminism, like *empowerment*, and have New Age–inspired guided meditations, "goddess newsletters," and bake sales, while rejecting the notion of actual magical practice.[35] When we see the group again in season seven's "The Killer in Me" (7.13), they have shed their former members' shallow ideas, are more open to magic, and seem to have sincerely embraced energetic healing. Though they remain mostly ineffective in the grander schemes surrounding the hellmouth, in both of their appearances the UC–Sunnydale Wicca group represents Willow's continual isolation. But with the mysterious British coven, a different dynamic occurs. First, these women are described as older, so presumably, Willow gets the mentoring she never received from her parents, her teachers, or even Giles. What they teach her is a sense of connection, not just with community, but in the sense of connection with nature, similar to some of the emerging patterns of Pagan theology. Returning to the notion of immanence, Starhawk defines the concept as a way of being in the world in relation to both divinity and community. She claims that "immanence is context, and so the individual self can never be seen as a separate, isolated object. It is a nexus of interwoven relationships, constantly being shaped by the relationships it shapes. Integrity also means integration — being an integral and inseparable part of the human and biological community."[36] The English coven teaches Willow this very concept, as Giles reiterates in "Lessons" (7.1) when Willow brings forth a foreign flower in the British soil. She tells us, "It's all connected. The root systems, the molecules ... the energy. Everything's connected." Giles urges Willow to accept her power, reminding her, "This isn't a hobby or an addiction. It's inside you now, this magic. You're responsible for it." Here, Whedon seems to be moving beyond previous manifestations of magic on the program and replacing them with a finally stable identity for Willow.

During the entire final season, Willow struggles with this responsibility. Her final test comes when she must use the mystical scythe that Buffy retrieves from the mysterious Guardian (an ageless woman who claims to have watched the watchers), to perform one last act of magic on the show.[37] Buffy's plan, which Giles concedes is "bloody brilliant," is to fly in the face of millennia of tradition by empowering all potential slayers, rather than just the one per generation that the entire show's mythos is based around. Buffy's plan, which she offers to the potentials in the aforementioned speech, hinges on Willow's ability to draw in power and connect to all the potentials around the world. Of course, she fears that she will revert to her dark self. However, when she performs the spell, the opposite happens. This time, we see Willow's hair go white as she is bathed in heavenly light and orgasmically exclaims, "Oh ... my ... goddess!" With this magical act, the show subverts its own mythology, the liturgical passage that introduced the show in its early seasons: "In every generation there is a chosen one. She alone will stand against the vampires, the demons, and the forces of darkness. She is the slayer."[38] Buffy's rebellion is, on one level, a textual one, an act that serves as a culmination of seven years of rejecting written tradition that has literally prescribed her life.[39] Greg Erickson describes the spell as "an act of antimyth which can be read as a dismissal of traditional religion, and a releasing of chaos upon a cosmic order."[40] Rather than chaos, I maintain that the undoing of the slayer line is similar to Naomi Goldenberg's rejection of Judaeo-Christian scripture as a crucial first step towards feminist thealogy. With the final spell Willow replaces scriptural authority with women's experiences, relying on the strength of the slayers to save the day. According to Goldenberg, "When feminists set up cornerstones for a new theology, the foundations of this theology need grounding in a place more earthly and immediate than those described by the old abstract terminology of transcendence — a place that allows for 'experience' to interact with 'Scripture, text, myth and history.'"[41] Further, Buffy and Willow's act undoes the patriarchal process of slayer creation, which we learn in "Get it Done" (7.15) is due to what amounts to a spiritual rape of the first slayer brought on by the earliest male watchers. This act could also be seen as having theological implications. Goldenberg further proclaims that "by challenging the authority of males on earth, feminists make effective onslaughts on male authority in heaven."[42] Perhaps to some, this act of rebellion might look like atheism, but for those committed to recasting religion in a feminist light, nothing could be further from the truth. Finally, by calling all the potential slayers, not just the warrior women fighting the climactic battle, but the timid softball player, the overweight abuse victim, and the submissive Asian daughter, the show fulfills Goldenberg's rejection of the feminine archetype in favor of a multiplicity of images for women.

Discussing feminist theology and globalization, Sheila Briggs praises popular culture which, like Buffy herself, "takes us beyond and outside the text." Briggs further argues that television, despite its complicity with corporate economic interests, is a "major site of global cultural contestation" and that these corporate entities "do not control how viewers perceive, interpret, and reshape what they see on the small screen."[43] One example of this is a 2008 study cited by the *Telegraph*, which apparently blames *Buffy* for lower church attendance in the UK, despite increased ordination of women. Dr. Kristine Aune of the University of Derby claims that women's dissatisfaction with traditional religion and its hierarchies are drawn to Wicca's message of empowerment. And *Buffy* is the conveyor of that message.[44] As the ritual I witnessed indicates, *Buffy the Vampire Slayer* does actually have the potential to influence spiritual practice, as it teaches valuable lessons about rewriting the script of patriarchal traditions. For contemporary practitioners of witchcraft and Paganism, especially teenage enthusiasts, the show has had an immeasurable impact on their exposure and interest in goddess religions despite the fact that most viewers are aware of the inaccurate portrayals of Wicca and magic on the show.[45] These audience responses seem to indicate that they did not read the show as an atheist program, but rather as a mythic narrative that can provide the tools to transform their approach to spirituality and religion. And in some cases, Joss Whedon's dialogue can actually work as a magic spell.

Notes

1. I use *Paganism* as an umbrella term for a distinct religious tradition which consists of contemporary practitioners who self-identify as "Pagans," as opposed to lowercase *paganism*, which refers to a wide range of polytheistic religions and traditions throughout history. For Pagan Studies scholars, capitalizing the term legitimizes traditions and movements that may not conform to traditional monotheistic definitions of religion in terms of organization and hierarchy, but nevertheless form a significant religious subculture in contemporary Western society. See Barbara Jane Davy, *Introduction to Pagan Studies*, 2.

2. Emily Nussbaum, "Must-See Metaphysics," 68.

3. Ken Plume, "An Interview with Joss Whedon," 2.

4. See especially J. Lawton Winslade, "Teen Witches, Wiccans, and 'Wanna-Blessed-Be's'"; Tanya Krzywinska, "Hubble-Bubble, Herbs, and Grimoires"; and Dominique Wilson, "Willow and Which Craft?"

5. And often, the show's writers can't seem to get the grammar right. Characters use the term *Wicca* as a catch-all, when *Wiccan* would be the proper term. For instance, when Willow says that she aspires to be a "bad-ass Wicca" ("Choices," 3.19), or when she refers to her "Wicca group" ("Hush," 4.10).

6. Other precursors to Gardner included anthropologist Margaret Murray, who espoused a theory, since debunked, that the witches persecuted in Europe during the 1600s were actual practitioners of an underground nature religion (*The Witch Cult in Western Europe*). Also, the poet Robert Graves's nonfiction prose work *The White Goddess*, which spoke of fertility cults and goddess worshippers, was popular in the midcentury. These are only a few of the cultural and literary influences on those poised to introduce contemporary witchcraft to the Western world. For more, see particularly Ronald Hutton, *Triumph of the Moon*.

7. Hugh Urban echoes a frequent criticism of Gardner, that he was "more interested in nudism and women's bodies than actual social reform." Indeed, Urban represents a critical take on post-Gardnerian feminist witchcraft that accuses the practice of essentializing gender roles, particularly that of women, associating women with nature, childbirth (even metaphorical), and emotion. Such discussions are relevant, but beyond my scope here. Urban, *Magia Sexualis*, 189.

8. Gardner's own "Book of Shadows" was rendered as if it were indeed antiquated, with deliberately archaic language and treated paper.

9. The origin of the term *Wicca* itself is highly disputed among scholars. One of the most popular theories put forth by practitioners is that it derives from the Old English *Wik*, which means *to bend or shape*. Berger, *A Community of Witches*, 11.

10. Ronald Hutton also notes the shift in political tone from British Wicca and ceremonial magic, which had a conservative, even monarchic bent, to American (particularly southern Californian) Wicca, whose feminist influences gave the practice a much more left-leaning socialist and activist tone. Hutton, *Triumph of the Moon*, 361.

11. Salomonsen, *Enchanted Feminism*, 292.

12. Stearns was a feminist, an unpublished novelist, high school history teacher, and founder of possibly the first high school chapter of Amnesty International. Her legacy inspired her former student, Jessica Neuwirth, to create Equality Now, a global charity organization that addresses gender issues in the human rights movement. This charity became the beneficiary of money raised by special viewings of the film *Serenity*, sponsored by the Browncoats, Whedon's ardent *Firefly* fans. http://www.cantstoptheserenity.com/dallas/charity.html.
13. Goldenberg, *Changing of the Gods*, 96.
14. Ibid., 41.
15. Ibid., 43.
16. Ibid., 77.
17. Ibid., 89.
18. Ibid., 91.
19. Kraemer, *Seeking the Mystery*, 5.
20. Ibid., 3–5.
21. While some of the trappings of Wicca were present, the film inexplicably created its own cosmogony, focusing on a fictional monotheistic entity, Manon, which supposedly gave the young witches their power.
22. For more discussion of these television trends and their impact on practitioners, see Aloi, "A Charming Spell."
23. Over one hundred twenty years after its initial publication, Frazer's magnum opus remains required reading for magical practitioners and, apparently, for Hollywood producers. Frazer introduced the notion that "like attracts like" and that an object once in contact with someone, like hair, for instance, maintains a connection with them. Though Frazer's ideas have been widely discredited by the academic community in the century since it was published, they remain the basis for most popular depictions of magic and voodoo. The classic voodoo doll encompasses both sympathetic magic (the doll is meant to look like the person being acted upon) and contagious magic (the doll contains hair, nail clippings, or other items connected to that person). Hutton, *Triumph of the Moon*, 117.
24. Both *Vampire Diaries* and *Secret Circle* are based on young adult novels by L. J. Smith and produced by Kevin Williamson of *Scream* fame.
25. Crowley, *Magick in Theory and Practice*, xii.
26. In that same episode, Willow utters "so mote it be" at the climax of the spell, one of the few phrases used in magical contexts on the show that is actually part of Wiccan liturgy. Hutton, *Triumph of the Moon*, 55.
27. Krzywinska points out that Amy's evocation of Diana instead of Venus, a goddess more readily associated with love spells, is "rather odd" ("Hubble-Bubble, Herbs and Grimoires," 187). But since the spell for Xander backfires and every woman does ultimately hunt him, it does make a kind of sense. Diana in her Greek form, Artemis, is actually associated with Hecate, who represents the underworld, according to Edith Hamilton's *Mythology*.
28. In this episode, we actually see a distorted image of the god, who Willow actually attacks magically, to what effect is unclear.
29. Sutin, *Do What Thou Wilt*, 126–127.
30. In another example of the rede in popular TV, the premiere episode of *Charmed* features Phoebe Halliwell explaining to her sisters that good witches follow the rede, which she quotes from her family's Book of Shadows.
31. The Threefold Law was used to literal effect in *The Craft*.
32. Curott, *Witchcrafting*, 180–181.
33. Starhawk, *Dreaming the Dark*, 13.
34. In the current season nine of the canonical comic books, Willow has joined a group of female creatures who are witches and goddess worshippers. It is implied by a supporting character that witches form covens to keep each other in a "self-sustaining contact high." Parker and Gage, *Willow: Wonderland*, 21.
35. I have written on this scene extensively and how it conveys a critique of commodified witchcraft in my 2001 essay, "Teen Witches, Wiccans and Wanna-Blessed-Bes."

36. Starhawk, *Dreaming the Dark*, 37.
37. Wiccan thealogy sees the Goddess in triple form as maiden, mother, and crone. While the show has plenty of maidens and a few mothers, the Guardian is the only example of a positive crone figure.
38. In the actual narrative that Giles quotes in the first episode, the passage is "Into every generation a slayer is born: one girl in all the world, a chosen one. She alone will wield the strength and skill to fight the vampires, demons, and the forces of darkness; to stop the spread of their evil and the swell of their number. She is the slayer."
39. As in Buffy's retort to the Master when he incredulously insists that her death has been written: "What can I say? I failed the written" ("Prophecy Girl," 1.13).
40. Erickson, "'Religion Freaky.'"
41. Goldenberg, *Changing of the Gods*, 23.
42. Ibid., 36.
43. Briggs, "What is Feminist Theology," 76–77.
44. Beckford, "Buffy the Vampire Slayer slaying church attendance."
45. Berger and Ezzy, *Teenage Witches*, 40.

Bibliography

Aloi, Peg. "A Charming Spell: The Intentional and Unintentional Influence of Popular Media upon Teenage Witchcraft in America." In *The New Generation Witches: Teenage Witchcraft in Contemporary Culture*, edited by Hannah E. Johnston and Peg Aloi, 113–127. Burlington: Ashgate, 2007.
Beckford, Martin. "*Buffy the Vampire Slayer* Slaying Church Attendance among Women, Study Claims." *The Telegraph*, August 22, 2008.
Berger, Helen A. *A Community of Witches: Contemporary Neo-Paganism and Witchcraft in the United States*. Columbia: University of South Carolina Press, 1999.
Berger, Helen A., and Douglas Ezzy. *Teenage Witches: Magical Youth and the Search for the Self*. New Brunswick: Rutgers University Press, 2007.
Briggs, Sheila. 2012. "What is Feminist Theology?" In *The Oxford Handbook of Feminist Theology*, edited by Mary McClintock Fulkerson and Sheila Briggs, 73–106. New York: Oxford University Press, 2012.
Crowley, Aleister. *Magick in Theory and Practice*. Secaucus: Castle Books, 1991.
Curott, Phyllis. *Witchcrafting: A Spiritual Guide to Making Magic*. New York: Broadway Books, 2001.
Davy, Barbara Jane. *Introduction to Pagan Studies*. Lanham: Altamira Press, 2007.
Erickson, Greg. "'Religion Freaky' or a 'Bunch of Men Who Died?': The (A)Theology of *Buffy*." *Slayage: The International Journal of Buffy Studies* 4, nos. 1–2 (October 2004). http://slayageonline.com/PDF/erickson.pdf.
Goldenberg, Naomi R. *Changing of the Gods: Feminism and the End of Traditional Religions*. Boston: Beacon Press, 1979.
Graves, Robert. *The White Goddess: A Historical Grammar of Poetic Myth*. London: Faber and Faber, 1948.
Hamilton, Edith. *Mythology: Timeless Tales of Gods and Heroes*. New York: The New American Library, 1942.
Hutton, Ronald. *The Triumph of the Moon: A History of Modern Pagan Witchcraft*. New York: Oxford University Press, 1999.
Kraemer, Christine Hoff. *Seeking the Mystery: An Introduction to Pagan Theologies*. Denver: Patheos Press, 2012.
Krzywinksa, Tanya. "Hubble-Bubble, Herbs, and Grimoires: Magic, Manichaeanism, and Witchcraft in *Buffy*." In *Fighting the Forces: What's at Stake in Buffy the Vampire Slayer*, edited by Rhonda V. Wilcox and David Lavery, 178–194. Lanham: Rowman & Littlefield, 2002.

Nussbaum, Emily. "Must-See Metaphysics." In *Joss Whedon: Conversations*, edited by David Lavery and Cynthia Burkhead, 64–70. Jackson: University Press of Mississippi, 2011.
Parker, Jeff, and Christos Gage. *Willow: Wonderland*. Vol. 3. Milwaukie, OR: Dark Horse Comics, 2013.
Plume, Ken. "An Interview with Joss Whedon." IGN.com, June 23, 2003. Accessed January 12, 2012. http://www.ign.com/articles/2003/06/23/an-interview-with-joss-whedon.
Salomonsen, Jone. *Enchanted Feminism: Ritual, Gender and Divinity Among the Reclaiming Witches of San Francisco*. New York: Routledge, 2002.
Starhawk. *Dreaming the Dark: Magic, Sex, and Politics*. Boston: Beacon Press, 1997.
Sutin, Lawrence. *Do What Thou Wilt: A Life of Aleister Crowley*. New York: St. Martin's Griffin, 2000.
Urban, Hugh B. *Magia Sexualis: Sex, Magic, and Liberation in Modern Western Esotericism*. Berkeley: University of California Press, 2006.
Wilson, Dominique. "Willow and Which Craft?: The Portrayal of Witchcraft in Joss Whedon's *Buffy the Vampire Slayer*." In *The Buddha of Suburbia: Proceedings of the Eighth Australian and International Religion, Literature, and the Arts Conference 2004*, edited by Carole M. Cusack, Frances Di Lauro, and Christopher Hartney. 146–158. Sydney: RLA Press, 2005.
Winslade, J. Lawton. "Teen Witches, Wiccans, and 'Wanna-Blessed-Be's': Pop Culture Magick in *Buffy the Vampire Slayer*." *Slayage: The International Journal of Buffy Studies* 1, no 1 (January 2001). http://slayageonline.com/PDF/winslade.pdf.

Apocalypse Now and Again

The Apocalyptic Paradigm and the Meaning of Life and (Un)Death in Buffy the Vampire Slayer

ROSLYN WEAVER

> *It's bills, it's money. It's pieces of paper sent by bureaucrats that we've never even met. It's not like it's the end of the world. Which is too bad, you know, because that, I'm really good at.*—Buffy, "Flooded"

Apocalypses become common season conclusions in Joss Whedon's *Buffy the Vampire Slayer* series. Much of the series involves gradual revelations to the human characters about powerful evil supernatural figures whose interventions in human affairs signal a cataclysmic rupture in history. Against such threats stand a supernaturally appointed savior of humanity and a small group of human followers. Increasing violence and chaos lead to a decisive confrontation between two groups representing good and evil, the salvation of humans, the restoration of the world, and the renewal of hope for the future.

The series' ongoing reliance on and attention to end-time scenarios provokes questions about how apocalypse is employed in *Buffy*. On a narrative level, apocalyptic scenarios are useful ways to add gravity to storylines and season arcs, even if they are often treated comically. Yet despite the humor, apocalypse in the series is used to engage with more serious issues. In this paper I aim to trace some of the ways in which *Buffy* negotiates the Christian and secular territories of apocalypse, which reflects to some extent how contemporary popular culture is engaging with apocalyptic and religious themes. Beyond the recurring apocalyptic scenarios found in the season conclusions, however, *Buffy* employs apocalypse as a means to explore teenage life and the process of maturity, where crises and disasters are just as often of friendships and romances and mundane realities of daily life than they are of supernatural battles against evil demonic forces.

Although the following discussion references the series as a whole, *Buffy*'s use of apocalypse is too broad a topic to cover in this space in any real depth, and therefore I have chosen to focus on several key episodes. In a paper dealing with apocalyptic thought, it seems fitting to focus on beginnings and endings, and accordingly I pay particular attention to the series' opening and closing episodes, all written by Whedon. These episodes are the opening two-part pilot episodes, "Welcome to the Hellmouth" and "The Harvest" (1.2), and the closing season seven episode "Chosen."

"Something's coming": Apocalyptic Patterns

From the opening episode of *Buffy*, the series is ensconced within an apocalyptic paradigm. Although *apocalypse* literally means *revelation*, it is commonly used in popular culture to simply denote the end of the world or even just widespread disaster. Stephen D. O'Leary describes apocalypse as a "discourse that reveals or makes manifest a vision of ultimate destiny, rendering immediate to human audiences the ultimate end of the cosmos in the Last Judgment. Apocalyptic eschatology argues for the imminence of this judgment, in which good and evil will finally receive their ultimate reward and punishment."[1] Much of our contemporary Western understanding of apocalypse is drawn from the New Testament, specifically the book of Revelation, and for this reason, as well as my own background, the following discussion is informed by the Christian biblical context, although I acknowledge that both the series and apocalypse have been read from other perspectives; one example being several *Buffy* scholars who have focused on the series with reference to its production of Jewish identity.[2]

Although there are some differences in apocalypse across the Old and New Testaments, there are nonetheless many similarities in biblical apocalyptic writings,[3] with the books of Daniel and Revelation in particular being influential in modern apocalyptic thought.[4] Generally, biblical apocalypse includes prophecies and visions of future destruction and salvation; increasing turmoil and persecution of the chosen people by hostile, oppressive forces; widespread devastation; the intervention of the messiah; and a new, restored world where the persecuted saints are victorious.[5] The purpose of such writing was often to provide hope for those who were oppressed and persecuted.[6]

Secular works often draw on biblical apocalyptic patterns, even while modifying or ignoring some aspects. In his work on apocalypse and American science fiction, David Ketterer describes how science fiction disaster narratives often contain elements of the apocalyptic pattern seen in Revelation; namely dystopia, the threat or reality of disaster, life following the disaster, and a new world.[7] Elizabeth K. Rosen suggests that secular versions exhibit "the basic three themes of judgment, catastrophe, and renewal" as well as "deity and New Jerusalem,"[8] although these can be considerably altered in postmodern apocalypses, which may give a more complicated treatment to themes such as judgment and notions of good and evil.[9] If we distil all these elements to several core features of a secular apocalyptic paradigm, what we can see is a pattern that recurs in *Buffy*: visions, disaster, a powerful malevolent supernatural character, a messianic figure who stands against the evil character to save the world, and restoration. Moreover, apocalypse in biblical and secular narratives is very much interested in time, not simply in terms of a heightened significance attached to numbers but also more generally involving a sense of imminence.[10] In the New Testament letters, for instance, Peter urges his fellow Christians to live holy lives in light of a looming apocalypse because "the end of all things is near" (1 Peter 4:7); while secular texts may highlight rapidly advancing disaster and a quick succession of catastrophes, as in the films *The Day After Tomorrow* (dir. Roland Emmerich, 2004) and *2012* (dir. Roland Emmerich, 2009), or more generally focus on the slow approach of the end of the world, as in Nevil Shute's *On the Beach*.[11]

These elements of an apocalyptic paradigm are, for the most part, replicated in *Buffy*. Following the opening scene in the series showing vampire Darla's attack on a human boy in Sunnydale High School, we see Buffy, asleep, having nightmares of vampires rising and of the Master, season one's arch villain. This component of visions is one of the gauges for Giles, Buffy's watcher, to decide if there is indeed an approaching apocalypse: "Perhaps there is no trouble coming; the signs could be wrong. It's not as though you've been having the nightmares." At this point, Buffy is still refusing to fully accept her role as the slayer and has not told Giles of her nightmares, but the dreams appear to be an external validation of not only her slayer identity but also the forthcoming end of the world. Fittingly, these initial visions are nightmares and focus on the rise of evil forces. The disaster element is a recurring feature in *Buffy*, evident in the multiple deaths and the repeated destruction of various parts of Sunnydale (or in its entirety) throughout the series. In each season we have a malevolent figure, the Big Bad, an orchestrator of evil whom Buffy must confront.

In addition to the visions, disaster, and evil figures, the series also gives us Buffy herself, a messianic figure, and it is worth giving this particular element more attention. Although scholars have discussed and disputed nuances and differences between Jesus- and Christ-figures in popular culture,[12] such refinements are beyond the scope of this paper. As with much popular culture, *Buffy* is less interested in faithfully adhering to biblical or Christian traditions than in drawing on particular motifs at regular points to serve its (secular) themes of Buffy as a savior for humanity. Even if we heed cautions against overreading parallels between secular characters and Christ,[13] the series rather obviously attempts to connect Buffy with Jesus in several ways. In more general terms, Buffy is (usually) the only one who can stand against evil: "Into each generation a slayer is born, one girl in all the world, a chosen one." This role is at times complicated by Buffy's death(s) and the emergence of other slayers, but her special identity as someone who "saved the world a lot" ("The Gift") is reaffirmed by others throughout the series. Drawing more explicit links between Buffy and Christ, Xander reframes the popular "What would Jesus do" expression into a secular version: "When it's dark, and I'm all alone, and I'm scared, or freaked out or whatever, I always think, 'What would Buffy do?' You're my hero" ("The Freshman," 4.1).

Much of Buffy's angst centers on her lonely destiny as humanity's savior. She also sacrifices her own life more than once to save the world; both times she is brought back to life: by resuscitation after drowning and resurrection after her sacrifice. Even this latter death has messianic imagery and themes. In the season five closing episode, "The Gift," when Buffy gives her life to save her sister and the world, she is depicted diving into the portal with her arms outstretched in a Christ-like manner. This occurs after the "death is your gift" voiceover, a saying that perhaps may recall for some viewers Christian ideas about the "gift" of eternal life brought about by Christ's death. Buffy's final voiceover in the episode also includes her realization that "This is the work that I have to do." Taken in conjunction with Buffy's later revelation to Spike in the next season that following her death she was in a dimension that she calls "heaven" and that she "was finished" ("After Life," 6.3), these ideas again recall Christ's words "It is finished" as he died (John 19:30), although Emily McAvan at least reads this as a Buddhist conception of nirvana.[14] Moreover, Buffy's exhortation to her sister and friends, just before her death, to "take care of each other" can be read as echoing Christ's words to his mother and John that ensure John will take care of Mary (John 19:26–27). Even when the final episode of the series sees Buffy lose her role as the "chosen one" because now there are many slayers, the narrative still relies on a messianic figure, one person to save the world. In this final episode that figure is Spike, a formerly evil vampire who has undertaken a journey of redemption to win a soul. These themes of sacrifice and redemption recur in the series.[15] Spike wears an amulet that is only to be worn by "the *right* person.... Someone ensouled, but stronger than human, a champion" ("Chosen," emphasis added); he then embodies light vanquishing all the darkness and the demons as he sacrifices his life by wearing the amulet.

In addition to these elements of visions, disasters, and figures of good and evil, Buffy's efforts are always successful in not only averting the end of the world but also bringing about some kind of restoration or hope for the future over the seasons. Finally, then, time is a major consideration in the series. For instance, Giles's language in the first episode underscores the sense of forthcoming doom, in a secular turn on the Apostle Peter's warnings of approaching apocalypse: "It's getting worse.... The influx of the undead, the supernatural occurrences, it's been building for years. There's a reason why you're here and a reason why it's now.... Something's coming ... something is going to happen here. Soon!... The signs, as far as I can tell, point to a crucial mystical upheaval, very soon. Days. Possibly less" ("Welcome to the Hellmouth"). This sense of history shifting towards a significant, catastrophic rupture permeates the series and provides urgency in the narrative.

Thus, *Buffy* in many ways adheres to the apocalyptic pattern found in the Bible, yet it is important to note that the series' use of apocalypse is often humorous. Lynn Schofield Clark writes that *Buffy*'s treatment of religion reflects its humorous take on life in general: "The program's irreverent approach to authority extends to its overt religious references. *Buffy the Vampire Slayer* is premised on the idea of an apocalyptic End Times, yet this point also becomes a source of humor."[16] *Buffy*'s ironic treatment of apocalypse reflects in some ways a contemporary postmodern sense of cynicism or skepticism towards apocalyptic themes.[17] As Claire Sponsler and Veronica Hollinger each write of cyberpunk, the great variety of apocalyptic predictions in recent decades — whether related to the millennium or to nuclear threats — can lead to indifference and boredom with such ideas rather than continued engagement.[18]

This cynicism about apocalypse is found to some extent in *Buffy*. The repetition of apocalyptic warnings throughout the seasons becomes part of the show's humor, as demonstrated in Riley Finn's oft-quoted quip when confronted with yet another threat: "When I saw you stop the world from, you know, ending, I just assumed that was a big week for you. Turns out I suddenly find myself needing to know the plural of apocalypse" ("A New Man," 4.12). Even Giles's attempts at solemnity are met with comedy by Buffy:

BUFFY: So, Giles, you got anything that can make this day any worse?
GILES: How about the end of the world?
BUFFY: Knew I could count on you.[19]

Buffy's own flippancy towards the gravity of their situation — "Well, we averted the apocalypse. Give us points for that" ("The Harvest") — is a recurring theme throughout the series.

Yet this does not mean that apocalypse is only a source of comedy in the series. If we turn to Frank Kermode's frequently cited work on apocalypse, *The Sense of an Ending*, Kermode suggests that part of apocalypse's enduring appeal is what he terms *resilience*, where skepticism allows apocalyptic predictions to be disconfirmed without being discredited.[20] Thus, repeated warnings of apocalypses may not negatively influence belief because apocalypse is open to multiple interpretations: if a prediction of apocalypse proves false, this is error on the part of the person making that prediction, not an error in apocalyptic belief itself.[21] Therefore, although we could dismiss apocalypse as simply a source of humor in *Buffy*, the series nonetheless does depend on it for much of its emotional resonance, particularly considering that several of the major characters lose their lives in attempts to avert just such apocalypses.

A Patchwork of Religious and Pagan Symbols

In following the basic pattern of biblical apocalypse and reproducing many religious symbols and imagery, the *Buffy* series demonstrates an ongoing interest in religious ideas that other scholars have discussed elsewhere.[22] Yet as much as *Buffy* confirms that contemporary popular culture continues to engage with religion, the series also deviates from Christian apocalyptic traditions in significant ways.

Given Whedon's own professed atheism, it might seem surprising that religious themes appear across the seasons of *Buffy* so regularly. Yet it is not uncommon to find deeply spiritual themes and imagery in works of fantasy. Novelists and academics such as C. S. Lewis and J. R. R. Tolkien believed that the fantasy mode could provide a highly appropriate space for religious issues because fantasy writing can absorb spiritual elements and allow religious issues to be recast in purer forms and reflect real-life beliefs.[23] Contemporary writers continue this engagement with spirituality, with perhaps the most well-known example of this being Philip Pullman's efforts to debunk religious institutions and practices in his fantasy series *His Dark Materials* in the 1990s.[24]

As others have pointed out, fantasy is one of the repositories for modern engagement with religious and spiritual matters. Although much has been made of the growing secularism of Western culture, with the scientific and industrial revolutions leading to what Max Weber has called the "disenchantment of the world,"[25] in more recent decades researchers have begun discussing a reenchantment of our culture. Peter Berger suggests that in some ways the secularization theory is "essentially mistaken"[26] because our culture continues to engage with religious ideas and practices on a societal and individual level. According to Richard Jenkins, "The historical record suggests that disenchantment — no less than power and discipline — provokes resistance in the shape of enchantment and (re)enchantment."[27] Jenkins cites examples such as millennial thought, neopaganism, religious fundamentalism, and science fiction and fantasy as symptomatic of reenchantments of our culture[28]; McAvan calls this kind of popular spirituality the *postmodern sacred*.[29]

This often highly individual approach makes *spirituality* a difficult term to define, but it often refers to a sense of supernatural reality.[30] Christopher Partridge describes the largely non–Christian milieu of contemporary society as *occulture*:

> Expanding the narrow, technical definition of the term "occult" to include a vast spectrum of beliefs and practices sourced by Eastern spirituality, Paganism, Spiritualism, Theosophy, alternative science and medicine, popular psychology and a range of beliefs emanating out of a general interest in the paranormal, occulture is the new spiritual atmosphere in the West; a large pool of ideas and theories feeding new spiritual springs; the environment within which new methodologies and worldviews are passed on to an occulturally curious generation.[31]

Another way to view this bricolage of different beliefs is as what Stig Hjarvard calls *banal religion*, which involves a mix of folk and institutionalized religion symbols, such as vampires and crosses.[32] This societal shift towards different forms of spirituality is especially evident in our popular fictions, which play a key part in the reenchantment of Western culture, both informing and informed by contemporary attitudes to religion.[33] As many others have noted, programs such as *Buffy* often include an array of good and evil figures with only a vague and undefined sense of divine authorities,[34] "in which a God called by that name is nowhere to be found."[35]

It is primarily in this way that *Buffy* deviates from Christian understandings of apocalypse; by removing a supreme deity from the scenario to instead focus on the humans and their role. Like most other secular apocalyptic narratives, "apocalypse" in *Buffy* more usually refers not to revelation but to widespread disaster, to the ending of the present order of the world. Unlike many secular apocalyptic narratives, however, *Buffy* retains supernatural dimensions with its host of undead creatures and demons, but terms such as *good* and *evil*, *heaven* and *hell*, *soul* and *salvation* remain rather abstract, ill-defined concepts in the show that do not constitute a particularly coherent worldview. The characters using biblical or religious language are usually evil, and Willow, a (usually good) witch, says "Oh my goddess" when she works the scythe spell to share the slayer powers in the closing episode of the series ("Chosen"). Greg Erickson writes that "the presence of traditional Christian symbols, churches, and divinity is generally lightly mocked" rather than endorsed in the series and even these symbols decline in their significance throughout the seasons.[36]

Moreover, although it is possible to interpret Buffy as a messianic figure, it is worth highlighting Christopher Deacy's point that such readings of secular characters fail to capture the full meaning of Jesus's redemptive act in reconciling humanity and God.[37] Thus, rather than attempting to find in *Buffy* a slavish adherence to Christian traditions, it seems more productive to note the occasional parallels and more importantly point to the series' patchwork of Christian, secular, and pagan symbols that represents a contemporary approach to individualized spirituality and religiosity. For instance, Giles's explanation in the opening episode is vague and employs terminology more commonly associated with esoteric philosophies, but then rejects Christian notions of paradise in the second episode: "Dig a bit in the history of this place and you'll find a steady stream of fairly odd occurrences. Now, I believe this whole area is a center of mystical energy that things gravitate towards that you might not find elsewhere" ("Welcome to the Hellmouth"). Elsewhere, Giles tells Buffy and her friends that "This world is older than any of you know, and contrary to popular mythology, it did not begin as a paradise. For untold eons, demons walked the earth and made it their home, their hell. But in time they lost their purchase on this reality, and the way was made for mortal animals, for man. What remains of the old ones are vestiges: certain magics, certain creatures" ("The Harvest").

Beyond this, however, Buffy herself repeatedly rejects the overtly mystical aspects of her identity, countering every supernatural aspect with irony and pragmatism:

> GILES: Even through this mass and this din, you should be able to sense them [the vampires].... Reach out with your mind. You have to hone your senses, focus until the energy washes over you, until you feel every particle of—
> BUFFY: There's one.
> GILES: Where?
> BUFFY: Right there, talking to that girl.
> GILES: You don't know—
> BUFFY: Oh, please! Look at his jacket. He's got the sleeves rolled up, and the shirt! Deal with that outfit for a moment.
> GILES: It's dated?
> BUFFY: It's carbon dated. Trust me, only someone living underground for ten years would think that was still the look.
> GILES: But you didn't *hone*.[38]

Buffy's refusal to invest too heavily in the supernatural dimension is a recurring theme in the series and signals the series' overall preference for multiple religious, pagan, and mythological symbols and ideas. Therefore, although in many ways the series incorporates Christian imagery and ideas around apocalypse, it is only part of a kaleidoscope of religious and pagan aspects.

The Meaning of Life and (Un)Death

Despite the often humorous approach to apocalypse in the series, scholars have pointed out that *Buffy* still uses apocalypse to make quite serious points about life. In "The End as Moral Guidepost," Greg Stevenson argues that the recurring apocalypses in the series add more than suspense because they function as "a moral guidepost in that they bring clarity to life and thereby inform moral decisions."[39] After all, as Kermode has noted of apocalyptic thought more generally, apocalypse can give a sense of purpose and meaning to our lives.[40] Stevenson describes *Buffy*'s use of an eschatological perspective — that is, "living one's life with an eye towards the end" — as a perspective that develops characters' appreciation of life, helping them prioritize tasks and clarify their decisions.[41] This last point has also been made by Clark, who writes that choice becomes one of the recurring themes of the show with respect to the apocalyptic events that unfold: "Thus, prophecies often set in motion the drama that results in confrontations between good and evil. At every turn, individual choice is emphasized, so that a person's (or monster's) actions can bring about or stop the prophecy."[42]

As the epigraph to this essay attests, although *Buffy* employs significant amounts of apocalyptic rhetoric for its narrative force, it is a rather more mundane concern that preoccupies Buffy for much of the series: how to navigate the journey into adulthood. In this closing section, I want to focus more closely on this theme of Buffy's own growth over the series as she comes to terms with her identity and her future, and read it with regard to the apocalyptic paradigm. That the series uses fantasy to address real-life issues is a reasonably obvious point that has been made by many others previously. For instance, Rhonda V. Wilcox and Stevenson have each pointed out that the fantasy monsters and scenarios of the series function as symbols or metaphors of social problems and teenage life.[43] Stevenson specifically links apocalypse with teenage life in his work and cites the second episode of the series for its famous quote from Buffy's mother, Joyce, which neatly conflates teenage and supernatural catastrophes:

> Apocalypses on *Buffy* often represent personal crises in life. The real problems teenagers face are blown up to apocalyptic proportions as a way of illustrating their emotional impact. While grounded, Buffy tells her mother how important it is that she be allowed to leave the house. Joyce replies, "I know. If you don't go out, it'll be the end of the world. Everything is life or death when you're a sixteen year old girl." The irony is that in Buffy's case, it may very well be the end of the world if she cannot leave. That emotional dilemma Buffy finds herself in reflects teenage reality where every decision feels like it has ultimate consequences.[44]

Stevenson also points to the show's ongoing use of apocalypses as metaphors for "personal endings," whether these endings relate to relationships, high school, childhood, or other aspects of teenage life[45]; while David Lavery also describes many types of endings in the show,[46] although I would suggest that new beginnings are just as much a feature as endings for these characters.

There are several obvious links, then, between adolescence and apocalypse in the series. Indeed, the supernatural apocalypse is not Buffy's real dilemma. She is a reluctant participant in it, but a capable one. The first episode highlights the teenage difficulties of accepting a special responsibility when Buffy tells Giles that no amount of preparation can assist in sacrificing a normal life: "[A watcher] prepares me for what? For getting kicked out of school? For losing all of my friends? For having to spend all of my time fighting for my life and never getting to tell anyone because I might endanger them? Go ahead! Prepare me" ("Welcome to the Hellmouth"). The adolescent apocalyptic disasters, then, are those faced by most teenagers: friendships, romances, family, and career decisions. When Buffy returns from the dead in season six, she finds herself having to take on adult responsibilities in the gulf created by her mother's death: bills, home repairs, loans. Compared to Buffy's experience in saving the world, these more human matters are daunting and challenging. Yet she is always reluctant to lose her sense of normality. The series begins in Sunnydale High School, and ends with the school's — and town's — total destruction. The school itself is directly over a hellmouth, and this tension between ordinary teenage existence and major supernatural dramas becomes a recurring theme. In a scene from the second episode of season one that is mimicked in the last episode of season seven, Giles is attempting to maintain gravity about apocalyptic events while Buffy and her friends determinedly focus on ordinary concerns:

> GILES: We are at the center of a mystical convergence here. We may in fact stand between the earth and its total destruction.
> BUFFY: Well, I gotta look on the bright side. Maybe I can still get kicked out of school.
> XANDER: Oh yeah, that's a plan. 'Cause a lot of schools aren't on hellmouths.
> WILLOW: Maybe you could blow something up. They're really strict about that.
> BUFFY: I was thinking of a more subtle approach, you know, like excessive not studying.
> GILES: The earth is doomed.[47]

Compare this with season seven's iteration of this scene, as Buffy and her friends plan their next day following the apocalypse:

> GILES: Well, are we going to discuss this? Save the world, go to the mall?
> BUFFY: I'm having a wicked shoe craving.
> XANDER: Aren't you on a patch?
> WILLOW: Those never work.

GILES: Here I am, invisible to the eye.
XANDER: See, I need a new look. It's this whole eye patch thing.
BUFFY: Oh, you could go with the full black secret agent look.
WILLOW: Or the puffy shirt, pirate sash —
GILES: The earth is definitely doomed.[48]

The series attempts a kind of reconciliation between these apparently competing forces, showcasing Buffy's progression throughout the seven seasons as she comes to accept her role in averting disaster while also steadfastly aiming for a "normal" life.

Although the parallels between apocalyptic disaster and teenage crises are obvious, it is also possible to see other elements of the apocalyptic paradigm that are used to illustrate how Buffy and her friends mature into adulthood and work through the meaning of their lives. For instance, rather than a simple delineation between good and evil figures, *Buffy* gives a more complicated treatment in its construction of several main characters. Angel, Willow, and Spike variously represent good and evil, but these shifts suggest that good and evil are not easy labels to separate people but can both be found in individuals. Also given more complexity is Buffy's attitude to time. Although teenage and young adult life is often characterized by concerns and impatience about reaching certain milestones, whether that is finishing high school or getting a first job or buying a first car, Buffy's conclusion in the final episode is just the opposite:

BUFFY: I don't see fat grandchildren in the offing with Spike, but I don't think that really matters right now. You know, in the midst of all this insanity, a couple of things are actually starting to make sense. And the guy thing. I always figured there was something wrong with me, you know, because I couldn't make it work. But maybe I'm not supposed to.
ANGEL: Because you're the slayer?
BUFFY: Because — okay, I'm cookie dough. I'm not done baking. I'm not finished becoming whoever the hell it is I'm gonna turn out to be. I make it through this, and the next thing, and the next thing, and maybe one day I turn around and realize I'm ready. I'm cookies. And then, you know, if I want someone to eat — or enjoy warm, delicious cookie me, then that's fine. That'll be then. When I'm done.
ANGEL: Any thoughts on who might enjoy ... Do I have to go with the cookie analogy?
BUFFY: I'm not really thinking that far ahead. That's kind of the point.

Coming as it does in this final episode, this is an important scene that captures Buffy's realization that her progress towards adulthood and mature identity cannot be rushed, nor does it need to be: she does not know the future, and must be content with the knowledge that she is still growing and is not yet at the end of childhood and young adulthood — "I'm not finished becoming whoever the hell it is I'm gonna turn out to be." Thus we have the idea that while Buffy lives she is in the process of forming her identity — she is neither "finished" nor "done" — and that this is a journey that can only find its ultimate fulfillment in death and a heaven dimension, which is a place where Buffy describes herself as being "finished, complete," as conceptualized in "After Life." Although Erickson finds this concept of heaven inauthentic in the series,[49] I think it is entirely appropriate given Buffy's realization that she is still a work in progress and does not need to have all the answers about life and relationships and the future now.

"I'm not really thinking that far ahead" seems to be a decidedly antiapocalyptic statement if we consider the importance of visions and time in apocalypse, but I think it is worth highlighting Buffy's visions in her development as a young adult over the series. Following Buffy's decision to stop worrying about the future and see her life as a process — of baking or otherwise — the series finally ends on a series of questions:

> WILLOW: The First is scrunched, so what do you think we should do, Buffy?
> FAITH: Yeah, you're not the one and only chosen anymore. Just gotta live like a person. How's that feel?
> DAWN: Yeah, Buffy. What are we gonna do now?

These questions perhaps mimic Xander's "What would Buffy do" saying earlier in the series, as the characters ask Buffy what they should do next, and in this instance it is telling that Buffy does not answer. She is no longer the messianic figure holding the power or the answers alone; many girls across the world now have slayer powers. In this same scene, Xander says, "We saved the world," and this also reinforces the theme that Buffy is no longer alone, especially in its inversion of Buffy's tombstone epitaph of "She saved the world a lot" ("The Gift"). More than this, however, the series ends in this scene with a focus on restoration and new worlds; as Willow puts it, "We changed the world." Willow's and Dawn's questions about the future do not remain unanswered; viewers have already been given a glimpse of the future, in an earlier collage of scenes featuring unnamed girls in scenes of sports, family, and abuse, who each discover their new slayer power and strength. As Willow tells the others in the final scene, "Slayers are awakening everywhere." It is a new world.

Conclusion

Ultimately, then, perhaps what is most apocalyptic in the series is this final revelation. As I noted earlier, the series opens with our first sight of Buffy asleep, having nightmares of the forthcoming apocalypse. The series ends similarly, closing with the last sight of Buffy, now a young adult, as she ponders visions of the life to come, but this time awake, and even smiling. Buffy's vision of a future where she is not alone but where every potential slayer has her power is a utopian dream compared to her nightmares that opened the series. Rather symbolically, and reinforced by Willow's reference to slayers "awakening," the sleeping Buffy first seen in the opening episode becomes the awakened Buffy in the final episode, eyes wide open as she looks into the future of the world, one that she has helped transform into something new.

Notes

1. Stephen D. O'Leary, *Arguing the Apocalypse: A Theory of Millennial Rhetoric* (New York: Oxford University Press, 1994), 5–6.
2. Jon Stratton, "Buffy the Vampire Slayer: What Being Jewish Has to Do with It," *Television & New Media* 6, no. 2 (2005); Matthew Pateman, "'That Was Nifty': Willow Rosenberg Saves the World in *Buffy the Vampire Slayer*," *Shofar: An Interdisciplinary Journal of Jewish Studies* 25 (Summer 2007).
3. John W. Martens, *The End of the World: The Apocalyptic Imagination in Film and Television* (Winnipeg: J. Gordon Shillingford, 2003), 7; Roslyn Weaver, *Apocalypse in Australian Fiction and Film: A Critical Study* (Jefferson: McFarland, 2011), 8–9.
4. Edward James, "Rewriting the Christian Apocalypse as a Science-Fictional Event," in *Imagining Apocalypse: Studies in Cultural Crisis*, ed. David Seed (Basingstoke: Palgrave, 2000), 46; Elizabeth K. Rosen, *Apocalyptic Transformation: Apocalypse and the Postmodern Imagination* (Lanham: Lexington, 2008), xiii.
5. Norman Cohn, *The Pursuit of the Millennium: Revolutionary Millenarians and Mystical Anarchists of the Middle Ages*, rev. ed. (London: Pimlico-Random, 1993); L. L. Morris, "Book of Revelation," in *The New Bible Dictionary*, ed. J. D. Douglas (London: Inter-Varsity Fellowship, 1962).
6. Martens, *End of the World*, 226; Rosen, *Apocalyptic*, 176.
7. David Ketterer, *New Worlds for Old: The Apocalyptic Imagination, Science Fiction, and American Literature* (Garden City: Anchor-Doubleday, 1974), 123–124.
8. Rosen, *Apocalyptic*, xxii.
9. Ibid., xxii–xxv.
10. Martens, *End of the World*, 67.
11. London: Heinemann, 1957.
12. Anton Karl Kozlovic, "The Structural Characteristics of the Cinematic Christ-Figure," *The Journal of Religion and Popular Culture* 8 (Fall 2004); Christopher Deacy, "Reflections on the Uncritical Appropriation of Cinematic Christ-Figures: Holy Other or Wholly Inadequate?" *The Journal of Religion and Popular Culture* 13 (Summer 2006).
13. Kozlovic, "Structural Characteristics"; Deacy, "Reflections."
14. Emily McAvan, *The Postmodern Sacred: Popular Culture Spirituality in the Science Fiction, Fantasy, and Urban Fantasy Genres* (Jefferson, NC: McFarland, 2012), 95.
15. Jana Reiss, *What Would Buffy Do?: The Vampire Slayer as Spiritual Guide* (San Francisco: Jossey-Bass, 2004).
16. Lynn Schofield Clark, *From Angels to Aliens: Teenagers, the Media, and the Supernatural* (New York: Oxford University Press, 2003), 49.
17. Rosen, *Apocalyptic*, xxvi.
18. Claire Sponsler, "Beyond the Ruins: The Geopolitics of Urban Decay and Cybernetic

Play," *Science-Fiction Studies* 20, no. 2 (1993); Veronica Hollinger, "Apocalypse Coma," in *Edging into the Future: Science Fiction and Contemporary Cultural Transformation*, ed. Veronica Hollinger and Joan Gordon (Philadelphia: University of Pennsylvania Press, 2002).
  19. "The Harvest."
  20. Frank Kermode, *The Sense of an Ending: Studies in the Theory of Fiction: with a New Epilogue* (New York: Oxford University Press, 2000), 8.
  21. Ibid.
  22. Greg Erickson, "'Religion Freaky' or a 'Bunch of Men Who Died?': The A(theology) of *Buffy*," *Slayage: The Online International Journal of Buffy Studies* 4, no. 1–2 (2004); Reiss, *What Would Buffy Do*; Greg Stevenson, "The End as Moral Guidepost," *Slayage: The Online International Journal of Buffy Studies* 4, no. 3 (2004).
  23. C. S. Lewis, "Sometimes Fairy Stories May Say Best What's to Be Said," in *Essay Collection and Other Short Pieces*, ed. Lesley Walmsley (London: HarperCollins, 2000), 527–28; J. R. R. Tolkien, *Tree and Leaf; Smith of Wootton Major, the Homecoming of Beorhtnoth Beorhthelm's Son* (London: Unwin, 1975), 68–71.
  24. Philip Pullman, *Northern Lights* (London: Scholastic, 1995).
  25. Max Weber, "Science as a Vocation," *Daedalus* 87 (Winter 1958): 133.
  26. Peter Berger, "The Desecularization of the World: A Global Overview," in *The Desecularization of the World: Resurgent Religion and World Politics*, ed. Peter Berger (Grand Rapids: Eerdmans, 2000), 2.
  27. Richard Jenkins, "Disenchantment, Enchantment, and Reenchantment: Max Weber at the Millennium," *Max Weber Studies* 1 (2000): 29.
  28. Ibid.
  29. McAvan, *Postmodern Sacred*.
  30. Peter Berger, Grace Davie, and Effie Fokas, *Religious America, Secular Europe? A Theme and Variations* (Aldershot: Ashgate, 2008).
  31. Christopher Partridge, "Alternative Spiritualities, Occulture, and the Reenchantment of the West," *The Bible in Transmission* (Summer 2005): 1.
  32. Stig Hjarvard, "The Mediatisation of Religion: Theorising Religion, Media, and Social Change," *Culture and Religion* 12 (June 2011): 128.
  33. Partridge, "Alternative," 2.
  34. Massimo Introvigne, "'There Will Be No Thomas Aquinas at This Table': Notions of God in the New Religious Consciousness" (paper presented at Expanding Concepts of God, Harvard University, April 7–9, 2000); Stevenson, "End as Moral Guidepost."
  35. Introvigne, "No Thomas Aquinas."
  36. Erickson, "Religion Freaky."
  37. Deacy, "Reflections."
  38. "Welcome to the Hellmouth."
  39. Stevenson, "End as Moral Guidepost."
  40. Kermode, *Sense*.
  41. Stevenson, "End as Moral Guidepost."
  42. Clark, *From Angels*, 50.
  43. Rhonda V. Wilcox, "There Will Never Be a 'Very Special' *Buffy*: *Buffy* and the Monsters of Teen Life," *Journal of Popular Film and Television* 27, no. 2 (1999); Stevenson, "End as Moral Guidepost."
  44. Stevenson, "End as Moral Guidepost."
  45. Ibid.
  46. David Lavery, "Apocalyptic Apocalypses: The Narrative Eschatology of *Buffy the Vampire Slayer*," *Slayage: The Online International Journal of Buffy Studies* 3, no. 1 (2003).
  47. "The Harvest."
  48. "Chosen."
  49. Erickson, "Religion Freaky."

Bibliography

Berger, Peter. "The Desecularization of the World: A Global Overview." In *The Desecularization of the World: Resurgent Religion and World Politics*, edited by Peter Berger, 1–18. Grand Rapids: Eerdmans, 2000.
Berger, Peter, Grace Davie, and Effie Fokas. *Religious America, Secular Europe? A Theme and Variations*. Aldershot: Ashgate, 2008.
Clark, Lynn Schofield. *From Angels to Aliens: Teenagers, the Media, and the Supernatural*. New York: Oxford University Press, 2003.
Cohn, Norman. *The Pursuit of the Millennium: Revolutionary Millenarians and Mystical Anarchists of the Middle Ages*. Rev. ed. London: Pimlico-Random, 1993.
Deacy, Christopher. "Reflections on the Uncritical Appropriation of Cinematic Christ-Figures: Holy Other or Wholly Inadequate?" *The Journal of Religion and Popular Culture* 13 (Summer 2006). http://www.usask.ca/relst/jrpc/art13-reflectcinematicchrist.html.
Erickson, Greg. "'Religion Freaky' or a 'Bunch of Men Who Died?' The A(theology) of *Buffy*." *Slayage: The Online International Journal of Buffy Studies* 4, no. 1–2 (2004). http://slayageonline.com/essays/slayage13_14/Erickson.htm.
Hjarvard, Stig. "The Mediatisation of Religion: Theorising Religion, Media, and Social Change." *Culture and Religion* 12 (June 2011): 119–35.
Hollinger, Veronica. "Apocalypse Coma." In *Edging into the Future: Science Fiction and Contemporary Cultural Transformation*, ed. Veronica Hollinger and Joan Gordon, 159–73. Philadelphia: University of Pennsylvania Press, 2002.
Introvigne, Massimo. "'There Will Be No Thomas Aquinas at This Table': Notions of God in the New Religious Consciousness." Paper presented at Expanding Concepts of God, Harvard University, April 7–9, 2000. http://www.cesnur.org/2001/buffy_march01.htm.
James, Edward. "Rewriting the Christian Apocalypse as a Science-Fictional Event." In *Imagining Apocalypse: Studies in Cultural Crisis*, ed. David Seed, 45–61. Basingstoke: Palgrave, 2000.
Jenkins, Richard. "Disenchantment, Enchantment, and Reenchantment: Max Weber at the Millennium." *Max Weber Studies* 1 (2000): 11–32.
Kermode, Frank. *The Sense of an Ending: Studies in the Theory of Fiction: With a New Epilogue*. New York: Oxford University Press, 2000.
Ketterer, David. *New Worlds for Old: The Apocalyptic Imagination, Science Fiction, and American Literature*. Garden City: Anchor-Doubleday, 1974.
Kozlovic, Anton Karl. "The Structural Characteristics of the Cinematic Christ-Figure," *The Journal of Religion and Popular Culture* 8 (Fall 2004). http://www.usask.ca/relst/jrpc/art8-cinematicchrist.html.
Lavery, David. "Apocalyptic Apocalypses: The Narrative Eschatology of *Buffy the Vampire Slayer*." *Slayage: The Online International Journal of Buffy Studies* 3, no. 1 (2003). http://slayageonline.com/PDF/lavery3.pdf.
Lewis, C. S. "Sometimes Fairy Stories May Say Best What's to Be Said." In *Essay Collection and Other Short Pieces*, ed. Lesley Walmsley, 526–28. London: HarperCollins, 2000.
Martens, John W. *The End of the World: The Apocalyptic Imagination in Film and Television*. Winnipeg: J. Gordon Shillingford, 2003.
McAvan, Emily. *The Postmodern Sacred: Popular Culture Spirituality in the Science Fiction, Fantasy, and Urban Fantasy Genres*. Jefferson, NC: McFarland, 2012.
Morris, L. L. "Book of Revelation." In *The New Bible Dictionary*, ed. J. D. Douglas, 1093–95. London: Inter-Varsity Fellowship, 1962.
O'Leary, Stephen D. *Arguing the Apocalypse: A Theory of Millennial Rhetoric*. New York: Oxford University Press, 1994.
Partridge, Christopher. "Alternative Spiritualities, Occulture, and the Reenchantment of the West." *The Bible in Transmission* (Summer 2005): 1–6.
Pateman, Matthew. "'That Was Nifty': Willow Rosenberg Saves the World in *Buffy the Vampire Slayer*." *Shofar: An Interdisciplinary Journal of Jewish Studies* 25 (Summer 2007): 64–77.
Pullman, Philip. *Northern Lights*. London: Scholastic, 1995.

Reiss, Jana. *What Would Buffy Do?: The Vampire Slayer as Spiritual Guide*. San Francisco: Jossey-Bass, 2004.
Rosen, Elizabeth K. *Apocalyptic Transformation: Apocalypse and the Postmodern Imagination*. Lanham: Lexington, 2008.
Shute, Nevil. *On the Beach*. London: Heinemann, 1957.
Sponsler, Claire. "Beyond the Ruins: The Geopolitics of Urban Decay and Cybernetic Play." *Science-Fiction Studies* 20, no. 2 (1993): 251–65.
Stevenson, Greg. "The End as Moral Guidepost." *Slayage: The Online International Journal of Buffy Studies* 4, no. 3 (2004). http://slayageonline.com/PDF/stevenson.pdf.
Stratton, Jon. "Buffy the Vampire Slayer: What Being Jewish Has to Do with It." *Television & New Media* 6, no. 2 (2005): 176–99.
Tolkien, J. R. R. *Tree and Leaf, Smith of Wootton Major, the Homecoming of Beorhtnoth Beorhthelm's Son*. London: Unwin, 1975.
Weaver, Roslyn. *Apocalypse in Australian Fiction and Film: A Critical Study*. Jefferson, NC: McFarland, 2011.
Weber, Max. "Science as a Vocation." *Daedalus* 87 (Winter 1958): 111–34.
Wilcox, Rhonda V. "There Will Never Be a 'Very Special' *Buffy*: *Buffy* and the Monsters of Teen Life." *Journal of Popular Film and Television* 27, no. 2 (1999): 16–23.

Who's Afraid of the Big Black Wolf?
Racial Identity and the Irrationality of Religious Belief in Firefly *and* Serenity

Desirée de Jesus

> *You ever been raped?*—Jubal Early (Richard Brooks), "Objects in Space" (*Firefly* 14)
>
> *I believe in something greater than myself. A better world. A world without sin.*—The Operative (Chiwetel Ejiofor), *Serenity*

Joss Whedon's popular but short-lived space western television series *Firefly* and its film sequel *Serenity* use the western genre's "civilization versus wilderness" dialectical thematic structure to prompt an examination of the relationship between faith and reason. The narrative follows the adventures of Captain Malcolm "Mal" Reynolds (Nathan Fillion) and his motley crew aboard the spaceship Serenity as they struggle to eke out a living in the vast wilderness of space, salvaging cargo from abandoned spaceships and transporting stolen goods and fugitives while evading capture by the interplanetary government, the Alliance. In this essay I will argue that while both texts narratively focus the tension between pragmatic empiricism and faith-based beliefs through their depiction of attempts to capture River Tam (Summer Glau), the psychic fugitive hiding on the spaceship Serenity, the force of their argument is dependent on the unconscious reproduction of a logic of representation that constructs black male figures onscreen as the negative image of heroic white masculinity. I suggest that the shared racial identity of River's pursuers, Jubal Early (the bounty hunter introduced in *Firefly*'s final episode "Objects in Space") and The Operative (*Serenity*'s main villain), create a visual link that invites comparison of their narrative function in relation to Mal, thus constituting a *de jure* objection against religious belief. Finally, by turning attention to the ideological function of stereotypes, I will demonstrate how the problematic of Whedon's cinematic treatment of faith, the stereotypical positioning of black masculinity, exposes a fundamental flaw implicit in his understanding of religious belief as irrational.

The Problem of Evil at the Battle of Serenity Valley

In "Serenity," *Firefly*'s pilot episode, Whedon introduces faith-based belief as an untenable position through his depiction of the Battle of Serenity Valley, the decisive encounter in the war between the Alliance government and the Browncoat independents. The shaky, handheld quality of the opening scene's consecutive shots of military combat are immersive and engaging, underlining the frenetic, disjointed experience of the Browncoat ground troops. Clearly, the Alliance forces outnumber Mal and the Browncoat ground troops. This becomes even more apparent when the camera follows Mal as he dodges enemy fire and narrowly escapes being hit by the blasts that kill key members of his team. Undeterred despite the increasing number of Browncoat casualties and reports of military reinforcements' reluctance to enter the fray, Mal stubbornly predicts that "just a little while longer and our angels are gonna soar overhead, raining fire on those arrogant clods. So you hold! You hold!" The goal of this opening scene is to introduce faith as irrational, particularly in the face of contrary evidence. This is accomplished not just through the religious imagery used by Mal in his descriptions of the imagined Browncoat victory, but also when he pauses to kiss the cross hanging around his neck, a gesture that grants religious specificity to the belief system undergirding his misguided predictions. When the military reinforcements unexpectedly abandon Mal's troops and recommend that they surrender to the Alliance, this narrative development underlines the incongruity between their inevitable loss and Mal's imagined victory.

Given the view of religious belief that this scene presents, the juxtaposition of Mal's baseless faith assertions and the Alliance's arrival in Serenity Valley vividly demonstrates a specific objection to the validity of Christianity. Through a series of shot-reverse shots, the sequence cuts between the landing of the Alliance spaceships and Mal's stunned response to the Alliance victory. Oblivious as a fellow Browncoat is killed beside him, Mal stares incredulously past the camera, his face illuminated by a bright light. It is worth noting that the stylistic discourse of this scene, particularly its use of an unsourced light that shines more brightly on his face than those around him, suggests that the real site of loss was internal. Whedon corroborates this idea in the "Serenity" commentary by identifying this as "the moment where Mal loses everything. It all falls apart for him. He gives up hope and becomes a bad man."[1]

Discussing the problem of evil in relation to Mal's loss of faith that the good guys always win, David Baggett identifies the disillusionment accompanying this loss as the catalyst for personal liberation and the creation of meaning.[2] He observes that Mal's "experience in Serenity Valley made him lose faith in a reliable providence. The problem of evil, we could say, was the undoing of his religious convictions."[3] If one operates on the premise that the good guys always win in the end, as Mal does, then the Alliance's victory at Serenity Valley temporarily destabilizes the category "good guys" and challenges the fixity of that perspective's inbuilt binary opposition.[4] Thus, implicit to this view is the challenge to Mal's faith: if God exists and is good and all-powerful, how could he let the *real* good guys lose? Or, more specifically, does the triumph of evil over good mean that there is no God? While a more detailed examination of the text's portrayal of the problem of evil is beyond the scope of this essay, it is my contention that the melodramatic narrative elements of *Firefly* and *Serenity* reestablish Mal's position as a good guy and make possible the conclusion that religious belief is irrational.

Moral Figures of the Melodramatic Mode

At first glance, situating the development of the western film genre within the American melodramatic imagination appears to be an exercise in futility, given the traditional association of westerns with masculinity and of melodrama with femininity. However, when considering the concept of melodrama as an expressionistic aesthetic with ethical dimensions, melodramatic features of the western film genre emerge that identify it as part of a narrative tradition preoccupied with the postulation of the moral occult.[5] In his study of nineteenth-century melodrama, Peter Brooks argues that within a postsacred world the melodramatic form provides moral legibility through the dramatization of "pure and polar concepts of darkness and light, salvation and damnation."[6] Furthermore, he posits that the destabilization of society's moral institutions provides this Manichaean modality with the opportunity to image a new morality through its fictional characterizations.[7] Most importantly, this imaging is consistent with David Lusted's claims about the western hero's function as a symbol of social status and masculinity in moral terms and the interconnectedness of the moral worlds of melodrama and the western film genre.[8]

In this regard, part of this narrative mode's achievement is its ability to construct an easily recognizable iconography that assigns virtue to suffering protagonists and villainy to the victims' oppressors. As Linda Williams notes in her article "Melodrama Revised," the emphasis on the presentation of moral truth through nonverbal means within the nineteenth-century melodramatic mode eventually resulted in the physical codification of a character's virtue or villainy.[9] By this account, the imaging of moral goodness through physical attributes within "a world where virtue has become hard to read" became an integral part of the melodramatic narrative mode in popular American cinema.[10]

To take an example pertinent to this project, *Firefly* and *Serenity*'s portrayal of River Tam's wronged innocence and exploitation by the Alliance establishes her as a suffering victim and provides the basis for the texts' narrative trajectory, thus situating both works within the melodramatic mode of storytelling. Accordingly, the narratives' villains are identified as those wishing to capture River and return her to the Alliance. However, most troubling is that the texts' foregrounding of the villains Jubal Early and the Operative as the agents posing the greatest threat to River's safety has meant that the gravity of her other pursuers' actions has been minimized in comparison.[11] Considering Williams's comments about the physical codification of morality in relation to Early and the Operative's shared racial identity begs the question: how does their appearance as black male figures onscreen typify a particular form of villainy within the American melodramatic tradition?

In "Race, Melodrama, and *The Birth of a Nation* (1915)" Linda Williams argues that as a racial melodrama, *Birth of a Nation*'s cinematic portrayal of an American national identity was dependent on linking the depiction of white women as suffering victims and the denigration of black male figures.[12] To make her point, she explains how the fear of miscegenation shaped the logic behind two popular nineteenth-century representations of the black male in American racial melodramas and defined black masculinity by the degree to which it posed a danger to the white female's purity. She notes that at one end of the narrative spectrum, the antebellum romantic racialism of *Uncle Tom's Cabin* feminized the "good negro" and removed the threat of miscegenation. At the other end was *The Clansman*'s "hypermasculine rapist who can only be stopped by lynching," a characterization that identified both the problem and solution to the black male's threat to white female virtue.

By contrasting the descriptive differences within both texts' portrayals of black masculinity, Williams notes how the authors' regard for the black male body influenced their view of his moral capacity. She links Uncle Tom's characterization as a good negro to the narrative emphasis of his moral qualities and the downplaying of his physical features, particularly through his depiction on stage as an old man.[13] Similarly, Robyn Wiegman discerns that Uncle Tom is "simultaneously deracialized as a corporeal entity and subsequently endowed with the moral superiority, heavenly religiosity, and spiritual self-sacrifice associated with an interiorized and subtly conquering feminine" in order to counter the inhumanity of his blackness and the patriarchal value of his masculine body. In other words, the logic of sexual difference underlying Uncle Tom's release from his strong, black male body defused his sexual threat and made him a mirror of the white female's moral sentimentality.[14] In the same manner, Donald Bogle traces the literature-to-film adaptation of the Uncle Tom character in early American cinema noting how his portrayal as a heroic character was constructed in the melodramatic narrative mode by emphasizing his ability to keep his Christian faith and avoid retaliating against his master despite the mental and physical assault he endured.[15]

By contrast, *The Clansman* contested the black male's capacity for rational thought by exaggerating his corporeality and constructing him as a figure unable to overcome his innate bestiality and latent villainy. Donald Bogle critically examines the pervasiveness of this mythic stereotype within American popular culture by using as a starting point *The Birth of a Nation*, D. W. Griffith's film adaptation of *The Clansman*. Crediting this film with the first onscreen portrayal of the "brutal, black buck" stereotype, Bogle anchors within the melodramatic narrative tradition the filmmaker's portrayal of the buck's unbridled rage and physical violence as the only outlet for his repressed excessive sexual desire for white women. He argues that Griffith creates a visual contrast between the pale, blond female victim and her attacker's dark skin in order to exploit the moral imagination of the American public and portray black masculinity as the greatest threat to the formation of a cohesive national identity. According to Bogle, "the black bucks of the film are psychopaths, one always panting and salivating, the other forever stiffening his body as if the mere presence of a white woman in the same room would bring him to a sexual climax. Griffith played hard on the bestiality of his black villainous bucks and used it to arouse hatred."[16]

The essence of Bogle's argument is that the film's moral legibility was dependent on its construction of the brutal black buck as an easily recognizable villain, the innately virtuous white woman as the suffering victim, and the white male as the protector of moral goodness. Bogle's approach here illustrates how the black buck's racial difference made visible his foreignness, provoking nativist attitudes and extending the moral and political implications of his sexual threat to white womanhood beyond the borders of the screen. While Bogle's project acknowledges the construction of other racially based mythic types like the tragic mulatto, coon, tom, and mammy in early American cinema, he maintains that they have persisted throughout American film history in varying forms. Significantly, Bogle concludes his analysis of this stereotype by noting the public's rejection of favorable modifications of the virile black male onscreen and its subsequent repackaging within the American melodramatic narrative tradition.[17]

Firefly *and* Serenity *as Racial Melodramas*

If we focus on this development of black male representation within American racial melodrama in relation to the white female figure's portrayal onscreen, then a parallel analysis of their Manichaean characterizations in *Firefly* and *Serenity* can hopefully demonstrate how Whedon uses racist stereotypes to illustrate the irrationality of faith-based belief. Ultimately, the interplay between Mal, River, and the texts' black males reenacts the pathos–action dialectic of the melodramatic mode and makes morally legible the guilt and innocence of its characters through easily identifiable physical codification.

The narrative trajectories of *Firefly* and *Serenity* are primarily driven by attempts to rescue and protect River from those pursuing her. As the reasons for the Alliance's pursuit of River emerge from her subconscious, her fragility and tenuous grasp on reality point to her wronged innocence. Ironically, Mal's ambivalence toward River's protection is governed by a quintessential trait of the American western hero: pragmatism. As Eric Greene notes, "Like many a pragmatic hero in the American Western, Mal is compelled almost exclusively by practical considerations, immediate survival needs, and personal loyalties. Mal is primarily instinctual rather than ideological."[18] This pragmatism, however, does not preclude the texts' portrayal of Mal as a moral and compassionate person. Most significantly, *Serenity* presents Mal's pessimistic philosophical anthropology, the impetus behind his decision to become personally involved in the Alliance's demise, in moral terms, and his hidden goodness and heroism are revealed through the highly stylized melodramatic aesthetics of astonishment.[19] David Lusted demonstrates how, even within the western genre, the rescue narrative enacts the overlapping moral sensibilities of the western and the melodramatic mode by making the hero's personal sacrifice a requirement for the revelation of his moral goodness.[20]

Brutal Black Bucks

What I find most telling about the introduction of Jubal Early in "Objects in Space" is the way that the episode's formal qualities differentiate him from those who have pursued River in earlier episodes. The lighting, framing, and musical score accompanying Early's onscreen presence recalls early American cinema's depiction of black male sexuality as monstrous, particularly in its transgressive and overwhelming desire for the white female body. Returning to our previous discussion of *The Clansman*'s simultaneous denial of the black male's capacity for rational thought and exaggeration of black male corporeality, I want to point out how low angle tracking shots and low key lighting cause the contours of Early's face and muscular body to appear both sensual and threatening. Further, his performance rehearses the brutal black buck stereotype of racial melodramas as he relentlessly pursues River Tam and threatens to rape and murder Serenity's mechanic, Kaylee (Jewel Staite).

To take a case in point, in what initially appears to be a point-of-view shot of the engine room, Kaylee's bottom pokes out from behind machinery as she kneels on all fours, her body partially obscured. Sensing someone's presence, Kaylee tentatively calls out for River and a reverse shot reveals an empty doorway. The camera follows Kaylee's movements as she reaches for her tools, stands, and is startled by Early's looming face. When she asks Early what he is doing there, Early describes himself as a kind of Santa Claus entering the ship by way of the chimney, and momentarily pauses to wonder whether he had always been there. When Kaylee asks what he wants, Early briefly turns his attention to spinning machinery and comments on the fragility of Serenity's "beating heart." Then, almost as if providing a delayed response to her question of what he wants, he asks Kaylee if she has ever been raped. A reverse close-up of Kaylee's startled face emphasizes the force of his troubling question. The subsequent low angle shots of Early, as he tells Kaylee that the crew is locked in their quarters, suggests that he is doubly violating Kaylee through his threat of rape and uninvited presence in *her* engine room. Furthermore, the frame's shallow depth of field and low key lighting erase the specificities of their environment, temporarily transforming the impact of this black man's threat to rape a white woman into a transhistorical cinematic event. When Early announces his intention to restrain Kaylee, the double entendre of his promise to "give her a present" and get rid of a problem she has "got" simultaneously recalls his self-description as Santa Claus and the savage black rapist of early American cinema. Most troubling is a shot of Early's face hovering behind Kaylee's hair as he restrains her and says, "Now tell me Kaylee. Where does River sleep?"

On one level, Jubal Early poses a challenge to Kaylee's nontraditional portrayal as a desiring subject (and mechanic of a spaceship) by threatening to punish and resubmit her to the patriarchal order onscreen. Certainly, his threat could be read purely as an antifeminist gesture. However, I would like to suggest that on another level, as a black male figure, Early's racial identity provides an additional layer of narrative subtext that recalls stereotypical cinematic portrayals of black men as the rapists of white women. There is a sense in which his excessive displays of violence and athleticism suggest that he relishes the brutality involved in disarming Mal and threatening Kaylee. Furthermore, his expression of interest in finding out where River *sleeps* after threatening to rape Kaylee crystallizes this very specific interpretation of black masculinity first introduced as Griffith's brutal black buck.

In "Music, Race, and Paradoxes of Representation: Jubal Early's Musical

Motif of Barbarism in 'Objects in Space,'" Neil Lerner links Early's musical theme to the musical motifs of black rapists in early American cinema.[21] Most significantly, his former study of musical themes in *The Birth of a Nation* discovered a relationship between the "motif of barbarism" and the onscreen presence of the film's black male characters that enacted a racist ideology through the use of musical binaries.[22] Although background music is absent during much of Kaylee and Early's exchange in the engine room, a few tentative chords of music accompany Kaylee's repetition of Early's claim that no one can help her, but they are quickly replaced by Early's ominous musical theme when he shares his belief in her body's inconsequentiality and availability for violation. In "Listening to *Firefly*," Jennifer Goltz suggests that musical signatures can enrich a viewer's understanding of character and notes how the similarities in River's and Early's musical themes reinforce the text's linking of the two characters.[23] Given the racial melodrama's traditional linking of the black male and white female onscreen as the embodiments of Manichaean polarities and the revelation of moral truth through a nonverbal system of signification, Goltz's remarks help us situate *Firefly* within the melodramatic mode.

Goltz also observes how the lack of music accompanying Early's disjointed verbal and physical exchange with River's brother Dr. Simon Tam (Sean Maher) emphasizes their disconnectedness. Adding to Goltz's argument, I would add that their interaction draws out the bounty hunter's brutal nature and the irrationality of his thinking as he tries to intimidate Simon. His misunderstanding of Simon's question of whether he works for the Alliance ("Am I a lion?") and philosophical musings about whether things have inherent meaning or purpose underline this irrationality and appear disjointed and nonsensical. Of note is Simon's questioning of Early's sanity only after hearing that he plans to violate Kaylee, not when Early tells Simon that he must help him find River. Early's response that the state of his mental health is a matter between himself and his mind serves to illustrate that he is not a man with whom one can reason.[24]

Lyle Zynda indirectly continues this exploration of Early's engagement with reality by examining the existential themes of "Objects in Space" and considering Early's relation to River.[25] While both River and Early share a sense of displacement that informs their ability to perceive physical objects as divorced from their meaning and their capacity to create new meanings for those objects, River's possession of this dissociative quality is best understood as a consequence of Alliance medical experimentation, whereas for Early, his "not-rightness" is a result of his sociopathic tendencies. Zynda notes, "Together, they form a contrasting pair, reflecting two distinct ways of responding to the contingency of existing things. For Early, it is a source of pain; for River, it is a source of joy."²⁶ This distinction between them is further emphasized when River makes Early an object of analysis. Relying on her psychic abilities and observation of items on his spaceship, River concludes that Early's claims that he is violent because his job requires it is a lie. Demonstrating a new forthrightness, she argues that it is his natural predisposition to violent behavior that makes him a violent bounty hunter. What this suggests, however, is that the ethical code governing Early's actions condones his violence. In this regard, the text creates a comparison between Mal and Early by contrasting the thought process that informs their decisions. Throughout the series, Mal's pragmatism calls into question the extent to which we can consider him morally good. By introducing Early, this question is resolved given the bounty hunter's adherence to a code that "allows him to threaten rape and murder, and to fulfill that threat."²⁷ While River's promise to accompany Jubal Early gets him to leave the spaceship, it is Mal's surprise assault that sends the villainous bounty hunter hurtling into space and insures River's protection. Also, by extension, the text's characterological comparison of Mal and Early provides a critique of religion that links wrong beliefs with unethical behavior. Although both characters are willing to do bad things in order to achieve their goals, it is the absurdity of the thought process informing Early's ethical code that constructs him as Mal's negative image.

Serenity uses a similar narrative strategy in its characterization of the Operative. Immediately following an action sequence depicting Simon's rescue of his sister River from the Alliance medical facility, the Operative walks through the paused holographic recording of the escape, his face temporarily merging with the image of River's face. When he is discovered in the records room by Alliance medical official Dr. Mathias (Michael Hitchcock), the Operative reveals that he is a nameless, rankless agent with high security clearance. Although initially deferential, the Operative quickly shifts the dynamic of their interaction when he reprimands Dr. Mathias for placing members of parliament in the same room with River, who may have used her psychic abilities to learn confidential information. While the Operative affirms that he is not interested in learning what these secrets are, he makes clear that he *is* interested in safeguarding the classified information, and offers death-by-sword as an honorable corrective to the doctor's folly. Indeed, after dispatching Dr. Mathias's bodyguards, the Operative immobilizes Dr. Mathias and kneels beside him, upturned sword in hand, waiting for him to fall onto it. As Dr. Mathias slowly slides down the sword's blade, the Operative affirms his commitment to the Alliance project of "making better worlds," thus establishing the motivation and epistemological framework informing his pursuit of River Tam. In this regard, *Serenity* makes clear that the Operative is unconcerned with discovering whether the Alliance's reasons for killing River are justifiable.

Rather, his commitment to helping them achieve their vision of interplanetary civilization and his belief in the goodness of their civilizing mission justifies his use of violence.

It is here that we see similarities between Early's and the Operative's characterizations as brutal, black bucks emerge most clearly. When we are first introduced to these characters, their violent behavior is presented within the context of their pursuit of River and the justification they offer for this behavior, their adherence to unethical ethical codes, appears illogical and disjointed. Crucially, their willingness to and the ease with which they commit these acts of violence as they seek to capture River recalls the idea that unbridled violence is the only outlet for the black buck's repressed and excessive lust for the white woman. Further, the unjustifiability of the black rapist's actions (he relentlessly pursues the white woman because of his inability to overcome his base nature) mirrors the irrationality of Early's and the Operative's ethical codes. It is against this stereotypical representation of black masculinity that Mal's rationality is constructed. Eric Greene agrees when he writes,

> Having so clearly defined Mal in *Firefly*, in *Serenity* Whedon gives him an adversary who is his diametric opposite. Mal, the pragmatist who reacts only to what he sees, is opposed by an agent known only as the Operative, a fanatic who blinds himself to the reality before his eyes and who, as Whedon says on the commentary, "believes so strongly that he would do anything." The Alliance and its Operative, unlike Mal, act almost exclusively in the name of abstractions like order, law, and morality. Yet these ideals have been severed from the true values that arise from lived human experience: the need for self-determination, the importance of dissent, the simple moral imperative that children should not be kidnapped, killed, or turned into killers.[28]

The essence of Greene's argument is that *Serenity*'s presentation of the Operative's faith as an oppressive belief in moral abstractions and the ontological transformation of humanity contrasts sharply with the empirical evidence of Mal's lived experience. In the same way, Gerald R. Butters, Jr., argues in *Black Manhood on the Silent Screen* that "Euro-American cultural superiority was stressed through film by pitting the positive, strong, rational nature of white men against barbaric, ferocious black men."[29]

Most significantly, both *Firefly* and *Serenity* suggest that the only way to keep River safe is to eliminate the threat posed by both Early and the Operative, a decision that mirrors *The Clansman* and *The Birth of a Nation*'s solution: the castration and/or lynching of the hypermasculine black male. Accordingly, both texts metaphorically enact this castration by having Mal strip Early and the Operative of their power; thus reestablishing his status as a good guy. Early's absurdist view of life makes him keenly aware of the contingency of human life and the things around him. While he marvels in the design of an object, he believes that it is the object's use that grants it meaning. In the same manner, Early's role as a bounty hunter gives his existence meaning within a seemingly contingent universe. And when Mal's surprise attack outside the spaceship propels Early through space, he divorces Early from his purpose.

Similarly, Mal disabuses the Operative of his purpose and philosophical anthropology when he forces him to watch the planet Miranda's final recording. Confronted with evidence of the Alliance's involvement in genocide, the Operative witnesses the effects of the Alliance's moral vision and must accept Mal's pessimistic view of human nature: people cannot be made better. No longer motivated and emboldened by his faith-based beliefs, the Operative, like Early, is divorced from his purpose and must fade into the proverbial background. As Eric Greene observes,

> "Was blind but now I see" is a classic statement of rebirth through faith, but here believing suggests blindness while seeing signifies being freed from the bondage of faith. And rescue from the horrors of faith comes at the hands of Mal, a man who has renounced his own. Shown the truth of his desired "world without sin" the Operative is stripped of the abstract beliefs that blinded him to his actual reality. He sees he is about to murder people for no reason and orders his soldiers to stand down. His faith shattered, the Operative loses his reason to be, ceases to exist, becomes merely a shadow.[30]

We could ask why Mal, as a pragmatist, fails to recognize the benefits of incorporating into his crew a skilled fighter with intimate knowledge of Alliance operations and whose recent loss of faith mirrors Mal's own experience. However, this question is problematic because it demonstrates how the inflexible Manichaean modality behind *Serenity*'s logic of racial difference exposes fundamental flaws in Whedon's understanding of religious belief as irrational. If the Operative no longer believes blindly, why is he still Mal's enemy? Perhaps the answer to this question is that the requirements for maintaining the film's narrative cohesion and moral universe preclude the possibility of the Operative's recuperation despite his rejection of an oppressive belief system. Further, from this perspective, it appears that the Operative's characterization as a brutal, black brute is the film's way of constructing and preserving Mal's heroic masculinity and status as River's protector. But what then, do we make of Shepherd Book (Ron Glass), *Firefly* and *Serenity*'s other black male character?

Something's Wrong with You and What You Think

Thus far we have explored how Whedon's characterization of Early and the Operative as brutal black bucks presupposes their irrationality in order to make his case against religious belief. Granted, his stereotypical representation of *Firefly* and *Serenity*'s villains confers a degree of fixity to the model of shifting antimonies of the western film, a move necessary for a cohesive presentation of his argument. However, it is the biased nature of his premise that concerns me; namely, his recourse to racial essentialism and the presumption that something is inherently wrong with these men. If not for the portrayal of violent behavior and irrationality as incontestably innate predispositions within their biological makeup, Whedon would have to do a bit more work to narratively cement their villainy and make them unsympathetic characters that affirm the rationality of white masculinity. Jubal Early, you may recall, had no qualms "finding all unseemly manners of use" for Kaylee's body if she got in the way of River's capture. Similarly, the Operative saw no harm in killing children if it meant reducing the number of places the Serenity crew could hide.[31]

Yet some readers will probably disagree with my argument by insisting that I have chosen to overlook the texts' portrayal of the preacher Shepherd Book in order to strengthen my case. To this I would say that while I think *Firefly* and *Serenity*'s depiction of Book is a welcome departure from the pervasive brutal black buck stereotype, in their foregrounding of his religious belief he is both feminized and deracialized in order to present faith as an untenable position. In this sense, Book serves as a double negative characterization because he is a neutered version of the brutal black buck and the reverse image of Mal's heroic masculinity. Eric Greene, discussing this portrayal in relation to the Operative, writes,

> The Operative stands not only in opposition to Mal but in opposition to Book as well. Book and the Operative embody two very different kinds of faith. Book's faith leads him to engage the world. The Operative's faith leads him to dominate it. Where Book might try to convince, the Operative, like the Alliance, seeks to control. That characteristic of the Alliance, the urge to control, is at the heart of its crime on Miranda. It is also a crime that Book likely would have objected to on theological grounds.[32]

Admittedly, as the most explicit representation of Christian faith in the television series and film, Book's character seems to be the most obvious target for Whedon's critique of religion. Thus, given my focus on Early and the Operative as examples of irrational belief it could be said that I am engaging with the texts selectively. But I would go on to point out that *Serenity* targets Book's depiction of Christian faith by removing him abruptly from the narrative in order to criticize a representation of faith more akin to religious fundamentalism.[33]

In this regard, we can see that Whedon views faith in all of its forms as dangerous because he physically codifies its villainy through negative representations of black masculinity. By linking Shepherd Book, Jubal Early, and the Operative visually, Whedon unconsciously reproduces a narrative Manichaean modality predicated on racial essentialism. Thus, at the heart of *Serenity*'s portrayal of faith-based belief as irrational is the claim that there is something wrong with the belief itself, and, ultimately, the believer.[34] The idea that "there is something inherently wrong with the believer of faith-based beliefs or he wouldn't hold those beliefs" seems to embody what is known as the *de jure* objection to Christian faith.[35] Eric Greene acknowledges this flaw in Whedon's understanding of religious belief:

> Throughout *Firefly*, *Serenity*, and his *Serenity* commentary Whedon seems to suggest that the very act of faith is inherently dangerous. Given the intimations of Book's Alliance past, he and the Operative seem linked, as if the capacity to murder is dependent on the capacity for faith, as if the Operative is merely a sociopathic version of Book, as if the Operative is where Book was inevitably headed had he not left the Alliance and become a Shepherd. The suggestion that Book did leave the Alliance holds out the possibility that faith need not become fanaticism but nevertheless, by the end of the film Whedon denies both Book *and* the Operative a place in *Serenity*'s community.[36]

It is important to note that the texts' aversion to religion is not just a product of Whedon's personal biases, but is also an integral part of the western film genre. Jane Tompkins in her study of westerns notes how the genre's inbuilt binary opposition is reflected in its view of religion as a part of the world of illusion. Given the antilanguage sentiment of the western genre, she observes its portrayal of the futility of religion and language ("Don't call on God; he's not there") to "express the truth of things." To make her point, she references John Wayne, an iconic western film hero who "not only challenges the authority of the Christian God but also expresses disgust at all the trappings of belief: liturgies, litanies, forms, representations, all of which are betrayals of reality itself."[37]

Along similar lines, we can discern how Mal's hostility towards belief in *Firefly* and *Serenity* stems from the idea that religion presents a false and oppressive view of human nature. When we first see Shepherd Book he is looking for passage on a spaceship. Significantly, his first interaction with a member of Serenity's crew is with Kaylee, a white woman. Nonthreatening and respectful, Book's demeanor recalls the deferential attitude of racial melodrama's feminized older black male as he explains that he has recently left an abbey and is in search of travel and adventure. Defined by his role as a shepherd, Book's interactions with Mal recall the captain's rejection of faith and provide opportunity for criticism. In particular, Mal's most memorable clashes with Shepherd Book have involved Book's desire to "say a few words," as grace over a meal or as parting words for the dead. After finding a lone survivor on a ship attacked by Reavers, the cannibalistic savages living on the borders of civilization, *Firefly* introduces a theme later developed in *Serenity* that I believe is at the core of the texts' examination of faith and reason: conflicting views about what it means to be human. As Mal and Book debate whether the Reavers' humanity has been destroyed or if they are men still capable of redemption, the text tries to construct this difference in opinion as pragmatic empiricism versus religious faith. Considering *Firefly* and *Serenity*'s hints about Book's past, particularly the idea that he was once associated with the Alliance, perhaps in a capacity similar to the Operative, it appears that Book's view of human nature is predicated on his own transformation.[38] Thus, it is my contention that despite the texts' characterization of faith as irrational, Mal and Book are both speaking from lived experience.

We're the Real Good Guys

Emboldened by the empirical evidence substantiating his previously held opinion about the destructiveness of the Alliance's civilizing mission, Mal passionately declares to his crew in Serenity's mess hall that it is their responsibility to speak on behalf of Miranda's dead and prevent the Alliance from again trying to change human nature. At first, the placement of the camera positions the spectator as a member of the crew listening to Mal's impassioned speech while a strong source of backlighting obscures him from view. As the camera tracks around the room to capture the crew's responses, Mal remains partially obscured by the light until his conclusion, when the camera's reframing causes the backlight to evoke an almost angelic aura around his face. It is in this moment that both the crew and the spectator are commissioned to join Mal in his fight against the tyranny of faith-based belief.

Significantly, the irony of this sequence is Whedon's decision to portray Mal's explicit critique of the Alliance's philosophical anthropology as a transcendent moment. Considering melodrama's focus on innocent victims and the recognition of their virtue, Mal's speech orchestrates the text's moral legibility by identifying River Tam and Miranda's inhabitants as victims of the Alliance's experimentation. According to Linda Williams, the recognition of virtue is accomplished through "an aesthetics of astonishment," a stylistic mechanism that provides "a way of crystallizing the dramatic tensions within a scene and of musically prolonging their emotional effects."[39] Clearly, implicit to this sequence is the conflict between the Alliance's attempts to civilize humanity and Mal's idea that human nature cannot be improved. In this manner, the sequence's stylistic qualities enable it to "put forth a moral truth in gesture and to picture what could not be fully spoken in words," chiefly the veracity of Mal's claims that the Alliance is wrong for imposing its view of humanity on others.[40] Whedon verifies this assessment of the Alliance in *Serenity*'s commentary when he argues, "the film is about the right to be wrong. You can't impose your way of thinking even if your way of thinking is more enlightened and better than theirs. It's just simply not how human beings are."[41] It is worth emphasizing at this point, however, that in making this comment Whedon fails to notice how Mal also imposes his way of thinking on his crew, or how he, as the writer and director of *Serenity*, does the same for his audience.

Conclusion

Inevitably, *Serenity*'s preoccupation with the demonstration of the irrationality of religious belief comes to its fullest realization during the final showdown between Mal and the Operative. Forced to watch the holographic recording which Serenity's crew discovered on the planet Miranda, the Operative learns the secret that the Alliance feared River knew: their involvement in the death of Miranda's thirty million inhabitants and the creation of the Reavers. In great detail, it reports how the Alliance's addition of G-23 paxilon hydrochlorate (or "Pax") to the planet's terraforming air processors destroyed life on the planet. Administered to decrease aggression, Pax also removed from Miranda's residents the basic drives necessary for human flourishing, like eating, drinking, and having sex. A small percentage of the population, however, became increasingly violent and uncontrollable, leading to the creation of the Reavers. Most significantly, this revelation challenges the Operative's belief system and prompts his loss of faith.

Of course, I can imagine someone challenging my view of this scene on the grounds that the Operative's violent behavior precludes the possibility that the death of Miranda's inhabitants would instigate a loss of faith. To this, I would respond that the Operative's loss of faith stems from the realization that human nature cannot be made better, not that the Alliance's actions led to genocide and the creation of the Reavers. Clearly, the Operative's beliefs caused him to be willing to go to any lengths to facilitate the Alliance's utopian vision of better worlds, even if that meant hurting women and killing children. This is apparent through his violent interactions with Inara (Morena Baccarin) and his massacre of the people living on Haven. Ultimately, like Mal, the Operative's crisis of faith is precipitated by the revelation that his actions were futile because they were motivated by misguided beliefs.

Although framed by the western genre's inbuilt binary oppositions, the texts' examination of the relationship between faith and reason relies heavily on the brutal black buck stereotype to give force to its argument about the irrationality of religious belief. It is my sense that the film, unable to neutralize the portrayal of racial difference as inherently irrational, had to forcibly remove Shepherd Book and the Operative from the narrative. This is the case because *Serenity*'s corrective for faith-based belief has been administered and while the Operative *should* be like Mal in the film's conclusion, he is not. In this way, Whedon's attempts to illustrate the irrationality of faith-based belief through racial stereotypes reveals that his understanding of religious belief is itself a stereotype and, as such, is unable to fully address the complexity of religious belief.

NOTES

1. As quoted in Cynthia Ryan, "'Serenity.' DVD Commentary," *The Encyclopedia of Buffy Studies*, accessed December 20, 2012, http://www.slayageonline.com/EBS/tables_of_contents/type/DVD_commentaries.htm.
2. David Baggett, "*Firefly* and Freedom," in *The Philosophy of Joss Whedon*, ed. Dean A. Kowalski and S. Evan Kreider (Lexington: University Press of Kentucky, 2011), 16.
3. Ibid., 13.
4. David Lusted, *The Western* (Essex: Pearson Education Limited, 2003). This negotiation of the binary oppositions of heroism and villainy continues later in *Firefly*'s pilot episode, six years after the Battle of Serenity Valley. An Alliance cruiser has discovered the Serenity crew looting an abandoned spaceship and refers to them as "vultures" and "scavengers." Mal, aware of the Alliance's self-identification as "the good guys," exploits their hubris and evades arrest by using a personnel ship decoy to send out dummy distress signals. While the Alliance cruiser attends to the rescue of the "distressed civilians," the Serenity crew escapes with their stolen cargo. However, their identification by the Alliance cruiser positions them as outlaws for the remainder of the series. Although illegal, the transport and sale of stolen cargo become the only means of earning a living available to the crew. Indeed, as outlaws, Mal and his crew must negotiate the tension between the criminality of their actions and their latent desire for justice and respectability.
5. Peter Brooks, *The Melodramatic Imagination: Balzac, Henry James, Melodrama, and the Mode of Excess* (New Haven: Yale University Press, 1995), viii.
6. Ibid., xiii.
7. Ibid., 15.
8. Lusted, *The Western*, 65–66.
9. Linda Williams, "Melodrama Revisited," in *Refiguring American Film Genres*, ed. Nick Browne (Berkeley: University of California Press, 1998), 78–79.
10. Ibid., 54–55.
11. I am thinking here of the "Blue Gloves" and of Lawrence Dobson, the undercover Alliance agent in "Serenity."
12. Linda Williams, "Race, Melodrama, and *The Birth of a Nation* (1915)," in *The Silent Cinema Reader*, ed. Lee Grieveson and Peter Krämer (London and New York: Routledge, 2004), 192.
13. Ibid., 244.
14. Robyn Wiegman, *American Anatomies: Theorizing Race and Gender* (Durham, NC: Duke University Press, 1995), 198.
15. Donald Bogle, *Toms, Coons, Mulattoes, Mammies, and Bucks* (New York and London: Continuum, 2002), 5–6.

16. Ibid., 13–14.
17. Ibid., 18.
18. Eric Greene, "The Good Book," in *Serenity Found: More Unauthorized Essays on Joss Whedon's Firefly Universe*. ed. Jane Espenson (Dallas: Benbella, 2007), 83.
19. B. Steve Csaki, "Mommas, Don't Let Your Babies Grow Up to Be Pragmatists," in *The Philosophy of the Western*, ed. Jennifer L. McMahon and B. Steve Csaki (Lexington: University Press of Kentucky, 2010), 55–68. Csaki's study of John Wayne's cowboy heroes as embodiments of American pragmatism is helpful because it presents the "code of the West" often depicted in the western film genre as a moral framework governed by situation ethics.
20. Lusted, *The Western*, 86–89.
21. Neil Lerner, "Music, Race, and Paradoxes of Representation: Jubal Early's Musical Motif of Barbarism in 'Objects in Space,'" in *Investigating "Firefly" and "Serenity": Science Fiction on the Frontier*, ed. Rhonda V. Wilcox and Tanya R. Cochran (London and New York: I.B. Taurus, 2008), 183–190.
22. Jane Gaines and Neil Lerner, "The Orchestration of Affect: The Motif of Barbarism in Breil's *The Birth of a Nation* Score," in *The Sounds of Early Cinema*, ed. Richard Abel and Rick Altman (Bloomington: Indiana University Press, 2001), 252–268.
23. Jennifer Goltz, "Listening to *Firefly*," in *Finding Serenity: Antiheroes, Lost Shepherds, and Space Hookers in Joss Whedon's "Firefly*," ed. Jane Espenson (Dallas: BenBella, 2004), 213–214.
24. His irrationality is further illustrated later when Early suggests that, as a doctor, Simon should have the experience of being shot, stabbed or "cut on" to inform his approach to healthcare, and also when Early strikes the companion Inara to silence her and stop her from "visiting" his intentions. In *Serenity* we also see the Operative physically assault Inara.
25. In his description of Jubal Early, Lyle Zynda writes, "Early seems both highly capable and somewhat damaged — not all is 'right' with him. He is a man of action (swiftly knocking out the captain and locking most of the other in their quarters as they sleep) and cunning (he deals with each crew member in a way most likely to achieve his aims). He also can be terrifying: in a disturbing scene, he coolly threatens to rape Kaylee, the ship's able and ever-positive engineer, if she gets in his way — and we believe him capable of it. Yet he also seems distracted by seemingly small and irrelevant features of his surrounding and digresses repeatedly into what appear to be meandering 'philosophical' questions. Perhaps, we surmise, his solitary life as a bounty hunter — as well as the violence his job requires — has taken its toll on him." Lyle Zynda, "We're All Just Floating in Space," in *Finding Serenity*, 86–87.
26. Ibid., 85.
27. Ibid., 94.
28. Greene, "The Good Book," 86.
29. Gerald R. Butters, Jr., *Black Manhood on the Silent Screen* (Lawrence: University Press of Kansas, 2002), 51.
30. Greene, "The Good Book," 89.
31. Significantly, in another scene immediately following Mal's fight with the Operative, Inara tells the crew that they should fear the Operative because he is a believer. It is not just his belief that killing River is the right thing to do that worries her, it is that he is methodical and devout in this belief. In other words, it is his position as a believer that makes him dangerous, not just the wrongness of his belief.
32. Greene, "The Good Book," 86–87.
33. Ibid., 93.
34. As Greene observes, "Whedon states on the *Serenity* commentary that 'the person who believes … is capable of terrible things,' and indeed, that conviction runs throughout both the series and the film." Greene, "The Good Book," 92.
35. Alvin Plantinga, *Warranted Christian Belief* (New York: Oxford University Press, 2000).
36. Greene," The Good Book," 92.
37. Jane Tompkins, *West of Everything: The Inner Life of Westerns* (New York: Oxford University Press, 1992), 48–53. Tompkins is referring to the film *Red River* (dir. Howard Hawks, 1948).

38. For instance, during the pilot episode of *Firefly*, when an undercover Alliance agent accidentally shoots Kaylee while attempting to arrest Simon, Shepherd Book quickly disarms the agent and renders him unconscious. In "Safe" (*Firefly* 5), while on an outer planet, Book is badly injured during a gunfight between those buying Serenity cargo and some local law officials. Unbeknownst to the crew, Simon is abducted by townspeople in desperate need of a doctor and the crew must turn to the Alliance for Book's medical help. Initially refused assistance by an Alliance cruiser, Book presents his identity card to a senior Alliance officer and is immediately granted special access to Alliance medical facilities. Most telling, however, is the exchange between Simon Tam and Jubal Early during "Objects in Space." When Simon rebukes Early for knocking a shepherd unconscious, Early replies, "that ain't a shepherd." Turning to *Serenity*, we find an important clue in Book's insightful description of the Operative and his in-depth knowledge about Alliance operations.
39. Williams, "Melodrama Revisited," 66–67.
40. Ibid., 52.
41. Greene, "The Good Book," 90.

BIBLIOGRAPHY

Baggett, David. "*Firefly* and Freedom." In *The Philosophy of Joss Whedon*, edited by Dean A. Kowalski and S. Evan Kreider, 9–23. Lexington: University Press of Kentucky, 2011.
Bogle, Donald. *Toms, Coons, Mulattoes, Mammies, and Bucks*. New York and London: Continuum, 2002.
Brooks, Peter. *The Melodramatic Imagination: Balzac, Henry James, Melodrama, and the Mode of Excess*. New Haven: Yale University Press, 1995.
Butters, Gerald R., Jr. *Black Manhood on the Silent Screen*. Lawrence: University Press of Kansas, 2002.
Csaki, B. Steve. "Mommas, Don't Let Your Babies Grow Up to Be Pragmatists." In *The Philosophy of the Western*, edited by Jennifer L. McMahon and B. Steve Csaki, 55–68. Lexington: University Press of Kentucky, 2010.
Gaines, Jane, and Neil Lerner. "The Orchestration of Affect: The Motif of Barbarism in Breil's *The Birth of a Nation* Score." In *The Sounds of Early Cinema*, edited by Richard Abel and Rick Altman, 252–268. Indiana University Press, 2001.
Goltz, Jennifer. "Listening to *Firefly*." In *Finding Serenity: Antiheroes, Lost Shepherds, and Space Hookers in Joss Whedon's "Firefly*," edited by Jane Espenson, 209–216. Dallas: BenBella, 2004.
Greene, Eric. "The Good Book." In *Serenity Found: More Unauthorized Essays on Joss Whedon's Firefly Universe*, edited by Jane Espenson, 79–93. Dallas: BenBella, 2007.
Lerner, Neil. "Music, Race, and Paradoxes of Representation: Jubal Early's Musical Motif of Barbarism in 'Objects in Space.'" In *Investigating "Firefly" and "Serenity": Science Fiction on the Frontier*, edited by Rhonda V. Wilcox and Tanya R. Cochran, 183–190. London and New York: I.B. Taurus, 2008.
Lusted, David. *The Western*. Essex: Pearson Education Limited, 2003.
Plantinga, Alvin. *Warranted Christian Belief*. New York: Oxford University Press, 2000.
Ryan, Cynthia. "'Serenity.' DVD Commentary." *The Encyclopedia of Buffy Studies*. Accessed December 20, 2012. http://www.slayageonline.com/EBS/tables_of_contents/type/DVD_commentaries.htm.
Tompkins, Jane. *West of Everything: The Inner Life of Westerns*. New York: Oxford University Press, 1992.
Wiegman, Robyn. *American Anatomies: Theorizing Race and Gender*. Durham, NC: Duke University Press, 1995.
Williams, Linda. "Melodrama Revisited." In *Refiguring American Film Genres*, edited by Nick Browne, 42–88. Berkeley: University of California Press, 1998.
_____. "Race, Melodrama, and *The Birth of a Nation* (1915)." In *The Silent Cinema Reader*,

edited by Lee Grieveson and Peter Krämer, 242–253. London and New York: Routledge, 2004.

Zynda, Lyle. "We're All Just Floating in Space." In *Finding Serenity: Antiheroes, Lost Shepherds, and Space Hookers in Joss Whedon's "Firefly,"* edited by Jane Espenson, 85–95. Dallas: BenBella, 2004.

"You're welcome on my boat, God ain't"
Ethical Foundations in the Whedonverse
DEAN A. KOWALSKI

Joss Whedon is renowned for his rich and complex characters. Malcolm Reynolds is a particularly striking example. Mal's complexity (in part) is grounded in the very fact that he wishes to be not complex at all. He looks to keep things simple without a lot of jabber. His basic principles, although sometimes pragmatically coarse, seem rather straightforward: "I do the job and then I get paid"; "If I ever kill you, you'll be awake, you'll be facing me, and you'll be armed"; "Someone tries to kill you, you try to kill 'em right back."[1] Furthermore, he no longer complicates his life with religion, seeing God (at best) as "a long wait for a train that don't come" (*Serenity*). The vampire with a soul Angel is another fascinating Whedon character who prefers self-reliance and simplicity, which only adds depth and complexity. Only slightly tongue-in-cheek, he asserts, "There are three things I don't do: tan, date, and sing in public" ("Judgment," *Angel* 2.1).[2] Angel tirelessly upholds his credo to "help the helpless," but will forever remain separated from humanity.

It will be argued that these two characters jointly serve as a microcosm for a distinctive ethical position that resonates throughout Whedon's corpus (or "Whedonverse"). The earlier parts of the essay will delineate how Mal, despite his rejection of theism, regularly (but not perfectly) acts from a principled ethical approach, one that is effectively characterized as a synthesis of Kantian and Aristotelian perspectives. The latter parts of the essay will explain how Whedon's portrayal of Angel can be interpreted as providing his implicit position on the conceptual adequacy of nontheistic ethical systems. It will be argued that if Whedon's position on the second issue satisfies, then Whedon provides the viewer important insights that go well beyond his fictive *Firefly* 'verse.

"Yeah — but she's our witch"

Sergeant Malcolm Reynolds was seemingly a devout theist until the Battle of Serenity Valley, the last stand for the Browncoats. Not only did the Browncoats lose the war, but Mal and his few remaining beleaguered troops were stranded while the powers that be decided upon terms.[3] In the six years that have passed, he has purchased a firefly-class transport ship in the hopes of regaining some semblance of his independence.

Although Mal has turned his back on God, religious influences persist throughout *Firefly* and *Serenity*. Shepherd Book, a preacher from the Southdown Abbey, boards spaceship Serenity in the first episode. Mal needs the fare, but not Book's "religiosity"; he can save that for the "Fuzzie Wuzzies." Yet Book soon becomes part of the crew. In "Heart of Gold" (13), the crew takes a job aiding Nandi, an old friend of Inara. Nandi, now running a bordello on a remote moon, has had various nasty disputes with local land baron Rance Burgess. Mal takes the job but soon chooses to run, explaining that Burgess will be relentless in getting what he wants because "there is nothing worse than a monster who believes he is right with God."

In "Safe," the crew delivers beef cattle to Jiangyn moon, but the drop is complicated when Dr. Simon Tam and his sister River are kidnapped by members of a destitute hill community. River's psychic abilities are soon discovered. One of the more learned among the hill folk thereupon recites, "And they shall be among the people, and they shall speak truths and whisper secrets — and you will know them by their crafts.... Thou shall not suffer a witch to live." The town elder, known as the Patron, announces, "She has had congress with the Beast! The witch must burn. God commands it." Simon lovingly stands with his sister at the stake, wrapping his arms around her. In the nick of time, Mal and Zoe appear, demanding that River and Simon be returned to them. But the Patron is resolute: "This is a holy cleansing. You cannot think to thwart God's will." Mal dismisses him, pointing to Jayne (Adam Baldwin) in Serenity's open cargo bay: "Y'all see the man hangin' out of the spaceship with the really big gun? ... Man's looking to kill some folk. So really it's his will y'all should worry 'bout thwarting." The Patron protests, "The girl is a witch!" Almost annoyed, Mal replies, "Yeah. But she is our witch. So cut her the hell down."

The religious elements in *Firefly* may be meant to remind us of the common belief that religion and ethics are somehow connected. Contemporary philosopher James Rachels asserts, "It is not unusual for priests and ministers to be treated as moral experts.... In popular thinking, morality and religion are inseparable: People commonly believe that morality can be understood only in the context of religion. So because clergymen are the spokesmen for religion, it is assumed that they must be spokesmen for morality as well."[4] Yet Whedon may remind us of this common assumption only to assess it. *Is* it obvious that ethics is groundless without religion? Whedon clearly holds that theistic belief is no guarantee of morally appropriate behavior. The wealthy Rance Burgess, infused with theistically inspired self-righteousness, is a misogynistic monster. The Jiangyn hill people, steeped in scripture, are quick to kidnap Simon and rush to murder River, despite the Tams' innocence. The Patron, moreover, presumably the spiritual leader of the community, murdered his predecessor for personal gain. Obviously, not all theists are morally dubious. Shepherd Book, despite his mysterious past, is an upright individual. Just as obviously, not all nontheists are morally suspect. Inara is also of strong moral fiber, but she is ostensibly Buddhist. Mal, an atheist, rescues River and Simon — a big damn hero he is — even if, pragmatically speaking, it would be easier for him and his crew if he didn't. All of this serves to cloud the presumed connection between religion and ethics.

That the hill people are prominently portrayed as hopelessly ignorant is possibly the result of lazy writing. But this seems unlikely given the obvious writing talents of Whedon and his staff. Alternatively, we might interpret Whedon as exploring some classic issues in religious moral philosophy. First, even assuming God's existence, it might be wondered whether God is the actual author of any scriptural injunction. The command to kill a witch seems particularly dubious. The actual existence of witches is incredibly unlikely, and God would know this. Second, the fact that we tend to gauge the validity of any biblical injunction by prior moral convictions speaks against a thoroughgoing scripture-based ethic. Any binding moral injunction requires following only well-accepted moral standards or principles. But would a morally perfect God ruthlessly command a fiery death for anyone? Third, great care must be taken when attempting to comply with a biblical command. Context must be taken into account. The assumed threat of witches to the authors of the Hebrew Bible is one thing, but is there any reason to believe that River Tam is a witch? Such questions must be carefully and conscientiously explored. If they are not, tragedy ensues, which is (in part) the dramatic force of "Safe."

Arguably, then, Whedon intimates that our efforts would be better spent following Socrates's example of determining for ourselves what we ought to do rather than mindlessly relying on ancient and not properly contextualized biblical injunctions. After all, sometimes when you look to the heavens for guidance you see only a large grizzled man aiming his frighteningly high-powered rifle at your chest. Careful reasoning might lead the hill people to the conclusion that even if River's psychic abilities resemble something like witchcraft, she is no witch and they have no right to burn her at the stake. Rather than execute her, the hill people should hand her over to the crew.

Mal asserts she is their "witch"—which is to say a troubled young girl who needs their help. The crew is praiseworthy for rescuing her (and Simon).

That Whedon portrays religiously steeped individuals dubiously but less religious characters in a positive moral light calls out for a closer examination of his implicit ethical views and the foundations upon which they rest. Analyses of Whedon's ethical views are not unprecedented.[5] But given Whedon's often ambivalent and sometimes cynical views of religion, it seems that interpretations stressing nontheistic approaches are preferable. A recent commentary by K. Dale Koontz often unfortunately uses unnecessary theistic motifs to interpret the Whedonverse, including *Firefly*. For example, she admits that Mal would "snort with derision" over her various argued parallels between the brigand's behavior and Christ's message.[6] One of the overarching goals of this essay is to provide an interpretation of *Firefly* (and perhaps the wider Whedonverse) that would not cause Mal—or Whedon—to "snort with derision."

"Wife or no, you are no one's property"

Exploring Whedon's ethical views, especially as conveyed in the 'verse, profitably begins with "Our Mrs. Reynolds." After a night of merriment, Mal finds a stowaway in the cargo hold. Her name is Saffron (Christina Hendricks)—Mal's new wife! But Mal doesn't remember getting married. The night before, Mal unknowingly participated in the marriage ceremony of the Triumph Settlers. Jayne feels immediately slighted, complaining, "All I got was that dumb-ass stick that sounds like it's raining. How come you got a wife?"

Mal doesn't want a wife. He would make a terrible husband. Jayne decides to trade up. He abruptly confronts Mal, declaring, "You got something you don't deserve." Jayne is carrying his favorite rifle; he reverently holds it out toward Mal. Bewildered, Mal asks: "Are you offering me a trade?" Jayne: "A Trade? Hell, it's theft! ... It's miles more worthy 'n what you got." Mal becomes incredulous, reminding Jayne, "*What* I got? She has a name." Jayne immediately retorts, "So does this! I call it 'Vera.'" Mal's incredulity turns to disdain. About Saffron, he explains: "She's not to be bought. Nor bartered, or borrowed, or lent. She's a human woman, doesn't know a damn thing about the world and needs our protection."

"Our Mrs. Reynolds" is a multilayered morality tale. First, there is the issue of whether the Triumph Settlers' practice of running a "Maiden House" is tantamount to slavery. Could any woman provide voluntary, informed consent to be involved in such a practice? Second, Jayne only makes matters worse by suggesting that because Saffron was a gift in lieu of payment, and one that Mal doesn't welcome, he would trade for her as he might a gun, horse, or floral bonnet. The very idea that Jayne believes "Vera" is equal in worth to Saffron is reprehensible. Third, as the episode unfolds, we learn that Saffron is actually a ruthless con artist. She plays Mal and crew so as to bring spaceship Serenity to a futuristic chop shop. Her dishonesty to the crew is tantamount to disrespecting them in the extreme. She places her selfish projects ahead of their wellbeing, putting their very lives in grave jeopardy.

That persons are not property but uniquely due moral respect is well attested in the 'verse. Recall Mal's reaction in "Serenity" when he discovered that Simon's blue cryochamber contained a young girl. Mal clearly thought (falsely) that River was some sort of sex slave, and Simon culpable for transporting her. A similar example occurs during the teaser of "Shindig" (4). Mal is playing pool with a smuggler named Wright. Wright announces his recent good fortune, a job transporting "labor" to border planets. Mal clarifies, "Labor? You mean slaves." Wright responds, "They wasn't volunteers, for damn sure." Mal unflinchingly steals Wright's money. Presenting it to Inara, he clarifies, "They earned that with the sweat of their slave-tradin' brows." The fact that Whedon has Mal take Wright's earnings clearly indicates that it was illicitly obtained, thereby reinforcing the belief that Wright acted impermissibly.

Later in "Shindig," Inara receives a lucrative and flattering business proposition from Atherton Wing. He wishes that she become his personal companion. Being a companion is a legal and rather well-respected profession, bordering on an art; however, it retains elements of prostitution. When Inara gives too much attention to Mal at a ballroom party the three are attending, Atherton becomes sour. He gruffly grabs Inara by the arm and affirms, "Excuse me. She's not here with you, Captain. She's mine." Mal chides him: "Yours? She don't belong to nobody." Atherton persists: "Money changed hands. Makes her mine tonight. And no matter how you dress her up, she's still —." Before Wing could finish his sentence, Mal punches him in the face, knocking him to the floor. Inara confronts Mal: "You have a strange sense of nobility, Captain. You lay a man out for implying that I am a whore, but you keep calling me one to my face." Mal explains: "I might not show respect to your job, but he didn't respect you. That's the difference, Inara, he doesn't even *see* you."

A fundamental moral point throughout *Firefly* seems to be that all persons are uniquely due respect. This ethical view closely approximates that of Immanuel Kant. For Kant, the conceptual differences between a person and a thing are crucial:

> Nonrational beings, [have] only a relative value as means, and are therefore called *things;* rational beings, on the contrary, are called *persons,* because their very nature

points them out as ends in themselves, that is as something which must not be used merely as means, and so far therefore restricts freedom of action (and is an object of respect). These, therefore, are not merely subjective ends whose existence has a worth for us as an effect of our action, but *objective ends,* that is things whose existence is an end in itself an end, moreover, for which no other can be substituted.[7]

Things are objects that have purposes put upon them. They are used as a means to achieve some project. Persons, however, are sources of value insofar as they (we) independently implement purposes into (or onto) the world. Persons, but not things, are able to recognize the difference between right and wrong as it applies to our purposes, and grasp the significance of that difference. Persons, but not things, can perform actions because they are right and refrain from actions because they are wrong (not that we always do). Persons, but not things, are appropriately praised or blamed given how they choose regarding the moral knowledge they possess. That persons possess such attributes grounds their moral importance, making them sources of moral behavior, and, in a way, of morality itself. A world without persons is tantamount to a world without moral worth. Kant labels these morally significant features of personhood "being autonomous." For Kant, the fact that persons are autonomous — rational agents, possessed of volition and foresight — is the crux of all moral value and ethically significant judgments.

Accordingly, whether a person is a wife or not, companion or not, or shepherd or not, she or he is not property and simply may not be treated as such. That persons possess *inherent* worth explains why murder, kidnapping, and slavery are impermissible. Human women and men may not be bought, bartered, or borrowed exactly because persons are not things. Treating persons in such ways fails to respect their inherent worth, which is to commit the gravest of moral errors. Mal recognizes this (which doesn't mean that he is always cheerful about it). Whedon's moral message seems to be that, apart from whether God exists, there are simply some things that we may not do.

"There's good people in the 'verse"

After Mal and the crew regain control of the ship in "Our Mrs. Reynolds," they track down Saffron to a remote moon.[8] Drawing his pistol, Mal declares, "You even think about playing me again I will riddle you with holes." She smugly replies, "Everybody plays each other. That's all anybody ever does. We play parts." Saffron's message seems to be that by playing "the part" properly, anyone can selfishly achieve whatever she wants regardless of the consequences. Mal replies, "Yet here I am with a gun to your head. That's 'cause I got people with me, people who trust each other, who do for each other and ain't always looking for the advantage."

This exchange between Mal and Saffron harkens back to Aristotle's view of the good life. Aristotle affirms that we are rational and social beings: "For the final and perfect good ... we do not mean a man who lives his life in isolation ... since man is by nature a social and political being."[9] Aristotle implicitly argues that whether a thing's life goes well invariably depends on what kind of thing it is. It's bad for fish to be separated from the water, and likewise bad for oak trees to be kept in a closet. If Aristotle is correct that we are naturally social, then it's bad for any human being to live in complete isolation, which explains why solitary confinement is such serious punishment. That Joss agrees with Aristotle's view fits well with his portrayal of Mal from *Firefly*. The only two times that Mal faces grave danger is in "Out of Gas" (8) and "War Stories" (10). In the former he is fatally wounded and near death; in the latter he dies, only to be revived by Niska so the crime lord can continue torturing him. On both occasions Mal was completely alone. He was rescued only upon the return of the crew, and most notably Zoe.

Having established that the good human life requires living in community, Aristotle further argues that it also requires friendship — living among those who wish one another goodwill and care about each other's interests. In support of this, Aristotle plausibly contends that friendship is universally valued; regardless of one's current station in life — young or old, wealthy or poor, powerful or disenfranchised — everyone desires friendship. Moreover, Aristotle asserts that "friends are the greatest of external goods" and "without friends no one would choose to live, though he had all other goods."[10] That is, if it's good to live in community, it's better to live among those who express mutual goodwill and concern about each other's interests.

Making this sort of connection minimally requires recognizing that the interests of others are no less important than yours. The value of such connections is enhanced by wishing goodwill onto others and conferring benefits to them simply for their own sake. They accomplish profound depths when others simultaneously seek your good, and all involved mutually work for the betterment of the other — simply for its own sake. Fostering this kind of reciprocal relationship requires time, familiarity, and trust. Once accomplished, one achieves a sort of second self, a true partner, such that one's interests are directly tied into that of the other. This is to enjoy the highest and best form of friendship, which is valuable for its own sake and for the benefits it confers.[11]

In some ways, spaceship Serenity can be interpreted as a small community and, arguably, a family. Each crewmember must be respectful of the other, and failing to do so (recalling Kant) is morally impermissible. In proof of this, recall how Jayne drew Mal's ire over a humiliating and rude comment about Kaylee at the dinner table in "Serenity." When the crew works together, respectfully, all goes well. When the crew does not, things go south. One of the more noxious examples of things going south again involves Jayne. In "Ariel" (9), recall that Jayne sells out Simon and River to the Alliance for the reward money. Not unlike Saffron, Jayne impermissibly decides to put his selfish interests ahead of the crew's. When Simon, River, and Jayne get pinched by the feds, making the hospital heist messy, Mal susses out Jayne's selfish intentions.

Whedon depicts the seriousness of Jayne's wrongful act in a tellingly novel, two-pronged way. First, Mal, fuming, threatens to blow Jayne into empty space. Jayne finally confesses, but remains confused: "Why are you taking this so personal? It's not like I ratted *you* out to the feds!" Mal barks back: "But you did. You turn on any of my crew, you turn on me." And note how closely Whedon's dramatic treatment mirrors Aristotle's assessment: "The duties of parents to children and those of brothers to each other are not the same nor those of comrades and those of fellow citizens, and so, too, with other kinds of friendship ... and the injustice increases by being exhibited toward those who are friends in a fuller sense; e.g., it is a more terrible thing to defraud a comrade than a fellow citizen."[12] Because the interests of the crew have grown together so tightly, harming one means harming everyone. That Mal is willing to end Jayne speaks to the severity of his misdeed. Mal relents only after Jayne exhibits genuine remorse, an emotion with which Jayne is unfamiliar.

Whedon frames a second response quite differently. Simon does not learn of Jayne's treachery until "Trash." At that time he neither threatens nor seeks retribution. Rather, he seemingly pardons Jayne, invites him to renew their relationship, and surprisingly offers to trust Jayne more. Simon tells Jayne, "No matter how you come down on us, I will never harm you. You're on this table, you're safe. I'm your medic, and ... we're on the same crew.... I don't care what you've done. I don't know what you're planning on doing, but I'm trusting you. I think you should do the same." By mercifully reminding Jayne of the importance of trust and friendship, concepts that Jayne has difficulty "wrapping his head around," Simon hopes to accomplish what Mal does albeit differently: bringing Jayne back into the fold, working for the common good, and strengthening the bonds of friendship.

Whedon further highlights the seriousness of Jayne's misdeed by what he expends to earn redemption. First, Jayne inexplicably spends some of his cut of the hospital heist on the crew in the form of fresh fruit — a rare and prized commodity in the 'verse.[13] Just as inexplicably, he throws the remainder of his hospital bounty into a kitty Zoe collects in the hopes of ransoming Mal and Wash (Alan Tudyk) from Niska's vengeful clutches. Second, Jayne is the first crewmember to follow Mal in his call to action upon learning the truth about planet Miranda in the film *Serenity*. This may require each of them to make the ultimate sacrifice. Jayne responds first, seemingly speaking for the crew: "Shepherd Book used to tell me, if you can't do something smart, do something right." He then takes a long swig from a whiskey bottle. That Whedon portrays him immediately sliding the bottle directly to Simon, who also drinks, intimates that Jayne's character arc is complete: through the efforts of Mal and Simon, Jayne has become a part of the crew, finally wrapping his head around the important ethical values of community and friendship.

Aristotle's wider ethical message is one of developing desirable character traits — the virtues — by constant mindfulness of one's current situation and acting appropriately in it. Overreacting (doing too much) and underreacting (doing too little) are both to be avoided. The proper course is somewhere in between:

> It is moral virtue that is concerned with emotions and actions, and it is in these we have excess and deficiency and the mean. Thus it is possible to go too far, or not far enough in fear, pride, desire, anger, pity, and pleasure and pain generally, and the excess and the deficiency are alike wrong; but to feel these emotions at the right times, for the right objects, towards the right persons, for the right motives, and in the right manner, is the mean or the best good, which signifies virtue. Similarly, there may be excess, deficiency, or the mean, in acts.[14]

Through regular mindfulness of appropriate behavior given the situation, we become courageous (rather than reckless or cowardly), honest (rather than boastful or deceptive), generous (rather than extravagant or stingy), loyal (rather than fawning or duplicitous), and temperate (rather than hot-headed or meek). We thereby acquire a morally desirable character, and such a stable character makes future moral choices less difficult. We thus approach the highest human moral good—*eudaimonia*. Jayne has a long way to go; however, by becoming more loyal and trustworthy, he is more likely to participate in the values of community and friendship. In this way, he is somewhat closer to becoming virtuous at the end of *Serenity*.[15]

Perhaps no one from the *Firefly* 'verse is very far along the path to *eudaimonia*. Arguably, Inara is the closest, with Book not too far behind. Furthermore, as noted, Mal and his crew don't always convey proper respect toward persons. Mal callously lies to Simon in "Serenity" about Kaylee's death, and he is far too quick to call Inara "whore." Mal is no moral saint. Koontz writes, "The character of Malcolm Reynolds is fascinating to contemplate *because* of his flaws ... rather than in spite of them. Malcolm often blunders, but like many of Whedon's characters ... he blunders *forward*."[16] The moral progress made, as argued here, is best interpreted along Kantian and Aristotelian lines.

A persuasive microcosm is Mal's ethical renewal in *Serenity*. It begins with his decision to not leave River in the Maidenhead, even though he "had every reason in the 'verse to leave her lay and haul anchor." It is solidified with the tragic loss of Shepherd Book, who never stopped being a part of Mal's crew. It reaches its zenith when he realizes something significant must be done about the tragedy on planet Miranda—"someone must speak for these people"— even though none of them were a part of his crew. Thus, core ethical themes pervading the *Firefly* 'verse do not require theistic moorings.

"Men of God make everyone feel guilty and judged"

Both Kant and Aristotle hold that there are true ethically significant moral judgments that are in some sense universally binding upon all moral agents, independent of what individuals may happen to believe. In this way, both are moral realists. Kant focuses on the issue of *rightness*. He holds that it is always wrong to disrespect persons by treating them as a mere means to an end; persons must be respected for the unique sources of moral behavior they are, and allowed moral space to make autonomous decisions. Aristotle focuses on moral *goodness*. He holds that there are better and worse ways for us to behave given the situation at hand and acting virtuously requires us to approximate the mean between overreacting and underreacting. Over time, acting virtuously will result in becoming a virtuous (that is, morally excellent) person.[17] Neither philosopher holds that God is required to determine rightness or goodness. In this, as noted, Whedon seems to agree. However, moral realism puzzles some scholars. How is it that moral judgments can be universally binding? What makes it true that one ought not to disrespect persons or that acting virtuously is commendable? Such questions seem to cast doubt on Whedon's implicit nontheistic moral message.

Inquiries into the most basic and general ethical concepts, including what makes any ethically significant claim true, fall under the subcategory of philosophy known as metaethics. Philosophers have been exploring metaethics for (at least) 2,500 years. In the *Euthyphro*, Plato recounts Socrates's analysis of the suggestion that ethically significant judgments must somehow be grounded in divine approbation.[18] After all, if moral judgments are to apply cross-culturally in some sort of universally binding sense, surely they spring from a suitable nonhuman source. Moreover, a universally binding moral judgment seems akin to a moral law, but because laws require lawmakers, it seems that universally binding moral judgments require an agency to legislate—and enforce—them. What better source than the divine? This sort of metaethical perspective, although sometimes differing in its details, is often called *divine command theory*. Typically cast in terms of theism, its most straightforward formulation entails that an act is obligatory (right) only because God commands it, and an act is impermissible (wrong) only because God forbids it.

In the *Euthyphro*, Socrates asks a deceptively simple question: Why would the gods command something of us? Socrates's dialogue with Euthyphro presupposed a polytheistic setting, but analogous questions can be asked of the divine command theory defender: Is an act right (merely) because God commands it, or does God command it because it is (already) right? If she answers affirmatively to the first and negatively to the second, then ethical behavior ultimately becomes arbitrary. Nothing is inherently right or wrong, but only becomes so once God decrees. On this account, murder, kidnapping, and slavery could be morally required of us simply upon divine whim. If one answers negatively to the first and affirmatively to the second, then ethical arbitrariness is avoided, but only to accept the existence of ethically significant truths that hold independently of God's decrees. These logically prior truths explain why God commands what God does, thereby being indicative of what is morally right to do. Either way, God's commands cannot play the sort of conceptual role in establishing ethical truth that divine command theorists intend. There seems to be more to establishing ethical truth than merely divine decree.

Some divine command theory defenders revise the classic view. They hold that even if God's commands do not create ethical obligation, God's essence or nature (somehow) serves as the necessary underpinning for ethical truth. On this revised account, God's commands are indicative of his morally perfect nature. This revision circumvents concerns about ethical arbitrariness. It is impossible for a morally perfect God to decree that murder, kidnapping, or slavery be obligatory. Nevertheless, this revision still falls prey to Euthyphroian inquiries. The issue becomes how to understand the metaethical status of the morally good properties God (essentially) possesses. Is it the case that a property is morally good merely because God possesses it, or does God, in his moral perfection, possess a morally significant property exactly because it is (already) good? Answering affirmatively to the first raises a host of new questions. Does God decide by fiat which of his properties are morally good or significant? Does it follow that if God were cruel and vindictive, these would be morally good merely because God possesses them? Both questions (again) raise the specter of ethical arbitrariness, this time about moral goodness.

Such Euthyphroian inquiries also serve to threaten the meaningfulness of God's moral perfection. If God remains morally perfect regardless of which morally significant properties he possesses, then God's moral perfection is rendered insignificant. Why praise God if he remains morally perfect possessing the properties of cruelty and vindictiveness? A natural response is to affirm that it is impossible for God to be cruel and vindictive exactly because God is morally perfect and such traits are moral imperfections. Rather, God is loving and forgiving exactly because to love and forgive are (already) good. If so, then some properties are *inherently* morally good and their being so explains why God, in his moral perfection, possesses them. But if some properties are inherently morally good, then they — all by themselves — can serve as the necessary conceptual foundation for a moral realist perspective. God's possessing them is not necessary.

This sort of critique is relevant to an example from "Bushwhacked" (3). Recall that the crew ponders whether they should investigate a derelict ship floating in space. Jayne doesn't see any profit in it so he thinks they shouldn't stop to look. Book suggests that there may be survivors in need of help and so reminds Mal of the Good Samaritan as a way to sway his decision. The relevant question is, Is it good that you provide aid to others, including strangers, in times of need simply because this behavior receives divine approbation, or does it receive divine approbation because it is good to provide aid to others in times of need? If the first, then there is nothing deeply profound about the Good Samaritan. It is (or would be) just as morally commendable to ignore others in need were that behavior to receive divine approbation. If the second, then divine approbation doesn't make helping others, including strangers, in times of need good. Rather, the fact that it is already good explains why it receives divine approbation.

Divine command theory is one popular way in which the presumed metaethical connection between religion and ethics manifests. But there are others. To note just one relevant example, some scholars affirm that the respect due persons requires that we are created in God's image. Louis Pojman writes, "Theism claims that God values us all equally. If we are his children ... we are family and ought to treat each other benevolently, as we would family members of equal worth.... But without the parenthood of God, it makes no sense to say that all persons are innately of positive equal value ... or any worth at all."[19] Pojman's position is clearly inconsistent with the (respective) nontheistic perspectives of Kant and Aristotle. It entails that in a Godless universe, fictional or not, human beings are merely animals. We are not due moral respect. In fact, without God, there cannot be any morally inappropriate behavior at all.

Although Pojman's basic point does not obviously rely on the truth of divine command theory, his position remains susceptible to Euthyphroian inquiries. We might ask why the moral worth of persons depends on God's creating us. Did God decide by fiat that we uniquely possess moral worth? If so, then God could have chosen otherwise, leaving open the possibility that (say) only monarch butterflies possess unique moral worth. In any case, on this account, there is nothing deeply profound about us that accounts for our unique moral worth; it results from mere divine whim. Alternatively, is our unique moral worth a result of possessing properties that in some sense (albeit imperfectly) resemble God's morally significant properties? If so, then there is something deeply profound about our moral worth, but it — being created in God's image — is secured by possessing a distinctive set of properties (that monarch butterflies lack). On this alternative, God may be ultimately responsible for the fact of our existence, but not the fact that we possess unique moral worth (similar considerations pertain to Pojman's views about familial relationships).

Some theistically inclined scholars also argue that without God, moral values and obligations are not sufficiently binding. Someone might escape the civil authorities, but no one escapes divine detection. God ensures that justice will be meted out for those who keep or fail their ethical obligations. In a world without God, all that ultimately ensures ethical compliance is personal conscience. Pojman finds this worrisome: "Conscience is very weak in the face of temptation and self-interest, and the rational amoralist or egoist can override it without insuperable difficulties.... In religion, the moral commands get their backing from the authority of God who backs them up with rewards and punishments."[20] So, in a world without God, if moral agents can eschew their obligations without detection, we will, especially if keeping them requires self-sacrifice. Some theistically driven ethicists have gone so far as to claim that self-sacrifice in a Godless world is simply foolhardy. William Lane Craig writes, "Acts of self-sacrifice become particularly inept on an atheistic worldview.... A firefighter ... or a policeman who sacrifices his life ... does nothing more praiseworthy, morally speaking, than an ant that sacrifices itself for the sake of the ant heap. On an atheistic view, this is just stupid."[21] Per theists such as Pojman and Craig, ethical considerations become impotent without the constant psychological force of guilt and judgment. Because it is often held that moral considerations are supposed to trump or override prudential, aesthetic, and etiquette considerations, but securing this feature is difficult in a world without God, many find this line of argument quite forceful. Any ethical perspective not requiring the truth of theism must take account of such concerns.

Concerns about how binding moral obligations are in a Godless world are not typically interpreted to entail that there cannot be any ethically significant truths without God.[22] This is one of the upshots of Euthyphroian assessments of theistically driven ethical systems. There seem to be ethically significant truths that are not legislated by God. In fact, they don't seem to be legislated at all.[23] Yet their existence is informative about what is intrinsically good, and, by extension (although not uncontroversially), what we ethically ought and ought not to do. For Kant, the supreme moral principle is the categorical imperative: everyone ought to respect persons (including oneself) as autonomous agents, ends unto themselves and not merely as a means to an end. Other often (less abstract) suggested moral principles include "Treat equals equally" and "Do not blame someone for circumstances completely beyond her control."[24]

Even assuming the existence of nonlegislated moral principles, what of their bindingness in a world without God? Theists who argue that moral principles alone are not sufficiently binding often do so from pragmatic or egoistic considerations. They do not, and cannot, provide moral reasons for keeping them. The implication is that without fear of punishment such theists would not behave ethically. This arguably signals moral defect in character, reminiscent of children who only do what they are told because they desire reward or fear punishment. But parents invariably wish for their children to do the right thing not just for the sake of rewards or punishments — more or less time playing Wii — but exactly *because* it is the right thing to do.[25] Similar considerations pertain to the alleged stupidity of self-sacrifice in a Godless world. Theists who countenance this controversial position have difficulty accounting for self-sacrifice at all. It seems that, ultimately and paradoxically, the only reason for selflessly acting on the behalf of another (even a loved one) is that you will be rewarded for it in heaven. However, at the risk of begging the question, it seems plain that the true nobility of self-sacrifice — and the coherence of the very notion itself— is to act on behalf of another without concern for reward.

Accordingly, there is some reason to believe that grounding the bindingness of moral principles and values squarely in God's existence runs the risk of adopting a dubious conception of the moral worth of our actions and character. Russ Shafer-Landau eloquently makes the salient point: "Fear of God has been a traditional way to get people to do their duty. But when it is effective, it undermines moral character, rather than supports it. People who deserve our praise and admiration are those who do their duty for its own sake.... This is an attitude of direct respect for morality.... Being well motivated requires a love and respect for the morally important things in life. Religion has often fostered such an outlook. But it isn't required to do the job."[26] Rather than merely relying on fear or simple guilt over being judged to motivate us to behave ethically, it is more valuable to develop our characters in ways that we better appreciate the significance of our choices. Striving to self-motivate, we harbor a healthy respect for ethics and become fully praiseworthy for doing morally good things. In this, Aristotle would agree.

"What's the math on that?"

Much more analysis is required regarding this difficult subject. However, perhaps these terse remarks and argument sketches are sufficient for setting up the relevance of Whedon's intriguing portrayal of Angel and, by extension, his implicit position on the debate. Angel is a striking example of someone who invariably does the right thing simply because it is right. His dialogue from "Epiphany" (2.16) has become Whedon lore: "If there is no great, glorious end to all of this and nothing we do matters, then all that matters is what we do. Because that's all there is—what we do, now, today. Because if there is no bigger meaning, then the smallest act of kindness is the greatest thing in the world." Apart from grand divine purpose or everlasting reward, Angel advises that we never forego an opportunity to help others. Nothing is more important than offering aid to those in need. Moreover, we should strive to develop a moral character that facilitates our regularly acting kindly. If we sometimes fail, then we should work harder to transform our character. Aristotle would again agree.

True, Angel occasionally acts for more self-interested reasons, especially in light of the discovered Shanshu Prophecy. His quest for redemption and atonement, especially as it seems tied to his becoming human again, sometimes clouds his motivations. However, near the end of "Judgment" he is quick to correct himself, symbolized by taking down the white board in Cordelia's apartment. The white board had quickly began to represent a scorecard, which compromised Team Angel's duty to "help the helpless" simply for its own sake. Moreover, it cannot be overlooked that Angel ultimately signs away his claim to the Shanshu Prophecy in season five to more effectively combat the rising forces of evil. His last words of the series are "Let's get to work" ("Not Fade Away," 5.22). That work is clearly not for personal gain; he and his comrades may not survive. Only a true champion would make such a decision and is testament to his (and their) exemplary moral character.

Of course, even the bravest of champions require some help from others occasionally. There are multiple examples from the series that convey self-sacrifice to aid Angel in his mission. Doyle gave his life in "Hero" (1.9) so that Angel could continue his mission. In "You're Welcome," (5.12) Cordelia, who was "owed one" by the Powers That Be, utilized that last wish, not to save her life, but to put Angel back on the champion's path. (And don't forget Buffy's extreme self-sacrifice at the end of *Buffy* season five; she saved the world a lot, remember.) Whedon portrays these characters and their choices with much nobility, which is testament to his position on whether doing something because it is right is more commendable than acting from egoistic or prudential reasons. If their choices are commendable, then they are not stupid, which serves as evidence of moral goodness apart from God's existence.

Of course, these choices were made by fictional characters. But Whedon's genius is making fiction seem so personally real. He helps us fully imagine, and in some ways feel, what it would be like to actually make choices similar to Angel, Doyle, and Cordelia. This arguably allows novel insights into the importance of those choices. Scholars such as Craig contend that such choices are stupid. The reader must decide for herself whether Whedon or Craig is closer to the truth regarding the connection, if any, between ethics and theism. If nothing else, how Whedon "figures the math" on this debate is rather clear. Angel is Whedon's champion exactly because he invariably acts ethically simply for its own sake, and Whedon invariably portrays instances of self-sacrifice with nobility, indicative of what champions do. That Whedon frames these choices in a positive dramatic light is some indication of his philosophical leanings in the relevant debate.[27]

"...intently at your own belly buttons"

Apart from his personal atheism, Whedon's corpus suggests an interesting reason for his rejecting the theistically driven ethical perspectives of Pojman and Craig. Consider the Watchers Council in England, the Wolfram & Hart senior partners, the Parliament of the Alliance, and the Rossum Corporation main office executives. Each of these organizations has a sort of phantom, faceless existence, and, although each is well publicized, their actual existence is occasionally questioned. If they do exist, each works behind the scenes very subtly and from a distance. Each serves the primary purpose of constraining behavior or providing obstacles to Whedon's characters. Because they inhibit autonomous and authentic existence, each is portrayed in a negative dramatic light. Buffy, Angel, Mal, and Caroline/Echo (Eliza Dushku) are portrayed as heroes exactly because each struggles against the influences of these organizations in the hope of leading a more autonomous and authentic life. But the full value of such a life cannot be realized unless it is guided by ethical ideals, including doing the right thing because it is right.[28]

Now recall how God is often interpreted or utilized by theistically driven ethicists. Among God's primary purposes is to ensure that we uphold our ethical obligations via the threat of everlasting punishment. But the world is religiously ambiguous; God's existence, despite the fact that it is well-publicized, is not abundantly clear. So, if God does exist, he works subtly, behind the scenes, and from a distance. Therefore, God's role in theistic ethics is eerily similar to the workings of Whedon's phantom, faceless organizations.

Because he portrays those organizations antagonistically — at odds with his protagonists — it is likely that he would also view theistic ethical systems antagonistically. From his perspective, it is better that we do the right thing simply because it is right, leaning on each other — and especially close friends — for support in our quest to become champions. God is arguably inimical to this. In this way, God isn't all that welcome on Whedon's boat, even if there is always room for one more dependable friend, shepherds included.

And what does the Whedonverse teach us about ethics? From Mal and the *Firefly* 'verse, Whedon expresses the importance of respecting persons, of community and friendship, and the character traits that facilitate respect, friendship, and community. However, Mal sometimes reverts to mere pragmatics; losing his moral rudder, he loses sight of doing the right thing. This explains his character arc in *Serenity*. From the *Angel* universe, Whedon expresses the importance of having a distinctive sort of moral character that facilitates the resolve to do good things simply because they are good, including noble acts of self-sacrifice. However, Angel occasionally overlooks the importance of friendship and community, with the Darla story arc of season two serving as a vivid example.[29] Viewers are led to believe that Mal and Angel could learn and benefit from each other and their respective perspectives. Putting together the strengths of each perspective overcomes their respective weaknesses. Putting them together also results in a potentially appealing perspective on ethics, one that does not directly rely on the truth of theism. If this is correct, then insights gained from the Whedonverse are applicable to the actual 'verse.

Is Whedon's implicit nontheistic Kantian-Aristotelian ethical synthesis conceptually adequate? This is a difficult question, one deserving of further thought. To that end, consider Angel's stirring words to his son Connor (Vincent Kartheiser) in "Deep Down" (4.1):

> Nothing in the world is the way it ought to be. It's harsh and cruel. But that's why there is us. Champions. It doesn't matter where we come from, what we've done or suffered. Or even if we make a difference. We live as though the world were the way it should be. To show it what it can be.

If you find Angel's words inspiring, this is some reason to think that you agree with Whedon's implicit ethical perspective. Perhaps you'll conclude that it is conceptually adequate. Consequently, you'll probably also acknowledge how Book is welcome on Mal's boat — even if God ain't — but none of that means that there aren't morally better or worse ways for them — for all of us — to interact. And, in this, Whedon gives us one more thing to ponder. Whether you do so with head bowed looking very intently at your belly button is up to you, but some may take it as a kindness.

Acknowledgments

I would like to thank my colleagues S. Evan Kreider and Joseph Foy for helpful comments on earlier versions of this essay. It was again a pleasure to "Whedonesquely" collaborate with them.

Notes

1. These quotations are from *Firefly*. The first is from "Serenity" and the second two are from "Our Mrs. Reynolds" (6). All quotes from *Firefly* are taken from Joss Whedon, *Firefly: The Official Companion*, vols. 1 and 2 (London: Titan Books, 2007). Most of this essay's section heading titles are also taken from *Firefly*. The first and fourth are from "Safe," the second and third are from "Our Mrs. Reynolds," and the fifth is from "Trash" (11). The sixth is from the film *Serenity*.
2. By the way, if "She" (*Angel* 1.13) is any indication, Angel probably shouldn't dance in public either.
3. Per a deleted scene from "Serenity," viewers are led to believe that Mal left his religious faith in that valley; it died just as so many of the soldiers under his command. Medical help doesn't arrive for weeks. When it does, with dozens of deceased soldiers strewn about, Zoe (Gina Torres) sighs and says, "Thank God." Mal simply (yet spitefully) mutters, "God? Whose colors he flyin'?"
4. James Rachels, *The Elements of Moral Philosophy* (New York: McGraw-Hill, 2003), 49.
5. For early interpretations of Whedon's ethical views, begin with James South, ed., *Buffy the Vampire Slayer and Philosophy: Fear and Trembling in Sunnydale* (Chicago: Open Court, 2003). For a more focused discussion, see Gregory Stevenson, *Televised Morality: The Case of Buffy the Vampire Slayer* (Lanham, MD: Hampton Books, 2003). For a more recent commentary, see J. M. Richardson and J. D. Rabb, *The Existential Joss Whedon* (Jefferson, NC: McFarland, 2007). While at times insightful, it is not entirely clear whether Whedon is the sort of thoroughgoing antirationalistic existentialist that Richardson and Rabb assert him to be.
6. K. Dale Koontz, *Faith and Choice in the Works of Joss Whedon* (Jefferson, NC: McFarland, 2008), 103. Despite imposing religious motifs onto Whedon, Koontz's text is erudite, impressively expansive of the Whedonverse, and often stimulating; it is worthy of careful consideration.
7. Immanuel Kant, *The Foundations of the Metaphysic of Morals*, trans. T. K. Abbott (London, 1873).
8. Some material from this section is adapted from Dean A. Kowalski, "Plato, Aristotle, and Joss on Being Horrible," in *The Philosophy of Joss Whedon*, ed. Dean A. Kowalski and S. Evan Kreider (Lexington: University Press of Kentucky, 2011), 71–87.
9. Aristotle, *Nicomachean Ethics*, trans. W. D. Ross (Oxford: Oxford University Press, 1925), 1097b8–10. By the terms *politics* and *political*, Aristotle didn't mean merely statecraft or some such, but something closer to the science of civilized human existence or perhaps simply society.
10. Ibid., 1169b9, 1155a5–6.
11. See ibid., 1156b25–28, 1166a30, and 1157b33–36 for textual support of the claims attributed to Aristotle in this paragraph.
12. Ibid., 1160a2–5. However, Aristotle should not be interpreted as implying we have no moral obligations to strangers, and Kant would agree.
13. Koontz wonders whether the apples symbolize the forbidden fruit in the Garden of Eden in terms of what Wash later comes to know about Zoe's wartime exploits (*Faith and Choice*, 77). If there is a deeper symbolic purpose to the apples, it rather seems to be the dangers of war and how even the most precious commodities (fresh fruit) can be harbingers of death and destruction (e.g., hiding bombs in them). This fits better with Whedon's penchant for exploring ethical ambiguities.

14. Aristotle, *Nicomachean Ethics*, 1106b15–25.

15. For more on Jayne's character arc via a Kantian and Aristotelian analysis, see Jason D. Grinnell, "Aristotle, Kant, Spike, and Jayne: Ethics in the Whedonverse," in *The Philosophy of Joss Whedon*, 88–102.

16. Koontz, *Faith and Choice*, 99. The italics appear in the original. Koontz's chapter on Mal ("I Got No Rudder") is often insightful, especially regarding Whedon's ethical commitment to the power of love.

17. There are numerous quality introductions to moral philosophy and ethical theory that include coverage of Kant and Aristotle (among other philosophers). See, for example, Emmett Barcalow, *Moral Philosophy: Theories and Issues*, 2nd ed. (Belmont, CA: Wadsworth, 1998) and C. E. Harris, *Applying Moral Principles*, 4th ed. (Belmont, CA: Wadsworth, 2002). For a text that includes coverage of Whedon's *Dr. Horrible's Sing-Along Blog* and *Serenity*, I (humbly) recommend Dean A. Kowalski, *Moral Theory at the Movies: An Introduction to Ethics* (Lanham, MD: Rowman & Littlefield, 2012).

18. *The Dialogues of Plato*, trans. Benjamin Jowett (New York: Oxford University Press, 1920), 2a–16a.

19. Louis P. Pojman, *Ethics: Discovering Right and Wrong* (Belmont, CA: Wadsworth, 2002), 205. Pojman more carefully defends this view elsewhere: Louis P. Pojman, "Is Contemporary Moral Theory Founded on a Misunderstanding?" *Journal of Social Philosophy* 22, no. 2 (1991): 49–59.

20. Pojman, "Contemporary Moral Theory," 50–51.

21. Paul Kurtz and William Lane Craig, "The Kurtz/Craig Debate: Is Goodness without God Good Enough?," in *Is Goodness without God Good Enough? A Debate on Faith, Secularism, and Ethics*, ed. Robert K. Garcia and Nathan L. King (Lanham, MD: Rowman & Littlefield, 2009), 33.

22. Admittedly, some theists remain firm that ethical obligations and, thus, moral rightness, require God. They invariably argue that ethical obligations are inherently social, laid down by and owed to (other) persons in distinctively pubic ways. See, for example, Robert M. Adams, *Finite and Infinite Goods* (New York: Oxford University Press, 1999), 13–82, 231–76. Yet if there are inherently good moral properties (or if morally good properties supervene on nonmoral properties), then acting contrary to them is evidence that one has acted wrongly. For a theistic version of this account, see Richard Swinburne, "What Difference Does God Make to Morality?" in *Is Goodness without God Good Enough*, 151–163. Without resolving this difficult debate, if there are inherently morally good properties, then it seemingly remains intelligible to at least speak of morally better and worse ways to treat one another that can be binding on all moral agents. For the sake of readability, and with all due respect to scholars such as Adams, the remaining pages of this essay use "right" and "good" more or less interchangeably when the context allows (even if the more cumbersome "right/good" would be more accurate).

23. For more on this, see Swinburne, "What Difference Does God Make."

24. For an accessible discussion of the former suggestion, see Theodore Schick and Lewis Vaughn, *Doing Philosophy* (New York: McGraw-Hill, 2003), 302–321. For an accessible discussion of the latter suggestion, see Dean A. Kowalski, *Moral Theory at the Movies*, 128–133.

25. Parents differ, of course, and some may wish to instill in their children the values of good citizenship or perhaps even friendship (by teaching, for example, the importance of sharing or empathy). However, a precocious child may ask why, say, citizenship is important. To avoid instilling egoistic tendencies, it seems the noblest tact is to stress the importance of doing the right (or good) thing simply because it is right.

26. Russ Shafer-Landau, *The Fundamentals of Ethics* (New York: Oxford University Press, 2012), 60.

27. For an influential account that filmmakers can be interpreted as philosophers given how they perform their craft, see Thomas E. Wartenberg, *Thinking on Screen: Film as Philosophy* (New York: Routledge, 2007). For an interesting take on how filmmakers convey philosophical insights even when they explicitly claim to remain neutral on an issue, see Joseph J. Foy, "Terrorism, Counterterrorism, and 'The Story of What Happens Next' in *Munich*," in *Steven Spielberg*

and *Philosophy: We're Gonna Need a Bigger Book*, ed. Dean A. Kowalski (Lexington: University Press of Kentucky, 2008), 170–187.

28. For more on this interpretation of authenticity in the Whedonverse, see Joseph J. Foy and Dean A. Kowalski, "Seeking Authenticity in the Whedonverse," in *The Philosophy of Joss Whedon*, 151–167.

29. The story arc extends from "Darla" to "Epiphany." Angel abruptly fires his team, largely cutting all ties with them. He subsequently goes through something of a transformation, allegedly becoming neither Angel nor Angelus. These facts, in turn, suggest an existential interpretation of the character, which fits well with Angel's comments to Lila near the beginning of "Blood Money" (2.12) that dealing with Wolfram & Hart is "actually kind of fun when you know the rules"—that is, "when you know there aren't any." However, he later admonishes Anne (Julia Lee; the same character from "Lie to Me" and "Anne") to avoid Wolfram & Hart involvement simply "because it's right." Furthermore, although he tells Anne that he no longer cares, the episode ends with Angel giving her all the charity proceeds, providing evidence that he actually does still care about "helping the helpless." This serves to temper a thoroughgoing existential analysis of Angel (and, arguably, provides a cautionary microcosm for interpreting Whedon's other characters).

BIBLIOGRAPHY

Adams, Robert M. *Finite and Infinite Goods*. New York: Oxford University Press, 1999.
Aristotle. *Nicomachean Ethics*. Translated by W. D. Ross. Oxford: Oxford University Press, 1925.
Barcalow, Emmett. *Moral Philosophy: Theories and Issues*. 2nd ed. Belmont, CA: Wadsworth, 1998.
Foy, Joseph J. "Terrorism, Counterterrorism, and 'The Story of What Happens Next' in *Munich*." In *Steven Spielberg and Philosophy: We're Gonna Need a Bigger Book*, ed. Dean A. Kowalski, 170–188. Lexington: University Press of Kentucky, 2008.
Foy, Joseph J., and Dean A. Kowalski. "Seeking Authenticity in the Whedonverse." In *The Philosophy of Joss Whedon*, ed. Dean A. Kowalski and S. Evan Kreider, 151–167. Lexington: University Press of Kentucky, 2011.
Garcia, Robert K., and Nathan L. King, ed. *Is Goodness without God Good Enough? A Debate on Faith, Secularism, and Ethics*. Lanham, MD: Rowman & Littlefield, 2009.
Harris, C. E. *Applying Moral Principles*. 4th ed. Belmont, CA: Wadsworth, 2002.
Kant, Immanuel. *The Foundations of the Metaphysic of Morals*. Translated by T. K. Abbott (London, 1873).
Koontz, Dale K. *Faith and Choice in the Works of Joss Whedon*. Jefferson, NC: McFarland, 2008.
Kowalski, Dean A. *Moral Theory at the Movies: An Introduction to Ethics*. Lanham, MD: Rowman & Littlefield, 2012.
_____. "Plato, Aristotle, and Joss on Being Horrible." In *The Philosophy of Joss Whedon*, ed. Dean A. Kowalski and S. Evan Kreider, 71–87. Lexington: University Press of Kentucky, 2011.
Plato. *The Dialogues of Plato*. Translated by Benjamin Jowett. New York: Oxford University Press, 1920.
Pojman, Louis P. *Ethics: Discovering Right and Wrong*. Belmont, CA: Wadsworth, 2002.
_____. "Is Contemporary Moral Theory Founded on a Misunderstanding?" *Journal of Social Philosophy* 22, no. 2 (1991): 49–59.
Rachels, James. *The Elements of Moral Philosophy*. New York: McGraw-Hill, 2003.
Richardson, J.M., and J. D. Rabb. *The Existential Joss Whedon*. Jefferson, NC: McFarland, 2007.
Schick, Theodore, and Lewis Vaughn. *Doing Philosophy*. New York: McGraw-Hill, 2003.
Shafer-Landau, Russ. *The Fundamentals of Ethics*. New York: Oxford University Press, 2012.
South, James B., ed. *Buffy the Vampire Slayer and Philosophy: Fear and Trembling in Sunnydale*. Chicago: Open Court, 2003.

Stevenson, Gregory. *Televised Morality: The Case of Buffy the Vampire Slayer.* Lanham, MD: Hampton Books, 2003.
Swinburne, Richard. "What Difference Does God Make to Morality?" In *Is Goodness without God Good Enough? A Debate on Faith, Secularism, and Ethics*, ed. Robert K. Garcia and Nathan L. King, 151–165. Lanham, MD: Rowman & Littlefield, 2009.
Wartenberg, Thomas E. *Thinking on Screen: Film as Philosophy.* New York: Routledge, 2007.
Whedon, Joss. *Firefly: The Official Companion.* Vols. 1 and 2. London: Titan Books, 2007.

Actives, Affectivity and the Soul

Interpreting Dollhouse *through the Phenomenology of Michel Henry*

J. LEAVITT PEARL

> *I am certain of nothing but of the holiness of the Heart's affections and the truth of Imagination.... O for a life of sensation rather than of thoughts!*— John Keats, in a letter to Benjamin Bailey

On February 13, 2009, Joss Whedon released his darkest television series yet, *Dollhouse*. Airing a meager twenty-seven episodes, the show was plagued by conflicts between Whedon and its network production team. As Whedon remarked in an interview shortly after the announcement of the program's cancellation, "basically, the show didn't really get off the ground because the network pretty much wanted to back away from the concept five minutes after they bought it."[1] Conceptual and production difficulties aside, the show was by no means a complete failure. Quite to the contrary, in its short run *Dollhouse* grew beyond its unsettling premise and developed into a complex analysis of the nature and meaning of consciousness, memory, affection, self-identity, and humanity. As Whedon remarks in his typical idiosyncratic manner, "we did manage to keep the questions about who we are and the interpersonal stuff."[2]

It is here — in "the questions about who we are and the interpersonal stuff" — that we might find resonance with this volume's theological project; for it is precisely these questions which must be addressed, not only to understand *Dollhouse* but, more significantly, to understand the nature of human individuality. Within this essay, we will ask if *Dollhouse* might permit us to consider the question of the soul. It is perhaps impossible, one might say, to seriously engage *Dollhouse* without opening oneself to the significant questions of rational psychology. Is there a core of human being or experience which might be called the *soul*? If so, what relationship might the soul bear to consciousness, memory, or personality? Faced with the disconcerting possibility of the total removal of everything that one knows about oneself, about one's history, and about one's friends and family, what trace could possibly remain? What could survive such a dramatic erasure?

Towards this end, this investigation will place *Dollhouse* in conversation with the French philosopher and theologian Michel Henry. Drawing upon his insightful phenomenologies of the soul and the affections, we will seek to bring to light theological and philosophical intuitions which may lie below the surface of *Dollhouse*'s complex narrative. Moreover, by drawing upon Henry and some of his primary influences, we will offer an interpretation of these insights which proposes not only that there may be an implicit concept of the soul undergirding *Dollhouse*, but that this concept may illuminate many of the most important events of the series. Before we dive into these questions and begin our philosophical and theological work, it may benefit us to refamiliarize ourselves with the basic outline of the show, its unusual premise, and its internal tension.

Setting the Scene

Dollhouse begins with a single foundational premise, a fact which clearly sets its fictional world apart from the world of the reader. In *Dollhouse*, this fact or given is the existence of a technology which has two functions: first, it can erase a human mind, including both memory and personality; second, it can upload or, as the show says, "imprint" an alternate one in its place. In Whedon's traditionally pessimistic vein, this technology is owned and operated by the corrupt and merciless Rossum Corporation, who maintains a series of underground facilities — dollhouses — to which individuals, often under heavy coercion or in states of desperation, can sell their bodies for a period of five years. These "dolls" or "Actives" are then wiped and repeatedly rented at an exuberant rate to various millionaires in order to fulfill a variety of roles: from sexual partner to bank thief, life coach to doctor. An Active, it might be said, is simply a made-to-order person: personality, language, sexual preference, technical skills, even martial arts training can be programmed as specifically as the customer desires. After the contractual period of five years, the Active awakes imprinted with her original personality and memories and is paid an impressive fee before being released back into the everyday world.

The Internal Dialectic

Were *Dollhouse*'s imprinting system to function flawlessly it might be inferred that Topher Brink (Fran Kranz)— the show's resident genius, cynic, and Active "programmer"— is correct; a mind is nothing more than a series of synapses, nothing more than the complex totality of electrical connections in the brain ("Omega," 1.12). We will call this perspective the *positivist hypothesis*, and it appears to be the primary intuition upon which *Dollhouse* is built. Drawing from the insights of the natural sciences, particularly neuroscience, this perspective argues for the total reduction of consciousness and its activities to material processes, specifically the neurochemical and electrical processes of the nervous system. One might say that, for this view, the human individual is *synthetic*: self-consciousness is the product of every memory, thought, and personality trait, all of which may be understood as physically present in the form of matter or energy— that is, as objectively determinable facts.

The positivist hypothesis, also called *physicalism*, has become increasingly popular throughout the last two centuries, and is often seen as a natural consequence of the Enlightenment. As the domain of the natural sciences has consistently expanded, it has become customary to look forward to a time when philosophical, theological, and psychological explanations of human reality will be subsumed under the natural scientific. Recent outspoken advocates of this perspective include Daniel Dennett and Sam Harris, although the historical roots of this tradition can be traced back at least as far as the German philosopher Ludwig Feuerbach, if not all the way to certain pre–Socratic philosophers of ancient Greece.[3]

If the positivist hypothesis might be taken as the foundational premise of *Dollhouse*, it does not reign unchallenged. Quite to the contrary, the movement of the show's plot is reliant precisely upon the consistent failure of the memory wipe system to adequately erase and imprint the Actives; perhaps, it might be suggested, upon the very failure of the positivist hypothesis itself. Subtle at first, the increasingly conspicuous difficulties faced by the dollhouse staff seem to hint at a fundamental flaw. Certainly, one might simply attribute this failure to the ineptitude of the staff, but such an analysis would hardly stand in resonance with the show itself, for *Dollhouse* adamantly (and incessantly) proclaims the absolute genius and technical proficiency of its primary programmer Topher Brink. Add to this the seemingly unlimited funds of the Rossum Corporation as well as its access to virtually unlimited technological resources, and it seems unlikely that simple human error could account for the persistence of these difficulties. Instead, it might be suggested that within *Dollhouse* there resides a challenge to its own founding premise, a contrary hypothesis. *Dollhouse*, it seems, is constructed upon an ambiguity — perhaps even a dialectic — between the positivist hypothesis and what we will call the *theological hypothesis*.

This theological hypothesis, what Topher Brink derisively calls "the whole 'God thing'" ("Instinct," 2.2), challenges the most basic presupposition of the positivist hypothesis, arguing that the living individual is not simply a synthesis of objectively observable processes. Instead, the theological hypothesis considers that there might be an essence to the human identity that is not entirely reducible to these electrical impulses or to the content of one's memories; that the individual may possess access to a subjective reality which is neither objectifiable nor physical.[4] If we have taken Topher Brink as the principal advocate of the positivist hypothesis, then perhaps we might similarly take Paul Ballard (Tahmoh Penikett), an FBI agent charged with uncovering the dollhouse, as the champion of the theological hypothesis. For it is he who simply states, "I still don't believe that you can wipe away a person's soul ... who they are at their core. I don't believe that goes away" ("Omega").

Of course, the precise nature of such a reality within *Dollhouse* is wholly ambiguous, as neither Whedon nor his writers are theologians or philosophers. Are we dealing here with the hylomorphic soul of Scholasticism or the soul-as-substance of Platonism, the divine soul of the Rhineland mystics or the purely logicostructural soul of Kantianism? Perhaps Whedon has in mind the bizarrely commodified soul of *Buffy the Vampire Slayer*, a soul which "you can trap ... in a jar."[5] In the end, it must be recognized that *Dollhouse* is above all else a narrative and that this soul or core is not primarily a philosophical concept, but a tool intended to move the narrative forward. As Whedon admits in an interview regarding *Buffy*, "I would love to give you a more in-depth coherent explanation of my view of the soul, and if I had one I would. The soul and my concept of it are as ephemeral as anybody's, and possibly more so."[6] Yet this ambiguity does not prevent us from delving into the narrative, attempting to piece together an *implicit* concept of the soul, and elaborating the way in which this concept may provide a helpful counterpoint or even challenge to the more prevalent positivistic hypothesis.

The Failed Wipes

Since we have already identified that our analysis will primarily be directed toward Active "malfunctions," those moments when the Active does not act in accordance with their programmed personality, it may now be helpful to provide a more thorough description of these glitches — a description which should provide a suitable groundwork for our later discussion.

If we might speak broadly, it could be said that traces of this tendency towards malfunction can be found in every major Active of the series, although their manifestation appears to be most clearly demonstrated within situations of intense emotional or physical stress and anxiety. Physical combat, particularly that which involves considerable head trauma, interactions with loved ones, and fear of death all appear to function as triggers. Although these triggers may result in the emergence of clear mental content — e.g., the memory of a past imprint or of life before imprinting — more commonly the content which arises takes the form of *ambiguous* feelings of love or trust and other nonconceptual content: the return of skills, muscle memory, or intuitions. There are two specific dynamics which most clearly manifest the ambiguous nature of these malfunctions: instinct and love.

Malfunction I: Instinct

Dollhouse primarily revolves around an Active designated "Echo," named Caroline Farrell before her tenure at the house. Unlike other Actives, Echo's physiology makes her particularly resistant to imprinting, eventually allowing her to access previous imprints at will, switch personalities on command, and even extract specific skills or knowledge from individual imprints.

In the appropriately entitled episode "Instinct," Echo is imprinted with the memories of a recent mother. Hired by a client, Nate, to replace his wife lost in childbirth, Echo's imprint is designed to interfere with her hormone levels, impersonating recent childbirth and stimulating lactation. However, as the engagement progresses Echo becomes increasingly paranoid that Nate intends to kill both her and "her" child and consequently begins to act erratically. Upon the cancellation of the engagement, the situation is further complicated by Echo's resistance to her trigger-commands and memory wipe,[7] resulting in her escape from the dollhouse and emotional confrontation with Nate. In what may be one of the most revealing scenes of the series, at least in regards to our search for an implicit notion of the soul, Ballard attempts to comfort Echo following the emotionally catastrophic confrontation. He remarks, "I know, Echo, I know you remember everything." But Echo responds curiously to this assertion, correcting Ballard and stating, "Not remember, *feel*.... I felt love and pain [and] fear, it's not pretend for me." Here, *Dollhouse* appears to be working within a dichotomy. On the one hand we have knowledge and memory; on the other, feeling or, if we might read into the episode's title, instinct. What possible distinction, we might ask, permits Echo to clearly demarcate these two? Moreover, what relationship do these two categories bear to the mental wipes? Why does one appear capable of remaining intact, while the other is erased? Before we engage these questions, let us first consider a second example of this phenomenon of Active malfunction.

Malfunction II: Love

What may constitute one of the most intriguing aspects of the series is the persistent relationship of Actives Victor (Enver Gjokaj) and Sierra (Dichen Lachman), a relationship which survives repeated wipes and personality imprints. Whether imprinted with alternate personalities, reduced to their so-called doll state (a childlike *tabula rasa* maintained between engagements), or returned to their original personalities, there exists an unmistakable force pulling the two characters towards one another. Increasingly throughout the series, the dolls Victor and Sierra (as well as occasionally Echo and November [Miracle Laurie]) begin to engage in "grouping": simply, they begin to prefer the company of one another and to intentionally seek one another at mealtimes and various other events. Such bonding tendencies should be, according to the positivist hypothesis and Topher Brink, impossible, as they emerge from each wipe with a brand new personality, a clean slate. Yet, throughout the show, there appears to be a growing unity between these two — a love which, even in the face of constant wiping, appears to intensify over time. By the second season episode "Meet Jane Doe" (2.7), the consistency of this grouping (including an impromptu kiss while programmed as scientists) leads Rossum executive Matthew Harding (Keith Carradine) to order their placement in different houses.

As with Echo, we here encounter a phenomenon whose essence is ambiguous and nonconceptual. As Sierra exclaims, professing her love for Victor, "I *don't remember* meeting him, or spending a moment with him, but I *can feel it* stronger than anything" ("Belonging," 2.4; emphasis added). Yet again we are faced with the recurring dichotomy: memory and feeling. If this feeling, this love, can be maintained across repeated wipes; if it can survive every imprint, including a return of the original identity; then there appears to be some trace, some feeling, emotion, or affection which has escaped every wipe — some core to this phenomenon which may not be reducible to memory and which might evade the positivist hypothesis. Before speculating upon the nature of this content or remainder, let us delve more deeply into this recurring dichotomy. Turning towards our primary interlocutor, Michel Henry, perhaps we might determine what truly differentiates concrete memory from the ambiguity of these feelings or instincts.

Intentional Consciousness

In order to understand the role of memory in *Dollhouse*, it may be helpful to recognize it as a subset of a more general mode of thought that Henry designates as *intentional consciousness*.[8] In phenomenology, intentional consciousness is recognized as the principal mode in which everyday experience appears to the subject. This type of consciousness is understood as the synthesis of two acts: the first is sensations or intuitions; the second is concepts or intentions.[9] Because it is the synthesis of both intention and intuition, intentional consciousness is marked by two defining characteristics. First, its experiences are always framed as subject opposed to object, the conscious objects always being *external* to the experiencing individual.[10] Second, objects are always received as *conceptually determined*.[11] That is to say, even if one does not possess the specific language to articulate it, every experience remains nonetheless meaningful to the extent that objects appear in the world. For example, although Actives in the doll state lack the language or knowledge to identify much of the world around them, objects nevertheless appear to them with distinct qualities (e.g., as colored, beautiful, etc.).[12] For phenomenology, and in particular Henry, these two facts—the externality and conceptuality of phenomena—are the two defining features of all intentional consciousness, and it is no different for memory.[13]

In the act of recollection, one brings to mind a certain definitive content: I remember this birthday party or that tree, this school day or that long trip.[14] Nonetheless, in an act of recollection one *can* pull apart the various objects, relationships, people, and events of the memory; e.g., "I remember climbing a fir tree at my childhood home on a cloudy day." Fir tree, my home, clouds: these all bear distinct conceptual meanings. In this way we can begin to recognize that, like all intentional consciousness, memory is conceptually determined. Likewise, we might say, all memory is external. It is certainly true that a memory is "in your head," in the sense that it is not physically present in the world; you can neither touch nor hold a memory. But this is not strictly speaking what Henry means by external. Instead, externality denotes the unmistakable difference between myself and that which I am remembering[15]; when I perceive, I am looking at "that out there"; when I remember, I remember "that memory there." Even in the first-person memory of an experience, there remains an undeniable distance. As Jean-Paul Sartre writes in his *Being and Nothingness*, in any act of perception (intentional consciousness) "there must be an immediate, noncognitive relation of the self to itself,"[16] a relation which is fully distinct from the object of perception. When Echo suddenly recalls experiences of past events, for instance her "terrorist" activity against Rossum, these play across her mind like a film projected upon a screen. On the one hand, these are undeniably *her* memories. But, as memories, they are not *her*; she is still present as a recollecting subject.

Affective Consciousness

Against intentional consciousness, Henry posits a second form of experience, *affection* or *affectivity*. If intentional consciousness is defined by its externality and conceptual determinacy, then affectivity may be understood as the direct reversal of these characteristics; affections are definitively marked by *internality* and *ambiguity*.[17] Since we have already described the internality/externality dichotomy as a claim concerning the very relationship between one's self and one's experiences, what form could an experience take if there were no distance, no difference between the subject and its object? Simply put, Henry argues that in an affective experience, the subject and object are one and the same: affection is always self-affection.[18] When one experiences pain, this pain is not external to the subject, it is one's very self which is pained; when one experiences joy or sorrow, anxiety or love, these affections are not external to the subject, but the facets of one's very life or — in Henry's reintroduction of theological language — facets of the soul.[19]

If there is, therefore, no difference between our selves and our affections, it stands to reason that these experiences should be transparent to us. Why then must we affirm that affections are fundamentally ambiguous? Our first evidence is phenomenological; that is to say, we must simply look at the experience of affection. At what precise moment did Sierra and Victor's love begin? How strongly did Echo feel her sense of maternal instinct? When we enter a doctor's office and are asked to assign a numerical value to pain, does this not strike one as an absurd request, a request which can be completed only with absolute uncertainty? Yet, on the contrary, if someone were to tell us that our anxiety was false, that we were not "really" anxious, this would seem equally absurd. Even if Nick was eventually able to convince Echo that the child was not her own, he could not talk her out of her experience; he could not make her stop feeling. Affection or affectivity, we might say, appears precariously perched between utter ambiguity and absolute knowledge; we can easily identify our affections, yet they resist clear demarcation and quantification. Is it simply that we are not adequately skilled to quantify our affections, or is it possible that the very nature of affectivity is itself ambiguous? As Merleau-Ponty writes of the "body-schema," the seat of "our affective life,"[20] "my awareness of it is not a thought, that is to say, I cannot take it to pieces and reform it to make a clear idea. Its unity is always implicit and vague."[21] Conversely, it is only when we are able to hold an object away from our self that we are able to quantify it, to clearly delineate its qualities and quantities.

Drawing upon Merleau-Ponty, Henry argues that contrary to our initial speculation, it is precisely the internality of affections which *prevents* their clarity; the internal cannot be encircled or encompassed by our concepts because there is no point at which the subject ends and the affection begins.[22]

The Priority of Affection

Although we have pushed intentional consciousness and affection away from one another, emphasizing their distinction, it is certainly undeniable that in common experience they feed and interact with one another. On the one hand, we fear *that* animal or *that* person out in the world; in some sense our affection appears to be driven by objects of our intentional consciousness. On the other, our anxiety, joy, or sorrow appears to affect our perception; our mood or state-of-mind directly orients our relationships to other people, even affecting the way in which we perceive their words or expressions. When November overrides her programmed directive to murder Paul Ballard, it is not simply her objective experience of Paul which changes, but more directly, it is her immediate affective experience of Paul. Whereas her programming appeared to direct her towards a starkly pragmatic and objectified perspective, Paul as target, the reemergence of a powerful affection, a deep love, radically changed the tonality of Paul's manifestation. Paul was no longer perceived in the mode of a target, but in the mode of an object of love and affection.

In the moment of pain there is just such a synthesis of affective and intentional consciousnesses; "my hand hurts (affective) because it has been cut (intentional)."[23] Yet, in the recollection of this painful event there is a split between this affection and its intentional object. As one recalls the injury (intention), one may *remember* that the cut hurt; perhaps this memory may even spark its own affection (e.g., nausea), but one does not *feel* the original pain of the injury (affection). If this were not so, then the memory of an injury and the injury itself would be equally painful. Is it not precisely the reemergence of the full affective tonality of his war-time experiences that marks Victor's post-traumatic stress disorder? Whereas a "normal" functioning memory is devoid of its original affective content, Victor's recollections are always experienced in an overwhelming manner to the extent of physical collapse.[24] In this way, we can recognize a certain, though not always absolute, independence of intentional and affective consciousness. The intentional object — "my hand has been cut" — can be separated from its initial affective tonality (pain) and presented as a painless memory.

But, is there a phenomenon in which either affective or intentional consciousness manifests alone? One possible answer to this question might be found in the work of Martin Heidegger.[25] In *Being and Time*, Heidegger attempts to understand the nature of human life as existence in the world. At the crux of this work, seeking a state of mind (affection) which would define the human condition, Heidegger stumbles upon the priority of anxiety. "In anxiety," Heidegger writes, "Dasein [human life] gets brought before itself through its own Being."[26] That is simply to say, in anxiety we find out who and what we truly are. How could anxiety provide such a self-revelation? In order to clarify this, Heidegger must distinguish anxiety from its phenomenological cousin, fear. Fear, Heidegger argues, is by its definition a fear of something: one is afraid of a cliff, a gun, a sound in the dark. Anxiety, on the contrary, is anxiety in the face of *nothing*. In a later work he writes, "Anxiety is basically different from fear. We become afraid in the face of this or that particular being that threatens us.... Anxiety does not let such confusion arise ... anxiety reveals the nothing."[27] To say that anxiety reveals nothing, or reveals *the nothing*, is simply to argue that anxiety is a phenomenon in which there is an affective consciousness (anxiety) but no corresponding intentional consciousness (an object one is anxious about). Here, in the face of pure affection, one becomes terrified of its utter indeterminacy. As Heidegger writes, anxiety is "no mere lack of determination but rather the essential impossibility of determining it.... The nothing reveals itself in anxiety — but not as a being. Just as little is it given *as an object*."[28] Analogously, we might consider Echo's experience of overwhelming maternal instinct. On the one hand, the objective content of her child (intentional) has been successfully erased by the dollhouse: "[I do] not remember" ("Instinct"). Nonetheless, the instinct or emotional draw (affection) remains; intentional and affective consciousness have in a meaningful sense been separated.

Yet, having discovered a phenomenon in which affectivity might act alone, we must ask if the opposite is possible: can intentional consciousness work alone? Such a possibility seems quite unlikely. A truly affectionless objectivity may have been the goal of many modern scientists, but it was the German philosopher Friedrich Nietzsche who showed that the "will-to-truth" (objectivity) was merely a "little instrument and toy" of the body, life, and the will-to-power (affectivity).[29] On the contrary, even the most placid scientist remains nonetheless affected by boredom, anticipation, or even curiosity. Moreover, "the fact that moods can deteriorate and change over means simply that in every case Dasein [human life] always has some mood. The pallid, evenly balanced lack of mood, which is often persistent and which is not to be mistaken for a bad mood, is far from nothing at all."[30] In this way, we can hypothesize with Henry that an intentional consciousness may never perform its work alone. While at the most extreme experiences of human life intentional consciousness may wane, affectivity is ever present.

Affectivity and the Soul

What do we mean by this word *soul*? If there is a soul, what would be its defining features? The answers to such questions are complicated by a constant redefining of soul throughout the history of theology; there is simply no consensus. For some a soul must be an eternal substance; for others it is nothing other than a misnaming of the mind, a mere epiphenomenon of the brain.[31] Yet, across these disagreements, there are certain attributes which appear with relative consistency. First, the soul is the self: it is my "I" in the most specific possible sense. It is not merely something that *belongs* to me as a possession, but is that very "I" which possesses attributes. Second, it is the subject of every activity, thought, and desire; it is the locus of the very experience of life. Third, the soul is persistent; as my body changes, as cells die, as interests wax and wane, the soul remains consistent, as though somehow beyond the grip of time. But can these characteristics of the soul be equally attributed to affectivity, as Henry argues?

First, as we have already seen, while intentional consciousness is built upon externality, affectivity is built upon internality; the affections are no different from that which they affect.

> The content of Life — what it experiences — is Life itself, [it] refers back to a more fundamental condition, to the very essence of "Living," to a mode of revelation whose specific phenomenality is the flesh of pathos, pure affective material, in which any cleavage, any separation, finds itself radically excluded.[32]

Because the internality of affectivity excludes all difference between subject and object, my affections are no different from the "I" which they affect. As Henry argues, all affection is autoaffection. Second, since affective consciousness is primordial, providing for the very possibility of intentional consciousness, affectivity is the seat of phenomenological life: "it concerns not what shows itself but the fact of self-showing, not what appears but the way of its appearing, not what is manifest but the pure manifestation."[33] Said differently, affectivity is life because it makes it possible for us to experience anything at all; if we did not first "feel" ourselves, we could never "see" or "know" the world.[34] "The second givenness (intentional), which is the ek-static givenness in the perception of the now, presupposes the first non–ek-static givenness in affectivity."[35] Third, affectivity possesses a relative permanence. On the one hand, it is in a constant state of flux, a permanent instability. Yet, one is never without affectivity. As Henry writes, "the movement by which life does not cease to come into itself and thus to enjoyment of itself— the movement of its own living, which itself does not cease, is never detached from itself but remains eternally within itself."[36] The permanence of affectivity, Henry seeks to illustrates, is absolute; not only when this affectivity is desirable, but perhaps more profoundly when it is not.

In this way, we might say, affectivity and its phenomena correlate to our three criteria of the soul. It is indistinguishable from the self or the "I"; it is the ground of all experience: "this 'feeling of oneself' is the first form of any conceivable phenomenality"[37]; and it is in some sense permanent or eternal, perhaps not in its content, but certainly *in its form*. Following from this correlation, might we then, with Henry, assert that this affectivity *is the soul itself*? Having taken this long tour through phenomenological philosophy, we are perhaps finally poised to return to our initial question, our thesis concerning *Dollhouse*, and to interpret *Dollhouse*'s implicit contrary hypothesis: that one cannot simply "wipe away a person's soul" (Ballard in "Omega").

The Soul in the Doll

If we reconsider our previously cited *Dollhouse* quotes about the priority of feeling over remembering, we can begin to recognize that this dichotomy which saturates *Dollhouse* bears a close relationship to Henry's distinction between intentional and affective consciousness. "I felt love and pain [and] fear": these are not the words of an external objective reality, they are the subjective language of affectivity, the internal language of the self. In its placement of memory and feeling in opposition, *Dollhouse* distinguishes between the affections of its Actives and their intentional objects. As Paul Ballard states in "Instinct," "[Echo] probably can't even remember his name, but she has to have him back." It is not an objective memory which drives Echo, but rather a deep feeling, an affection. What *Dollhouse* intuitively presents through the consistent malfunctions of its Actives is simply the fact that experience is in some sense bifurcated: on the one hand we experience that which is outside of ourselves, that which is rationally cognizable, and on the other hand we experience that which is internal, the ambiguous reality of our subjective life which nonetheless drives our actions: "all these things that have happened to me, I feel them" (Echo in "Instinct"). The Actives of *Dollhouse* illustrate a primordial ontological reality, a division which separates what we feel from what we know, what we see from who we are. While the positivist hypothesis might always be maintained and the failure of the wipes might simply be attributed to an underdeveloped technology, *Dollhouse* continually pushes towards a dialectical alternative, towards its theological hypothesis: that the failure of the wipes results not from a scientific failure, but from a philosophical one; or, what Henry might call the failure to recognize an ontological difference between what we see and what we feel. By reducing human existence to the materially and conceptually identifiable, specifically to memories and traits which could be eliminated by the wipe technology, the positivist hypothesis misses the single most important human characteristic — the very mode by which we experience ourselves and the world, our affective consciousness, or, if we follow Henry's theological turn, our soul.

Yet, even if we follow Henry's distinction between affective and intentional consciousness, as well as its use in the interpretation of *Dollhouse*, is it fair to make this further step of applying the distinctly theological terminology of *soul* to this recurring theme, particularly given Whedon's own outspoken atheism? Initially it must be recognized that although Whedon may not be philosophically or theologically trained, the philosophical and theological depth of his creations is not coincidental, but rather an important part of his writing process. As he states in a *New York Times* interview, "we think very carefully about what we're trying to say emotionally, politically, and even philosophically while we're writing it."[38] It is not merely by chance that numerous works have already been published analyzing the philosophical character of Whedon's productions, for this is an essential and intentional aspect of Whedon's works. That is simply to say, the search for the theological in Whedon's work is by no means futile, but rather true to the character of this work itself. Furthermore, although Whedon himself is an atheist, this does not indicate a closed response to the question of the soul. As he states, "can I say that I believe in the soul? I don't know that I can. It's a beautiful concept, as is resurrection and a lot of other things we have on the show that I'm not really sure I can explain and I certainly don't believe in."[39] Although his own religious beliefs may not include a concept of a soul, this does not necessitate its absence in his work. Quite to the contrary, Whedon's recognition of the aesthetic character of the soul makes it perfectly suited for his complex narratives, particularly that of *Dollhouse*.

With this in mind, it may perhaps be more suitable to turn finally to the show itself and attempt to determine the role that this recurring theme plays within the structure of the narrative. As we have already seen, the clearest appearances of this feeling/memory (affection/intention) dichotomy is within the context of Active malfunction. But where do these malfunctions appear within the narrative? First, and most conspicuously, they are the simple catalyst for the action of the individual episodes. In fact, the trigger of or resolution to nearly every major confrontation of the series is an abnormally functioning Active. Yet, this is merely the small-scale or narrow function of these malfunctions. Taken *in toto* they serve a much more important function. For Echo, these malfunctions stand as important markers in the development of her increasing self-consciousness and individuality; for Victor and Sierra, they mark the emergence of a love, not merely for their respective personalities, but for the other person himself or herself; for November, in the series finale "The Hollow Men" (2.12)[40] malfunction allows her to break through her programmed personality and to recover some sense of herself, to reemerge as someone distinct from and possibly greater than her programming; and lastly, in a darker vein, malfunction permits the psychopathic core of Alpha's (Alan Tudyk) personality to reemerge with violent consequences. In every instance, that which emerges from the malfunction is in some sense the core or essence (if we might use uncomfortably substantial language) of the individual, some important piece of what makes them who they are. But, in what is perhaps the most remarkable insight of *Dollhouse*, this core is not reducible to any one personality, not even an Active's original personality. Instead, this core transcends these individual imprints and appears to reach into the depth of the totality of the character's lived experience. Echo's sense of justice is problematically present in her original life. She is enraged by the inhumanity of the Rossum Corporation and the death of her boyfriend, and openly engages in "terrorist" activity in her attempt to stop the disturbing experiments that she discovers. But it is only after her imprints, as Echo, that this justice reemerges in full clarity and that she is able to overcome her own tendency to use people, and eventually stop Rossum. For Victor and Sierra, their love continues to strengthen even in the face of repeated wipes and imprints. Bouncing between personalities, they not only remain drawn toward each other, but more strongly, fall deeper in love at every meeting, even though they *appear* to each other at every instance as mere strangers. Most dramatically reflecting that this affective core (or soul) is *not* simply an Active's original personality, November's love for Ballard is fostered entirely while a programmed Active. Yet, at a key moment, this love for Ballard manifests in order to save his life. Even Alpha's sadism, clearly manifest in his original life as a serial killer, cannot remain below the surface. Rather, his dark soul is always present, even when reduced to the docile doll state. This sadism allows him to viciously disfigure Whiskey's (Amy Acker) face, while seemingly unaware of his actions (in an ethical sense). In essence, the true core or reality of these individuals does not stand outside of their imprinted experiences, waiting on a hard drive until their "real personality" is reinstalled, but rather incorporates both who they were *and* who they are.

In the end, our investigation must simply ask if this core of human individuality, which continually reemerges regardless of imprint, is to be called anything, should it not be called a *soul*? What other name could be given to this unified self, that factor which simultaneously determines what kind of person an individual will be, but which is also determined by the experiences of that life? *Dollhouse* seems to be asking us to consider the possibility that below the superficial changes in accent, skills, and memory there might exist a "true" self, an internality which resists reduction to what one knows, sees, or even thinks — an internality which, as much as it may be repressed or printed over, continually forces itself to the surface. Perhaps we might even boldly venture that, against its own positivistic foundation, *Dollhouse* proposes a soul.

In conclusion, let us turn to the dramatic series finale, where two Actives are forced to face the reality of their existence, the fact that they have both been generated by a computer, products of a bizarre technology. "I'm a program!" cries out November. But Paul Ballard, responding in a moment of clarity, states, "so am I, [but] I decided it doesn't matter anymore. *We feel what we feel*" ("The Hollow Men"). In the end, *Dollhouse* appears to betray its initial intuition, its positivist hypothesis. It appears to side with the wisdom of Paul Ballard against the genius of Topher Brink. In the midst of its Active malfunctions, *Dollhouse* appears to recognize that the core of human life and human value does not exist solely in the objectifiable world of externality, in that which can be programmed with a computer, but in the deepest ambiguities of our feelings, instincts, and affections.

NOTES

1. As quoted in Maureen Ryan, "Sex, Secrets and *Dollhouse*: Joss Whedon Talks about the End of His Fox show," *Chicago Tribune*, December 3, 2009, http://featuresblogs.chicagotribune.com/entertainment_tv/2009/12/dollhouse-fox-joss-whedon.html.
2. Ibid.
3. Certain of the pre–Socratic philosophers, notably Thales and Democritus, are noted for their abandonment of mythological explanations of reality and are, for this reason, often designated as the founders of Western science and early proponents of materialism, or as we have termed it, the positivist hypothesis.
4. For this alternate perspective, we will be primarily turning to the work of Michel Henry, most clearly articulated in *I am the Truth: Toward a Philosophy of Christianity*, trans. Susan Emanuel (Stanford: Stanford University Press, 2003).
5. Joss Whedon, "10 Questions for Joss Whedon," The New York Times, May 16, 2003, http://www.nytimes.com/2003/05/16/readersopinions/16WHED.html?pagewanted=all.
6. Ibid.
7. Throughout the show, "Are you ready for your treatment?" functions as a trigger-code, creating a sense of absolute trust and complacency within the Actives.
8. This term is borrowed from the founder of phenomenology, Edmund Husserl, who uses it to describe the "directedness" or "act character" of conscious activities towards their respective objects. That is to say, consciousness is always consciousness of something.
9. As Kant once famously stated, "thoughts without content are empty, intuitions without concepts are blind." Immanuel Kant, *Critique of Pure Reason*, trans. Paul Guyer and Allen W. Wood (New York: Cambridge University Press, 1998), 193–194. Also, for intentions and intuitions, see Edmund Husserl, *Ideas*, trans. W. R. Boyce Gibson (New York: Routledge, 2002), 174–178.
10. Henry describes this as the *ek-static* (meaning *to stand out from*) character of intentional phenomena. Michel Henry, *Material Phenomenology*, trans. Scott Davidson (New York: Fordham University Press, 2008), 25.
11. "In so far as we think of it and say something about it, we have made it into an object in the sense of something apprehended.... In the act of valuation we are turned towards values,

in acts of joy to the enjoyed, in acts of love to the beloved, in acting to the action, and without apprehending all this. The intentional object rather, that which is valued, enjoyed, beloved, hoped as such, the action as action, first becomes an apprehended object through a distinctively 'objectifying' turn of thought." Husserl, *Ideas*, 69.

    12. According to Kant and more recent phenomenology, this characteristic is a product of human consciousness's reliance upon transcendental categories (quality, quantity, modality, and relation), categories into which all conscious phenomena must be placed in order to appear within the horizon of visibility (that is, the subjective world). See Kant, *Critique of Pure Reason*; and Jean-Luc Marion, *Being Given: Toward a Phenomenology of Givenness*, trans. Jeffrey L Kosky (Stanford: Stanford University Press, 2002).

    13. For more information on intentional consciousness and phenomenology, see Kant, *Critique of Pure Reason*; Husserl, *Ideas*; Martin Heidegger, *Being and Time*, trans. John Macquarrie and Edward Robinson (New York: Harper & Row, 1962); Maurice Merleau-Ponty, *Phenomenology of Perception*, trans. Colin Smith (London: Routledge and Kegan Paul, 1958); Henry, *Material Phenomenology*.

    14. The relationship between these memories and the "actual event" is in a certain sense irrelevant. One can question, for instance, whether a memory is historically accurate or in some sense invented, but this does not bear upon the object or conceptual character of the memory itself. Just as the act of imagination has an associated content, the imagined as such, the content of recollection is present to consciousness regardless of its empirical validity.

    15. A notable exception may be Merleau-Ponty, who argues in *Phenomenology of Perception* that "objective thought is unaware of the subject of perception" (240). However, even this claim is later expanded and clarified in ways which may find commonality with our analysis.

    16. Jean-Paul Sartre, *Being and Nothingness*, trans. Hazel E. Barnes (New York: Pocket Books, 1956), 12.

    17. For more information on affective consciousness, see Merleau-Ponty, *Phenomenology of Perception*; Michel Henry, *Material Phenomenology*; Michel Henry, *I am the Truth*; and Jean-Luc Marion, *Being Given*.

    18. "Life is a self-movement that is self-experiencing and never ceases to be self-experiencing in its very movement — in such a way that from this self-experiencing movement nothing is ever detached: nothing slips away from it, away from this self-moving self-experience." Michael Henry, *I am the Truth*, 56.

    19. Michel Henry, "Le concept d'ame a-t-il un sens?" *Revue philosophique de Louvain* 64 (1966): 5–33.

    20. Merleau-Ponty, *Phenomenology of Perception*, 178.

    21. Ibid., 231.

    22. For Merleau-Ponty, Henry, and later Jean-Luc Marion, this ambiguity is distinguished from the ambiguity of intentional objects (e.g., the mysterious creature of our previous discussion) by its inability to be categorized by the Transcendental Categories. The experience of the affective body, for instance, "is torn from the category of relation.... The flesh is defined as the identity of what touches with the medium where this touching takes place (Aristotle), therefore of the felt with what feels (Husserl), but also of the seen and the seeing or the heard and the hearing — in short, of the affected with the affecting (Henry)." Marion, *Being Given*, 231.

    23. Perhaps it might also be argued that, in extreme pain, affective consciousness reigns alone, overwhelming any possibility of objective consciousness: "I was in so much pain I couldn't think." But this would take a more rigorous phenomenological analysis to establish.

    24. See "Echoes" (1.7) and "Belonging."

    25. Perhaps the most important implicit interlocutor of Henry, both negatively and positively.

    26. Martin Heidegger, *Being and Time*, 229.

    27. Martin Heidegger, "What is Metaphysics?" in *Basic Writings* (New York: Harper & Row, 1993), 100–101.

    28. Ibid., 101–102 (emphasis added).

    29. Friedrich Nietzsche, *Beyond Good and Evil*, trans. Walter Kaufmann (New York: Cam-

bridge University Press, 2001); and *Thus Spoke Zarathustra*, especially book I, "On the Despisers of the Body," in *The Portable Nietzsche*, trans. and ed. Walter Kaufmann (New York: Penguin Books, 1976).

30. Heidegger, *Being and Time*, 173.

31. For classic arguments for the eternality of the soul, see Plato's *Phaedo* and John Calvin's *Institutes of the Christian Religion*, especially book I, chapter XV. For theories of the mind as epiphenomenon of the brain, see note 6 above.

32. Henry, *I am the Truth*, 30.

33. Ibid., 23.

34. Here Henry stands, most importantly, in opposition to many common readings of the dialectical tradition inaugurated in Jacob Boehme and epitomized in the German Idealists. For these thinkers, one must first experience the "Not-I" (or other) before one can be constituted as a "self."

35. Henry, *Material Phenomenology*, 25.

36. Henry, *I am the Truth*, 56.

37. Ibid.

38. Whedon, "Ten Questions."

39. Ibid.

40. Excluding the unusual epilogue "Epitaph Two: Return" (2.13).

BIBLIOGRAPHY

Heidegger, Martin. *Being and Time*. Translated by John Macquarrie and Edward Robinson. New York: Harper & Row, 1962.

———. "What Is Metaphysics?" In *Basic Writings*, edited by David Farrell Krell, 89–110. New York: Harper & Row, 1993.

Henry, Michel. *I Am the Truth: Towards a Philosophy of Christianity*. Translated by Susan Emanuel. Stanford: Stanford University Press, 2003.

———. "Le concept d'ame a-t-il un sens?" *Revue philosophique de Louvain* 64 (1966): 5–33.

———. *Material Phenomenology*. Translated by Scott Davidson. New York: Fordham University Press, 2008.

———. *Words of Christ*. Translated by Christina M. Gshwandtner. Grand Rapids: Eerdmans, 2012.

Husserl, Edmund. *Ideas*. Translated by W. R. Boyce Gibson. New York: Routledge, 2002.

Kant, Immanuel. *Critique of Pure Reason*. Translated by Paul Guyer and Allen W. Wood. New York: Cambridge University Press, 1998.

Keats, John. John Keats to Benjamin Bailey, 22 November 1817. Accessed February 3, 2013. http://www.john-keats.com/briefe/221117.htm.

Marion, Jean-Luc. *Being Given: Toward a Phenomenology of Givenness*. Translated by Jeffrey L. Kosky. Stanford: Stanford University Press, 2002.

Merleau-Ponty, Maurice. *Phenomenology of Perception*. Translated by Colin Smith. London: Routledge and Kegan Paul, 1958.

Nietzsche, Friedrich. *Beyond Good and Evil*. Translated by Walter Kaufmann. New York: Cambridge University Press, 2001.

———. *Thus Spoke Zarathustra*. In *The Portable Nietzsche*. Translated and edited by Walter Kaufmann, 103–439. New York: Penguin Books, 1976.

Sartre, Jean-Paul. *Being and Nothingness*. Translated by Hazel E. Barnes. New York: Pocket Books, 1956.

Whedon, Joss. "10 Questions for Joss Whedon." *The New York Times*, May 16, 2003. http://www.nytimes.com/2003/05/16/readersopinions/16WHED.html?pagewanted=all.

Whedon, Joss, and Maureen Ryan. "Sex, Secrets and *Dollhouse*: Joss Whedon Talks About the End of His Fox Show." *Chicago Tribune*, December 3, 2009. http://featuresblogs.chicagotribune.com/entertainment_tv/2009/12/dollhouse-fox-joss-whedon.html.

Just to Love and Be Loved in Return
Identity and Love in the Dollhouse
JULIE CLAWSON

In 2009 Joss Whedon introduced viewers to the world of *Dollhouse*. The show centers around a secret organization that controls individuals called "dolls" by programming (or "imprinting") them to serve the needs and desires of others. These dolls have had their own personalities erased so as to become a *tabula rasa*, in a rather Lockean sense, upon which a new personality can be imposed. For a price, a doll can be programmed to be a perfect lover, expert negotiator, or devoted confidant. When the engagement is over, the doll has all memories of the encounter erased and is then returned to the blank-slate state in which they are described as being as innocent as children.

In the two short seasons that *Dollhouse* ran, Whedon explored the implications of this ability to create perfect people for others to use. Questions of identity, the nature of love, and what it means to be truly human were raised as the story progressed and the highly structured hierarchy of the dollhouse began to unravel and its secrets led to devastating consequences. With his trademark brilliance, Joss Whedon offered in *Dollhouse* not just an edgy science-fiction narrative, but a show which wrestled with the very idea of what it means to be human. While it would be difficult to argue that *Dollhouse* is an intentionally religious show given that Joss Whedon, its creator, is a self-proclaimed atheist, the questions it addresses *are* common spiritual concerns for people of faith. In many ways the show serves as one of the dominant myths or images of the age which, as theologian Amos Wilder describes, function as carriers of meaning for society and reveal "the contemporary quest patterns of a changing world."[1] In exploring issues of love and identity, *Dollhouse* reveals the deeper longings and uncertainties that resonate with the viewing audience and which are, for many, ultimately issues of spiritual significance. From a Christian theological perspective, therefore, these questions and concerns have poignant religious implications for contemporary Western culture. With those implications in mind, this essay explores how the journey of the dolls from a life of subjugation to discovering their underlying identities parallels recent theological developments in relational conceptions of what it means for humans to be created in the image of God.

The premise undergirding the world of the dollhouse is the assumption of an essential mind–body dualism within persons. The body is viewed as an empty shell, a mere object that the mind can ultimately control. To have power over the mind or to be able to rewrite the mind like a blank slate is the primary goal, while the body is merely pretty packaging to be used as needed. Within the world of the dollhouse, this division is strictly emphasized. The dolls are seen as minds to be programmed to meet the expectations of each client, yet often the client requests certain programming so that he can simply use the body of the doll as he desires. Where the drama develops within the narrative arc of the show is in demonstrating how this dualistic view of the mind and body ultimately breaks down. The supposedly perfect system of the dollhouse simply does not work because people, even wiped and imprinted people, cannot exist as mere bodies or minds to be used. The dolls are not just bodies upon which various personalities and minds can be imprinted. Over the course of the show, they manifest biologically and psychologically an inherent need to have a holistic identity and to move beyond objectification to relationship that cannot ultimately be suppressed by even the most advanced technology. It is through the show's exploration of the natures of identity and love that the failure of the dualistic view of human nature is revealed.

Not restricted to science fiction television, the presumption of a mind and body dualism is pervasive in Western culture. This dichotomy between the mind and body has historically placed the center of consciousness or personality in the mind and derided the body as the center of the purely animal. Descartes's famous *cogito ergo sum*, "I think therefore I am," establishes the existence of the self based on the reality of one's own thought processes.[2] Such observable processes provided an objective means of understanding and therefore mastering the self. This ability to master both the self and by extension the world resonated with the emerging Pietistic and Puritan movements in the Enlightenment period because of its implications in affirming the human role of stewarding God's creation. The subsequent dominance of such religious traditions in the Western world as well as the Evangelical awakenings they sparked served to establish this Cartesian conception of the self as the primary popular view.[3] Despite contemporary challenges to this dualistic conception, it remains deeply rooted in Western religious (and cultural) consciousness, especially in the Evangelical streams of the church. This view assumes that a person is a person because he or she has an individual identity and knows, acts, intends, decides, and asserts a will based on the interior working of the mind. Experience of the world is mediated through the physical senses, but it is how the mind reflects upon and responds to those experiences that is seen as primary. Such a conception of the self led philosopher John Locke to even propose that the mind is a sort of *tabula rasa*, a blank slate, to be written upon through one's self-reflected experience of the world.[4] A person constructs his or her own identity by sheer assertion of the will.

The premise of the technology of the dollhouse is that it is possible to repeatedly return people to a blank slate and then imprint a new identity upon that person. The dolls that have been contracted to the various dollhouses around the world have had their original identities copied and removed and an infrastructure constructed inside their minds that allows for them to be constantly reborn as new people. As their mind is reprogrammed so goes their body. When the doll Echo is programmed with the identity of a crisis hostage negotiator in "Ghost" (1.1), she manifests symptoms of asthma just like the imprint of her new identity. Similarly, in "True Believer" (1.5), when she is imprinted as a religious convert in order to infiltrate a cult, her mind is programmed to not only have her believe that she is blind, but to also physically manifest blindness. Creating dolls requires a complete acceptance of the Cartesian conception of the self being located in the mind and the Lockean conception of the mind as a blank slate upon which a complete identity can be written.

From a Christian perspective, the approaches of Descartes and Locke are problematic, although they are often embraced by theologians. In such a world of isolated selves, God becomes just another self with whom other individual selves interact. The Augustinian view that the image of God exists in the interior of a person's self further supports this isolation and separation.[5] If to be human is to be a self-reflective thinking mind and humans are created in the image of God who is similarly a separate self, one accesses and reflects that image of God solely through introspection. The image of God as an individual self, therefore, is to be found in individual creatures who resemble that which they image. Not surprisingly, when God is seen as a powerful self who exists in transcendent isolation from the creation, ideas of how this divine character should be reflected in the lives of followers are easily corrupted.

For instance, despite confessing the doctrine of the Trinity, many Christians conceive of the Father as primary and the ruler of the other two persons, a view which has served to justify many forms of domination in both the church and culture. God the Father becomes the ruling king within the Trinity while the Son, the Spirit, and all of creation are subordinated to his authority and rule. Intentional or not, this theological position has direct practical implications. As Miroslav Volf writes, "Given the conflictual nature of all social realities, the church not excepted, a hierarchical notion of the Trinity ends up underwriting an authoritarian practice in the church."[6] Subsequently, this presumed hierarchy in the Trinity is assumed to be mirrored in creation and is frequently used to justify hierarchies of male over female, master over slave, and human over nature. When God is seen as an isolated self existing as the reigning monarch even within the Trinity, it is easy for humans to mirror that hierarchy in systems that enforce the subordination of others through acts of injustice and oppression. As Jürgen Moltmann reminds readers, the term *hierarchy* implies a "holy rule," and is easily used to justify all sorts of "earthly domination."[7]

In the course of post–Cartesian Western history the affinity for an isolated hierarchic God has resulted in many Westerners being unwilling or unable to identify the image of God in people of other cultures. If the self is formed through introspection, then those persons from cultures who do not value or think in the same ways must not yet have developed selves and, therefore, do not possess the image of God. Some people, it follows, are thought to be like the dolls, blank slates ready to have selves imprinted upon them by their "superiors," people who already reflect God's image. Locke's ideas therefore held great sway during the colonial era as Westerners encountered and conquered the lands, bodies, and minds of other peoples.[8] As postcolonial scholar Musa Dube comments, "Colonial subjugation was not just a simple geographical control of black African lands by white people. It was a complex networking of the molding of black African minds and spaces according to and for the material benefit of the West."[9]

The effects of this dominance of powerful selves over others are revealed in *Dollhouse* as the series progresses and the viewer gains insight into the original personalities of the dolls and what led them to become part of the dollhouse. One discovers that for the main character, Echo, the choice was not entirely voluntary. Her original personality is that of Caroline, a college student and animal activist intent on exposing the mysterious Rossum Corporation for animal testing. When she and her boyfriend infiltrate one of their labs, they discover that Rossum not only tests on animals but also on humans. After her boyfriend is shot and killed by Rossum security as they attempt to escape, she becomes a sort of terrorist intent on bringing down the Rossum Corporation. When she is finally caught by Rossum, she is confronted by the director of the Los Angeles dollhouse, Adelle DeWitt (Olivia Williams), and given the option of having all her memories erased by becoming a doll within the Los Angeles dollhouse (also run by the Rossum Corporation). Preferring this zombie-like existence to death, Caroline enters the dollhouse and becomes the doll Echo.

While other dolls may have willingly entered service in the dollhouse to have their personalities removed,[10] it soon becomes apparent within the narrative of the show that there are serious problems with the very premise of this Cartesian/Lockean conception of the self. Historically, the cultural manifestation of the Cartesian method of defining the self based on internal thought processes has been the idea, prevalent in popular conceptions of personhood, that "the self can be a self by itself, apart from relationship with anything or anyone else."[11] Individuals might interact with and experience others, but it is in introspection and not relationship that personhood is established.

In this contractual system where clients express the desire of their internal selves by having a person created to meet their unique desires, their interaction is merely transactional: the consumption of goods instead of the mutual respect and vulnerability which characterize healthy relationships. The clients are able to use the imprinted dolls as objects for their pleasure without the complications of having to exist in relationship with them. The dolls in their imprinted personalities might believe they are in a real relationship, like Echo does after an engagement in the first episode. She rambles on about how she thinks she might have finally found "the one," but as soon as her handler brings her back to the dollhouse for her treatment, that identity is wiped and the feelings forgotten. The clients are able to consume the bodies and imprinted selves of the dolls without the consequences that might come from having to consider the needs or desires of the doll they have engaged.

In the first few episodes of the series, the dolls engage in fun and altruistic assignments. They provide companionship for the lonely, help rescue kidnapped children, and protect a pop star from a stalker. While it initially appears that their lives fulfill a good service to the world, it is one that, like slavery, they have no choice but to accept. As the show progresses, however, it becomes increasingly evident that the dolls are commodities to be prostituted out by the directors of the dollhouse. As pretty bodies holding blank minds that can be manipulated at will without the consequences of intimate or genuine relationships, the dolls are perceived as mere objects to be used by the rich and the powerful.

Through the revelation of the doll Sierra's backstory in the season two episode "Belonging," viewers finally see the full extremity of the objectification of the dolls into mere bodies to be used as playthings for the wealthy. Sierra's original personality was that of Priya Tsetsang, a young carefree artist who had moved to Los Angeles from Australia. Nolan Kinnard, a rich doctor, encounters her selling her art on the boardwalk and becomes obsessed with her. Priya repeatedly rejects his attempts at a relationship, and he becomes increasingly violent in his interactions with her. In light of his growing obsession with Sierra, Kinnard has her hunted down and admitted to a hospital where he has her pumped full of drugs that make her appear to be a paranoid schizophrenic suffering from severe hallucinations. Kinnard uses his connections in the dollhouse to manipulate them into turning Priya into a doll as a seeming act of altruism. He then requests that the dollhouse create an imprint of a docile version of Priya who is devotedly in love with him. He engages this false imprint of Priya on numerous occasions, essentially raping her on each encounter.

Kinnard did not want the complications of being in a relationship with another individual who could choose to reciprocate or withhold love, and so he reduced Priya to a mere body. This issue is similarly dealt with in the episode "A Spy in the House of Love" (1.9) where viewers discover that Los Angeles dollhouse director Adelle DeWitt secretly has the doll Victor imprinted in order to engage in a love affair with him. As the director of the dollhouse, she bears a responsibility for the wellbeing of the dolls in her care, people who are often described as childlike and innocent; yet out of her extreme loneliness she behaves as a sexual predator toward one of those very childlike dolls. However, even in this extreme objectification of the dolls as bodies to be used for sexual gratification, there is evidence of the underlying need for relationship in both Kinnard and DeWitt. They desire love and yet feel like they can only fulfill that desire by asserting dominance over others. Nevertheless, their twisted attempts at meeting their felt needs parallel a healthier development among the dolls themselves.

Over the course of the first season, the dolls Echo, Victor, and Sierra are shown to be developing a friendship while in their doll state. They regularly eat meals together and participate in activities together in the dollhouse. In their blank-slate state, they should not have the memory or the self-awareness to develop something as permanent as friendship. Topher Brink, the programmer of the dolls' minds, initially dismisses their behavior as a sort of herd mentality. He perceives them as bodies with blank minds and so therefore assumes that they are simply behaving like other unreflective animals. Yet the relationship is shown to be more than mere herd mentality when the staff at the dollhouse notices that the doll Victor develops a physical, sexual response to the doll Sierra when they are in the shower (something a doll should not be able to do). Echo, Victor, and Sierra also begin to worry about each other's wellbeing and, in the limits of their simple-minded doll state, do what they can to protect each other. Despite repeated mind wipes, all three of them continue to be drawn to each other, their relationship extending deeper than the attempted eradication of their selves. From this relationship, all of them, especially Echo, form new identities that supersede any attempt to imprint or wipe their minds. Memories of imprints remain after they are wiped and they even begin to recall their bond from the dollhouse after being imprinted with new personalities.

The inability of the mind wipes to create a truly blank slate in the dolls emerges in "Man on the Street" (1.6) when Sierra starts displaying signs of fear and panic in her supposedly innocent and childlike doll state. When Victor touches Sierra on the shoulder, she reacts by screaming in panic. Echo also mentions that she can hear Sierra crying herself to sleep at night. Wiping her mind and returning her to the default *tabula rasa* doll state does nothing to overcome this unexplained fear and pain. It is later discovered that Sierra's handler had on multiple occasions raped her while she was in her doll state. The physical violation of her self could not be erased with a mind wipe but affected her on an emotional level even though she was unable to articulate why she was experiencing feelings of sadness, fear, and panic. Similarly, Sierra's trauma from being repeatedly raped as Kinnard's love slave becomes increasingly difficult to erase, even in her blank-slate state. The objectifying violation of her body has an impact on her that reveals a connection between the mind and the body that cannot be overwritten.

Relationships, both good and bad, affect the dolls despite what the reigning assumptions about the nature of the self may be within the world of the dollhouse. The dolls are not simply blank slates within bodies, but people who are drawn into relationships and somehow manage to create identities out of those interactions. The need to find companions and develop friendships directs even those bodies that possess what are supposedly empty minds. This development within the show illustrates recent critiques of the Cartesian conception of the self which argue that a person cannot simply be defined as a "being-in-itself or being-by-itself" but must be understood as a "being-in-relation-to-another."[12] In this way of conceiving human identity, people are fully human only when they are in relation with others. As theologian LeRon Shults describes it, one's "sense of self is called into being and formed through interaction with other persons."[13] To be fully human, one needs relationships. These relationships are not the sorts of interactions where the other is used as an object, but a reciprocal relationship where love is offered and given in return.[14]

This relational definition of identity is similar to the African concept of *ubuntu*, which Desmond Tutu describes as the realization that "my humanity is caught up, is inextricably bound up, in yours. We belong in a bundle of life.... I am human because I belong, I participate, I share."[15] Unlike the individual introspective self or blank slates existing apart from bodies, relationships require a holistic presence. People exist as physical entities in the world and that presence shapes them. Volf reminds his readers of this when he refers to Jeremy Bentham's critique that Locke seemingly forgot that individuals do not appear in the world having already come of age. Volf writes that "a person cannot arise, develop, and live apart from her relationships with others" and is instead shaped by that very experience of being in reciprocal relationship.[16] Even the dolls with their wiped minds cannot help but develop relationships which come to define their very identities. Others attempted to assume superiority over them and imprint constructs onto their minds as they use their bodies, but the ironic twist of the narrative is that it is the dolls who through relationship demonstrate the healthiest depictions of self and identity. As theologian Stanley Grenz comments, the "who" of the self "emerges communally rather than in isolation; that is, it emerges together with other 'whos' and from within a conversation of persons-in-communion."[17]

Over the course of the *Dollhouse* narrative, this grounding of identity in reciprocal relationship is revealed through the journey of Topher Brink. A common description of the dolls is that in their wiped state they are as innocent as children, but it is Topher — the seemingly amoral programmer who installs and wipes the various personalities of the dolls, thereby repeatedly returning them to a childlike state — who actually appears to be the most childish. Topher is usually shown drinking juice boxes and keeping his work area full of items like gaming systems and a bubblegum machine. "Haunted" (1.10) depicts him on his birthday imprinting one of the dolls with his idea of the perfect girlfriend with whom he then spends the evening playing games, eating junk food, and talking about his favorite hobbies. Topher does not imprint the doll with a true person with whom he must interact, but instead narcissistically creates "the perfect girl," a female mirror of himself. While those who are supposedly wiped into a childlike state are able to realize their deep need to be in relationship with others, Topher is stunted in his inability to move outside of his isolated self.

It is when Topher starts to develop true relationships with the dolls that he begins to form a moral conscience and move beyond his self-absorption. As the genius programmer for the dollhouse, he was fascinated with the possibilities of what one could do with the human mind. He saw the dolls as true blank slates that he could manipulate as objects with the technology he developed. Topher's first moral dilemma arises in "Belonging" when he discovers the truth about Priya's admission to the dollhouse. He truly had thought that he was helping a mentally disturbed woman by giving her infrastructure upon which more stable personalities could be imprinted. Once he discovered the truth that she had been drugged into that state so she could be imprinted and repeatedly raped, Topher was horrified by his complicity. When Kinnard's deception is revealed and he is not punished but instead able to use his influence to insist that Priya be released to him permanently imprinted with her docile love-slave personality, Topher is ordered to comply with this demand. Instead, Topher chooses to restore Priya's original personality and tell her the truth about what has happened to her. She is returned to Kinnard as her original self and murders him when he tries to assault her again. Topher then has to help her clean up the mess of the murder and is appalled by his actions throughout the entire ordeal. He claims that he does not know if he can live with what he has done. From that point on, he becomes more protective of the dolls and begins to treat them more like real people instead of blank canvases upon which he can impose his imprints.

What ultimately awakens Topher to his moral responsibility and connection to others is the realization that his technology is not amoral as he had assumed and has in fact been used to evil ends. When the shady Rossum Corporation that runs the dollhouse obtains Topher's remote wiping and imprinting plans, they begin modifying them for use on nondolls. While Topher had intended to use the technology to help imprinted dolls when they needed to be rescued from an imprint gone wrong, Rossum wants to use it to imprint personalities onto whomever they desire (willingly or not). This technology would grant them complete control over governments, militaries, and other corporations, essentially giving them the ability to take over the world. After Topher discovers their plans for his technology, he joins Echo in her fight to take down the Rossum Corporation. Their attempts to destroy the technology fail and Rossum starts making use of it. As viewers see in "Epitaph One" (1.13), this technology spirals out of control and ultimately destroys civilization. The abuse of this technology allows a few Rossum executives to live in luxury, inhabiting multiple bodies while the streets have become wastelands as people are imprinted and wiped in guerrilla warfare settings.

Topher eventually experiences a complete mental breakdown because of his part in developing this destructive technology. The Rossum Corporation kidnaps him and coerces him into working on the technology for a more powerful remote wiping device by shooting someone in front of him for each day that he fails to complete it. This experience drives him insane as he is repeatedly confronted with direct evidence of how his work affects the lives of real people. It is no longer just a puzzle for him to solve and people are not just objects to be manipulated or blank slates to be written upon, but real people who are being hurt because of him. After Echo rescues him, he returns to the Los Angeles dollhouse so he can develop a way to reverse the effects of the mass wiping and imprinting technology. He thus turns his genius abilities, which had allowed him to create the technology that destroyed the world, to create a system that will hopefully restore it. Implementing this final reversal requires someone to trigger a massive explosion. Topher, the once childish and self-absorbed amoral genius, willingly sacrifices himself to undo the harm his imprinting technology had wrought on the world. In the end, the communal good of humanity became his motivation, even at the cost of his life.

This innate need for relationship and the implication of *Dollhouse*'s narrative that ultimately one's identity is determined by such relationships challenge the concept of a binary division of mind and body that reduces the body to a mere commodity to be bought, sold, and controlled by those with wealth and power. The dolls, although at times programmed to be the perfect companion, cannot sustain existence devoid of true relationships and, as shown through Topher and Adelle, neither can the dollhouse staff. For Christian theologians, this pull towards relationship and defining of self in connection to others is explained by the belief that the self is a reflection of the image of God. Instead of viewing the Trinity as a practical monotheism that sets up a hierarchic, controlling God who can be used to justify the oppression and subjugation of others, theologians that recognize the importance of relationships in the development of identity have turned to a truer trinitarianism in their understanding of God.

Recent discussions of the Trinity suggest that "what is mined from understanding God as Father, Son, and Spirit in relationship bears directly upon our social existence."[18] That the relationship within the Trinity has been used as a justification for oppression seems to contradict the call for Christians to love others and exist in right relation with all. For this reason, some theologians are calling Christians to embrace a social concept of the Trinity. Instead of assuming that God is the authority imposing his rule on all, the emphasis on a truly triune God places the focus instead "on dynamic interrelationship among persons."[19] The mutual indwelling and equality of the members of the Trinity reveal that even God exists in perpetual relationship, constantly giving and receiving love. Although the voices of those advocating for such social understanding of the Trinity have grown in influence in recent years, this emphasis on divine interrelationship is nothing new within Christian theology. John of Damascus in the eighth century referred to this relationship within the Trinity as *perichoresis*, a sort of divine dance where three distinct persons draw life from one another. In this dance "each divine person is irresistibly drawn to the other, taking his/her existence from the other, containing the other in him/herself, while at the same time pouring self out into the other."[20]

Understanding the Trinity as a manifestation of relational love rather than as an abstract idea of God existing in isolation from everything except Godself helps Christians better understand not only their relationship with God but also their relationship with others. Often Christian discourse on the Trinity fails to take into account this relational aspect of the Trinity and its subsequent real-life applications, defaulting instead to speculations on the inner life of the Trinity, assuming "a Trinity locked up in itself and unrelated to us."[21] Those who believe that God exists in the perichoresis of never-ending reciprocal love — always giving and receiving love within the relationship of the Trinity — hold that human identity is similarly shaped by relationships. To be human is to image God, and when God is seen as a relationship of ever giving and receiving love, it follows that human identity can only emerge from similar interconnections among persons.

Far from being isolated introspective minds or blank slates within bodies, this view of the self holds that human beings are image bearers who, to be fully human, must both give and receive love in ways similar to the relationship within the Trinity. It serves as a critique of the failings of the Cartesian and Lockean views of isolated selves that were used to justify acts of domination and oppression in God's name. Joss Whedon's imaginative narrative in *Dollhouse* reflects this shift in conceptions of the self and thereby can serve to illuminate relational understandings of God and what it means to relationally bear the image of God. The Western world experimented with philosophies of the isolated, thinking self, and the result was disastrous for those around the globe upon whom some Westerners attempted to narcissistically imprint versions of their own selves. Other people became just one more thing to mold, shape, and consume for one's personal pleasure instead of real people with whom to be in mutually respectful and vulnerable relationship. That Western culture has devolved into a consumer culture where people are not only objects to be consumed, but are also defined by what they consume, reveals the broken effects of such conceptions of human identity. Whedon's *Dollhouse* narrative brilliantly reveals the shortcomings of those philosophies and consumeristic tendencies and the subsequent necessity of turning towards relational understandings of identity. He shows that those who are truly human do not see the dolls, or fellow human beings, as merely bodies to be used or minds upon which to imprint new identities, but as beings whose humanity is inextricably caught up in the humanity of others. *Dollhouse* is a reminder that it is not thought or domination that make us human, but learning to love and be loved in return.

NOTES

1. Amos Niven Wilder, *Theopoetic: Theology and the Religious Imagination* (1976; repr., Lima, OH: Academic Renewal Press, 2001), 25.
2. See Descartes's *Meditations on First Philosophy.*
3. Stanley J. Grenz, *The Social God and the Relational Self: A Trinitarian Theology of the Imago Dei* (Louisville: Westminster John Knox Press, 2001), 78.
4. See Locke's *An Essay Concerning Human Understanding.*
5. Catherine Mowry LaCugna, *God for Us: The Trinity and Christian Life* (1973; repr., New York: HarperCollins, 1991), 14.
6. Miroslav Volf, *After Our Likeness: The Church as the Image of the Trinity* (Grand Rapids: Eerdmans, 1998), 4.
7. Jürgen Moltmann, *The Trinity and the Kingdom*, trans. Margaret Kohl (Minneapolis: Fortress, 1993), 192.

8. Beyond the influence of his ideas, as a secretary to the English Council of Trade and Plantations (1673–1674) and a member of the Board of Trade (1696–1700), Locke directly supervised the acquisition of land from Native Americans and the system of slavery in the British colonies. For more information on Locke's role and the influence of his ideas on colonialism, see James Farr, "'So Vile and Miserable an Estate': The Problem of Slavery in Locke's Political Thought," *Political Theory* 14, no. 2 (May 1986): 263–289.

9. Musa Dube, *Postcolonial Feminist Interpretation of the Bible* (St. Louis: Chalice Press, 2000), 19. For instance, introspective selves who believed that they and those like them best reflected God took it upon themselves to use the bodies of the African peoples even as they attempted to mold their minds. The conquered people were shaped into what their conquerors preferred them to be in an attempt to not only ignore but utterly rewrite their selves. What were the colonial project and the slave trade but attempts to create a sort of dollhouse out of conquered lands that white Euro-Americans saw as blank slates upon which to inscribe their ways and construct new empires?

10. For example, the doll November entered the dollhouse in exchange for help in erasing the crippling memory of her daughter's death.

11. LaCugna, *God for Us*, 251.

12. Ibid., 250.

13. F. LeRon Shults, *Reforming Theological Anthropology: After the Philosophical Turn to Relationality* (Grand Rapids: Eerdmans, 2003), 2.

14. LaCugna, *God for Us*, 292.

15. Desmond Tutu, *No Future Without Forgiveness* (New York: Image Books, 2000), 31.

16. Volf, *After Our Likeness*, 178.

17. Grenz, *Social God*, 12.

18. Quentin P. Kinnison, "The Social Trinity and the Southwest: Toward a Local Theology in the Borderlands," *Perspectives in Religious Studies: Journal of the National Association of Baptist Professors of Religion* 35, no. 3 (2008): 263.

19. LaCugna, *God for Us*, 269.

20. Ibid., 270.

21. Ibid., 2.

BIBLIOGRAPHY

Dube, Musa. *Postcolonial Feminist Interpretation of the Bible*. St. Louis: Chalice, 2000.

Farr, James. "'So Vile and Miserable an Estate': The Problem of Slavery in Locke's Political Thought." *Political Theory* 14, no. 2 (1986): 263–289.

Grenz, Stanley J. *The Social God and the Relational Self: A Trinitarian Theology of the Imago Dei*. Louisville: Westminster John Knox Press, 2001.

Kinnison, Quentin P. "The Social Trinity and the Southwest: Toward a Local Theology in the Borderlands." *Perspectives in Religious Studies: Journal of the National Association of Baptist Professors of Religion* 35, no. 3 (2008): 261–81.

LaCugna, Catherine Mowry. *God for Us: The Trinity and Christian Life*. 1973. Reprint, New York: HarperCollins, 1991.

Moltmann, Jürgen. *The Trinity and the Kingdom*. Translated by Margaret Kohl. Minneapolis: Fortress, 1993.

Shults, F. LeRon. *Reforming Theological Anthropology: After the Philosophical Turn to Relationality*. Grand Rapids: Eerdmans, 2003.

Tutu, Desmond. *No Future Without Forgiveness*. New York: Image Books, 2000.

Volf, Miroslav. *After Our Likeness: The Church as the Image of the Trinity*. Grand Rapids: Eerdmans, 1998.

Wilder, Amos Niven. *Theopoetic: Theology and the Religious Imagination*. 1976. Reprint, Lima, OH: Academic Renewal Press, 2001.

"There's no place I can be"
Whedon, Augustine and the Earthly City
Susanne E. Foster *and*
James B. South

Though Joss Whedon and Augustine may differ with regard to the ends of their works (their underlying religious and metaphysical commitments), the juxtaposition of the works that we will be pursuing in this paper is founded on a set of shared concerns and commitments about the role of the individual within society, the ends of society, and the ends of humans. At the root of the juxtaposition is the view, shared by both, that human beings as they actually exist in the world are flawed, restless, prone to lust (both sexual and political), and desirous of a happiness that cannot be fulfilled in earthly life.

One key point of agreement between Whedon and Augustine concerns the relationship between the individual and the government. Whedon clearly seems to think that the appropriate role of the state is negative — to protect citizens from harms that stem either from within the state or those external to the state. In fact, when the state tries actively to further the good of its citizens, its actions quickly become as bad as or worse than the ills it seeks to eliminate. Consider, for example, the interplanetary government from *Firefly*, the Alliance. In an attempt to better the lives of its people, the Alliance experiments with releasing a gas, g23 paxilon hydrochlorate (or "Pax") — designed to remove aggressive tendencies from the populace — into the atmosphere of Miranda, one of its planets. The ends of the government are noble — the "comfort and enlightenment" of its citizens. But the state's paternalism results in the deaths of the vast majority of Miranda's population by making them overly passive, and the few remaining inhabitants have the opposite reaction to the drug, devolving into hyperviolent monstrosities.

One way of understanding why the government's interference with the people on Miranda is wrong is provided by *contractarian theory*. On this view, individuals surrender their right to respond to aggression (beyond the point of self protection) in exchange for protection from the state. Any activity of the state beyond protecting its citizens is thereby an infringement of their freedom since the activity transgresses the bounds of the agreement. Neither Augustine nor Whedon would think contractarianism provides an adequate account of the relation between the individual and her communities, including the state, or of the wrongness perpetrated by the Alliance on Miranda. The reasons Whedon offers us to believe that governmental interference is wrong go well beyond its being a violation of the social contract. Government is ill-suited to further the good of people — both individually and collectively. When in an early scene in *Serenity* River Tam states that people don't like being meddled with, she is not referring to a simple contractual fact, but pointing to a characteristic aversive tendency deeply embedded in human nature. Whedon repeatedly shows that the aversion is well justified. When governments meddle, the outcomes are catastrophic — not just in terms of general social consequences, but also in the individual physical and psychological harm caused by the meddlesome activity. Consider the scene in which River makes this observation. At the beginning, she is a small child in class being addressed by her teacher.

> TEACHER: Everyone can enjoy the comfort and enlightenment of true civilization.... It is true that there are dangers on the outer planets. So with so many social and medical advancements we can bring to the independents, why would they fight so hard against us?
>
> RIVER: We meddle. People don't like to be meddled with. We tell them what to do, what to think. Don't run. Don't walk. We're in their homes and in their heads and we haven't the right. We're meddlesome.
>
> TEACHER: River, we're not telling people what to think. We're just trying to show them how.

At this point, the teacher jabs a pencil at River and the action flashes forward to River as a young woman seated in a government laboratory. The pencil has been transformed into a metal probe entering her head, and she is screaming.

While these initial examples represent extreme cases of government "meddling," they are indicative of a direction of thought present in both Whedon's and Augustine's works. Even something as apparently benign as a teacher trying to correct a disruptive student by the intellectual enforcement of a political ideology is shown to be a grave violation of River's personal integrity by its visual juxtaposition with a scene of intrusive bodily violence. One might think that this is merely a case of Whedon thinking, in the words of Stanley Cavell, that "it is a very poorly kept secret that men and their societies are not perfect."[1] What Whedon's work goes on to describe are the deeply corrosive effects that societies can have on individuals. Before pursuing some additional examples in Whedon, though, it will be helpful to bring out some themes in Augustine's thought to help situate Whedon's critique. As the quote from Cavell suggests, these issues are not merely political ones; they extend to various forms of association. The relation between political order and various kinds of associations is one that is helpfully explored by Augustine.

While Augustine believes that humans are naturally social, he believes that political order is the result of original human sinfulness and has as its primary aim the mitigation of the corrupt motives of the self-involved citizens living within that legal framework. In their fallen state, individual humans are predestined either for heaven (and thus are citizens of the "heavenly city") or predestined for hell (and thus are citizens of the "earthly city"). Any polity comprises members of both, so no historic or current polity can be identified with either city. Hence, it falls prey to the same insufficiencies that characterize fallen human nature. These insufficiencies Augustine refers to as forms of *cupidity*, a lusting after wealth, pleasure, and power over others or even the desire to do ill simply because one can. One of Augustine's famous examples of such cupidity is shown in book II of his *Confessions* in his story of the theft of pears. He and his youthful friends saw fit to steal pears that they neither wanted nor needed. Indeed, once stolen, they were simply cast aside. According to Augustine, there was no good brought about in the theft of the pears and there is no obvious way to read the theft as a merely akratic action, that is, one done because one is overwhelmed by some competing good or strong passion.[2]

Augustine notes that in Greek philosophy, the ultimate end sought by a rational being is happiness, the welfare of a rational individual such that he or she is living a flourishing life that other virtuous people would find enviable. In Greek philosophy, however, what constitutes the flourishing life differs from school to school. Augustine counts close to three hundred different possibilities, but he believes none of the answers provided by philosophical schools can be adequate. Each has a secular conception, a happiness to be aimed at in this life. Unlike the Greek philosophers, Augustine thinks that there is no earthly answer to the question "What is happiness?" that will satisfy a human being. For Augustine, the happiness of a human being lies in an end beyond this life, when the restless heart rests in God.[3]

Human societies, then, have inadequate conceptions of the good. Insofar as a political order pursues the good for its citizens it seeks to provide citizens with earthly goods like wealth, medical care, and "the comfort and enlightenment of true civilization," as River's teacher explains. It is also true that, where the ends of action are bad, the means to those ends may also be bad. Any society whose ends and means of obtaining those ends are strongly deformed by cupidity Augustine places on a continuum. A robber baron has his end in common with an earthly political order: secular happiness. The real difference between the baron and a society that we may call a *polity* is that the robber baron may be made to pay for his evils. The political order, by contrast, is powerful enough to have impunity from punishment.[4] Given the corruption of any earthly political arrangement, the only legitimate role of political authority is to shelter its citizens from the worst harms that might befall them, so that individuals may work out their happiness in their own terms.

Within governments, groups of individuals form societies, and it is within these groups that individuals pursue their varied conceptions of happiness. Augustine's formal definition of a *people*, whether a polity or any other community, is "the association of a multitude of rational beings united by a common agreement on the objects of their love."[5] Augustine's analysis provides a strikingly realistic picture of what binds people together in groups. So, it is not surprising that people in the Whedonverse band together to pursue their ends.

In the Whedonverse we find varieties of people banding together to pursue their own ends. In *Buffy the Vampire Slayer*, the Watchers Council has existed for millennia. Their purpose is to train slayers who in turn go out and, in the words of the opening of the early episodes of *Buffy*, fight "vampires, demons, and the forces of darkness; to stop the spread of their evil and the swell of their number." We might say, then, that the council has the cohesiveness necessary for a society. They share in their desire to train potential slayers, thereby working to protect the world from significant dangers. And, of course, the Scooby Gang is brought together by their desire to protect the citizens of Sunnydale from the monsters that prey on the city, situated as it is on a hellmouth. In *Dollhouse*, the Rossum Corporation is a large international business that uses their pharmaceutical discoveries and brain scanning technologies to develop "dolls," people who contractually consent to have their minds wiped and reprogrammed so that they can perform various tasks for clients of the corporation. These tasks range from sexual encounters to industrial espionage, from protection services to fulfilling people's wishes. What draws the employees of the Rossum Corporation together is a strong profit motive, coupled with various employees' desires to develop and perfect the technology used by the company. In *Angel*, Angel and the people who associate with him at Angel Investigations — Cordelia, Wesley (Alexis Denisof), Gunn (J. August Richards), Lorne (Andy Hallett), and Fred — are united around the Agency's motto, "We Help the Helpless." The crew of the Serenity is bound together by their outsider status, exemplified by their unwillingness to work within the system of laws and agreements as set forth by the Alliance.

One distinctive feature of Augustine's thought relevant to a consideration of the Whedonverse is brought out in his practical activities after an instance of civil unrest in a town over which he had jurisdiction as bishop. The city had experienced several days of rioting between pagans and Christians. As things calmed down and civic officials tried to restore order, Augustine argued that the guilty pagans should be made to pay hefty fines while the Christians involved in the riots should be allowed to confess their role and do penance. The pagan civic leader rather understandably saw a double standard at work in Augustine's recommendation. After all, pagans, too, could recognize their wrongdoing and make restitution. In writing his reply, Augustine stressed that what the Christian's penance might achieve would be a true change of heart, a conversion, while the pagan's acknowledgment of complicity would not. It is easy to read this Augustinian claim as merely special pleading for Christians.[6] However, in an insightful discussion of this incident, the Augustinian scholar Robert Dodaro has strikingly shown what is really at stake in the debate. Rather than seeing Augustine's position as rooted merely in a view of the moral superiority of Christianity over paganism, Dodaro argues that Augustine is really trying to get his reader to see certain prideful elements present in various pagan conceptions of civic virtue that revolve around earthly honor, glory, and renown. Those pagan conceptions had as their goal "an accomplished, autonomous moral and spiritual perfection." By contrast, Augustine wants to place the stress of his thought on the idea that that "true pardon and reconciliation ... can only be produced between individuals who continually recognize themselves as sinners in need of God's pardon."[7] In short, Dodaro sees in Augustine's position an awareness of the depths in a human's soul and he urges that what is required is recognition of the soul's "captivity to external influences" and its need to reject "the seductive premise that such weakness, and the self-deception that inevitably disguises their presence, might be rooted out of the soul."[8]

We have lingered at some length on this point because it seems especially pertinent to Whedon's view both of the fragility of the human personality and the ease with which a self-satisfied and self-righteous group can find themselves in the position of doing harm while intending to do good. In this way, characters in the Whedonverse all operate under conditions similar to those humans Augustine sees as subject to original sin. Though Whedon would not use the term *sinfulness*, all of his characters are broken in the same sorts of ways, being subject to selfish motives, conflicting desires, and acting in ways that undermine their attempts to connect with other human beings. Fred and Connor are psychologically scarred from having spent years in hell dimensions; Buffy's childhood has been usurped by her destiny as slayer; Angel has had his soul thrust back into his body after a demon has used it to rampage for over two hundred years; and Mal has had his ideals crushed by the tragic loss of a war against the Alliance. Accordingly, it is possible to translate these various broken characters into an Augustinian idiom as though they were living under the condition of original sin, which, for Augustine, means that they "live by the standard of a falsehood" and not by God's standard, the truth.[9] Since, as we saw above, Augustine cannot hold that we can recognize now those future citizens of the heavenly city, the only standard he can provide in assessing groups of people is a comparative and qualitative one; namely, the better the object(s) a group loves, the better the group; the worse the object(s) a group loves, the worse the group.

Augustine's definition of a society raises two significant questions. The first has to do with the nature of love, as Augustine thinks about it; the second has to do with how we assess the objects of love. In the *Confessions*, Augustine states, "The weight moving me is my love."[10] In other words, we reveal ourselves in what it is that we love. At the same time, of course, not all objects of love are on par. One criterion that Augustine uses to distinguish the relative values of objects of love is whether they are "fleeting," and thus in a sense unreal, or "everlasting," and thus in a sense as real as something can be. Hence, Augustine writes:

> I say there is no one who holds that there is nothing she or he ought to worship, who is not the slave of carnal pleasures, or seeks vain power, or is madly delighted by some showy spectacle. So, without knowing it, they love temporal things and hope for blessedness therefrom. Whether one wills or not, one is necessarily a slave to the things by means of which one seeks to be happy. One follows them wherever they lead, and fears anyone who seems to have the power to rob one of them. Now a spark of fire or tiny animal can do that.... Time itself must snatch away all transient things, those who think to escape servitude by not worshipping anything are in fact the slaves of all kinds of worldly things.[11]

Augustine scholar Herbert Deane has glossed Augustine's thought nicely:

> Since fallen man has set his love on earthly things rather than on God and since his body no longer obeys all the commands of his soul, it is clear that he sinks to the level of the beasts, and, indeed, in his ferocity and malice toward other men he often sinks below the level of the animals. Even the good man, the pilgrim on this earth who yearns for his true home in heaven, is hardly able to live in this world without seeking some tangible, material goods as a place where his soul may pause to rest, if only temporarily.[12]

Important distinctions can be drawn between the various communities in the Whedonverse based upon the goals they pursue. Some goals are more divisive and ephemeral; others foster cohesion and offer a deeper sense of fulfillment. The Rossum Corporation and Wolfram & Hart are built around the desire for wealth and power and, like the organization itself, the employees are motivated by a desire for these goods. Not only do wealth and power not last in the Whedonverse, they are competitive goods. For one to be powerful, others must lack power. Moreover, neither good ever satisfies. The powerful want more power. The wealthy want more wealth. As a result, communities and individuals dedicated to these goods are at war, and war leads to destruction. For instance, the heads of the Rossum Corporation, Lilah (Stephanie Romanov) and her bosses, and even the ancient power embodied as a little girl in the White Floor of Wolfram & Hart's Los Angeles branch office are all destroyed in their pursuit of power and usually by members of their own community.

Even communities whose ends do not seem divisive can be undermined if they lack sufficient commitment to the welfare of their members. The Initiative portrayed in season four of *Buffy* has as its mission the advancement of scientific knowledge and the control of demons, but it sacrifices the welfare of its members, giving them drugs that increase their performance at the expense of long-term health. They implant behavior control chips in the bodies of some of their soldiers and ultimately create a human/demon/machine hybrid that wreaks havoc and destroys the Initiative itself.

Even the Watchers Council is not above reproach in its pursuit of its shared object of love. While the watchers provide the world with significant protection from the dangerous monsters that threaten it, they are prone to violence and not just the sort of violence that protects others. To create the first slayer, a group of men brutalize a young woman by forcing her to submit to the implanting of a demon in order to enhance her physical prowess as well as her sensitivity to the demonic elsewhere. That is, at the common origin of both the council and the first slayer, there is a primal violence and deformation of another human being to advance its goals. This patriarchal power endures for centuries until Buffy shows how corrupt the council is in its ways of enforcing slayerhood. For example, on a slayer's eighteenth birthday, the council secretly administers a drug to her that removes her powers and then forces her to confront an especially vicious vampire. Giles, Buffy's watcher, interferes in this ritual, thereby protecting Buffy. While the male protector model is itself a bit patriarchal, the council's ruthless test of a young woman shows that it perceives the slayer as little more than an interchangeable piece in the ongoing battle between vampires and slayers.

The patriarchy of the council lasts until Buffy, the last in the line of slayers, realizes that, in fact, the watchers need her more than she needs them. That is, there would be no purpose for watchers were there not a slayer. She reclaims much of her own power, forcing the council to reinstate her watcher, Giles, and to cease interfering with her. At the end of season seven, Buffy repudiates the patriarchic Watchers Council completely. A shadow organization of women has been passing down a powerful weapon, a scythe. The last of them hands the weapon to Buffy, who subverts the primal watcher/slayer paradigm with the help of Willow's "female" magic (by which we mean that it clearly stands in contrast to the patriarchal system of the council). Thanks to the cooperative efforts of Willow's magic and Buffy's inherent slayer power, Buffy is able to share her power with a large number of what up to then were only potential slayers. Each potential is given the choice of whether to accept the power or not. The reconfiguration of power and emasculation of the Watchers Council is graphically represented by the destruction of the council headquarters at the instigation of a particularly ruthless character, Caleb, who dresses like a priest and is clearly shown to use biblical imagery that denigrates women.

This example of the Watchers Council serves as a reminder that for Augustine, too, it is the city of a patriarchal God, via the mediation of a male priesthood and male savior, that opposes the power of hell, the earthly city. By and large, in Augustine's world it is males who play the major roles within both governments and societies. The point of the discussion of Buffy and the Watchers Council is to stress the following aspect of Whedon's worldview. The patriarchic model of the council concentrates power in the hands of the few, that is, the watchers. Buffy's matriarchal model, by contrast, passes power on to any woman willing to bear the responsibility of wielding it. So, while the watchers attempt to keep their power to themselves for their own elite purposes, Buffy's act is one that provides potential slayers with a choice that brings with it a genuine responsibility to use the power for good ends and to do so in ways that do not involve the oppression of others. While Whedon may use patriarchy to symbolize self-serving power and matriarchy to symbolize other-serving power, in Whedon's world the key players in societies (both good and ill) are as often women as men. As Gunn leads a band of vampire killers in Los Angeles, Anne heads the shelter protecting the dispossessed kids on Los Angeles's streets. The voices of Buffy, Echo, Willow, River, and Inara are as important to their communities as those of Angel, Wes, Mal, and Wash. Where Augustine's works are shaped by sexist assumptions, Whedon's work subverts and thus opposes sexism in critical ways.[13]

Nonetheless, those communities that aim at fostering the welfare of their members (e.g., the crew of Serenity, Anne's shelter, the Avengers, and the Los Angeles dollhouse) and those that also aim at helping others (e.g., Angel Investigations and the Scooby Gang) fare better because their goals can be and are pursued cooperatively. While it is true that the members of Angel Investigations and the Scoobies sometimes violate the goods to which they and their communities are dedicated, at the end of the day they realize they have done wrong.[14] They return to the group, apologize, and do penance, much as Augustine suggested was appropriate to those who can achieve a true change of heart. This analysis of social repair is perhaps one of the most interesting elements in Whedon's work. Though in a healthy community social repair is possible, it is never easy. Characters have to show by their actions as well as their words that they have mended their ways and it is a genuine question whether they will be allowed to return to their group. In fact, Buffy is voted out of her position as leader of the potential slayers and asked to leave her community and her own home. Angel is not permitted to return to Angel Investigations until he offers to return under the leadership of Wesley. Even when straying members are accepted back into the group, the damage caused by their lapse remains. Xander is still blind in one eye. The man Willow killed is still dead. The characters return with fresh wounds that develop into deep scars and the group dynamic is permanently altered. A striking example of this dynamic occurs after Willow has "done penance" and is supposedly ready to reintegrate with the group. She recognizes that she is in some real sense still the same person who flayed someone alive and initially avoids reintegrating. The graphic representation of her inability is that she inhabits the world being invisible to those around her. Not only must she realize she has been forgiven, she also must acquire the humility to permit others to see her brokenness. It is when she realizes that the others love her, knowing that she is broken, that she finally becomes visible to them.

It is also worth stressing that societies are not monolithic and individual allegiances of the members can shift. Their ends can come into conflict with those of the group or their conception of the good and hence their own ends can change. At the beginning of *Dollhouse*, it seems clear that the Los Angeles branch shares the goals of the Rossum Corporation. They are willing to exploit their operatives, are committed to researching and improving the technology necessary to carry out the company's goals, and the leader of the Los Angeles branch, Adelle De Witt, certainly seems to be a model corporate citizen. Nonetheless, as certain aspects of the corporation's activities and goals become clear to her and her employees, they are willing to risk their own place in the corporation, indeed their lives, in order to prevent the dire consequences of the company's technology being used. Indeed, by the final episode, the Los Angeles branch has, through the various sacrifices of its members, become a kind of bastion against the destruction of much of the world and will provide, in due time, the resources necessary to rebuild from the ruins caused by the Rossum Corporation's technology. Other characters whose commitments to the ends of the groups they inhabit are unclear include Jayne, Wesley, Lilah, Boyd Langton (Harry Lennix), Lindsey McDonald (Christian Kane), Kate Lockley (Elisabeth Röhm), and Dr. Horrible (Neil Patrick Harris). Each of these characters performs actions that are both intrinsically ambiguous and leave them in a complex relation to their communities. So, for example, Dr. Horrible's metamorphosis into a truly deserving member of the Evil League of Evil is not predetermined by his character at the beginning of the show. After all, he thinks he is trying to make the world a better place by exposing the failure of his government and showing Captain Hammer (Nathan Fillion) to be a "corporate tool." Likewise, Jayne's allegiance to the crew of Serenity is persistently at odds with his desire to acquire wealth, and after Jayne sells out the Tams, Mal threatens to expel him from the group. It is not clear to the viewer which "city" these characters inhabit until the character's demise or the end of the series.

The limited fulfillment of life in a well-functioning community is all that is available to the characters in the Whedonverse. Though Buffy and Cordelia both attain a kind of heaven, perfect contentment in a life beyond this one is not expected. Indeed, Willow performs a ritual of the blackest magic to bring Buffy back from the dead because she believes Buffy's soul is suffering in a hell dimension. The state of bliss is not permanent for either Cordelia or Buffy; each is returned to a world that needs her. While Buffy suffers from being forced to take up her life again, Cordelia finds heaven boring and looks for help to escape her higher plane.

As Whedon sees no future state for humanity after death, but rather that heaven and hell are here and now, so too he conceives of no uncorrupted state for human beings and so a good or just community will never be better than a community comprising genuine, flawed human beings. These human beings may strive for justice, and when they fall short they may confess their flaws and try to make amends, but they will never become good in the Augustinian sense. Thus, like Augustine's Christians, and unlike the pagans he describes, Whedon's characters act within the constraints of a self that they have achieved but which is at the same time fragile, so they must guard against self-complacency and self-righteousness.

While Whedon rejects the idea of "a true home in heaven," as Herbert Deane called it in the quotation above, he nonetheless gives us various images of characters whose lives are full of turmoil seeking to find some rest in the world. The name of the ship in *Firefly*, Serenity, thus operates as a kind of enigmatic signifier. It is what the character thinks he wants and it is also what actually will satisfy him, but the character will only discover the latter through his journey. In *Firefly*, for example, Mal's way of achieving "serenity" is to "keep flying." This continuing journey, though, is not to any specific resting place, but rather the very act of continuing brings a kind of peace to Mal. Mal's "pilgrimage" is an image of finding a kind of peace in accepting transience. Likewise, Cordelia finds peace not in a perfect existence on a higher plane, but when she uses the last moments of her life to help Angel get back on track fighting for the values they had both held dear in the early seasons of the series ("You're Welcome").

So, what are we to make of the relation between the Whedonverse's idea of the individual/communal and Augustine's? We have seen that both share a sense that humans are fallen or broken creatures. As fallen or broken, humans are prone to acts of violence and avarice in pursuit of power and wealth. At the same time, though, humans can become aware of their finitude. For Augustine, that means recognizing that the things one has loved are ephemeral and transient and, with God's help, trading up, as it were, to the true love of God, who is timeless truth itself. For Whedon, the "angry atheist," there is no path to God. Hence, his characters must find other ways to acknowledge their suffering as a fact of life and, in the face of that suffering, come to see in it some value.

The contemporary philosopher Stanley Cavell can be of use here in helping us understand what is at stake in the preceding discussion. In his essay "Thinking of Emerson," Cavell has noted that one legacy of Emerson's work is the way in which he urges us to move beyond nihilism, and more specifically "beyond the curse of human depravity and its consequent condemnation of us to despair." This is not to say that the world is a rosy place — Cavell approvingly concedes with Emerson that we make way for a "more-than-tragic emotion of thankfulness."[15] That is, we need to cultivate an attitude in which we can accept the pain and suffering of the world, the brokenness of individuals, the secret and not so secret societies defined by their loves, without succumbing to false hope. This is what Emerson calls "onward thinking," and Cavell characterizes it as "knowing how to go on" even when there is no prespecified way to do so as there is for Augustine. That is, for Cavell, there is no place our onwardness stops — no place where we are not restless. As he writes, "Were philosophy to concede such a place [i.e. an Augustinian resting place], one knowable in advance of its setting out, philosophy would cede its own autonomy."[16] Another notion Cavell borrows from Emerson is *abandonment*: "the achievement of the human requires not inhabitation and settlement, but abandonment, leaving."[17] Cavell clarifies: "For the significance of leaving lies in its discovery that you have settled something, that you have felt enthusiastically what there is to abandon yourself to."[18] In effect, if one does not abandon one's place, if one settles for staying where one is, one dies.

Whedonverse characters do not settle down, they do not find permanent peace or stability. Many end up dead. They end up dead not because they hoped for another world beyond this one, but because they hoped for a better world than this one. Buffy changed the world, after all. She didn't redeem it. The extraordinarily poignant moment at the end of the *Angel* episode "Shells" (5.16) deals with the aftermath of the death of Fred. As we see the characters reacting to Fred's death, we also see flashbacks of her leaving home to set out for college as the Kim Richey song "A Place Called Home" plays on the soundtrack. The song speaks to the richness of a life spent exploring possibilities and avoiding feeling regret, even if the path traveled is not a straightforward one. It was Fred's leaving home that led to her suffering for five years in a hell dimension before doing good work with Angel Investigations that, in the end, led to her death.

Similarly, the theme song to *Firefly* speaks to the loss of love, home and a place to belong. If there's no place one can be, then there's nothing else to do but keep becoming. The characters in the Whedonverse that we recognize as "good," as having formed societies that love in such a way that they can move forward, don't always meet with good ends. But they have good journeys. They may not be citizens of the city of God, but their refusal to settle also keeps them from being citizens of the earthly city. As Mal says in "Out of Gas,"

> I tell ya, Zoe, we find ourselves a mechanic, get her running again. Hire a good pilot. Maybe even a cook. Live like real people. Small crew, them as feel the need to be free. Take jobs as they come — and we'll never be under the heel of nobody ever again. No matter how long the arm of the Alliance might get, we'll just get ourselves a little further.

Notes

1. Stanley Cavell, *The Claim of Reason* (Oxford: Oxford University Press, 1979), 23.
2. Augustine, *Confessions*, trans. Garry Wills (London: Penguin Books, 2006), book II, 9–18.
3. Augustine, *City of God*, trans. Henry Bettenson (London: Penguin Books, 2003), book XIX, chapter 1, 846.
4. Ibid., book IV, chapter 4, 139.
5. Ibid., book XIX, chapter 24, 890.
6. The correspondence between Nectarius and Augustine has been translated in *Augustine: Political Writings*, ed. and trans. E. M. Atkins and R. J. Dodaro (Cambridge: Cambridge University Press, 2001), 1–21.
7. Robert Dodaro, "Augustine's Secular City," in *Augustine and His Critics: Essays in Honor of Gerald Bonner*, ed. Robert Dodaro and George Lawless (London: Routledge, 2000), 248.
8. Ibid., 249–250.
9. Augustine, *City of God*, book XIV, chapter 4, 552–554.
10. Augustine, *Confessions*, book XIII, chapter 10, 318.
11. Augustine, *On True Religion*, XXXVIII, 69, cited by Herbert Deane in *The Political and Social Ideas of St. Augustine* (New York: Columbia University Press, 1963), p. 41. We have modified slightly the translation Deane uses. This entire paragraph is shaped, as is the paper as a whole, by Deane's work on the psychology of the fallen human and the impact of that fact on society and political order.
12. Deane, *Ideas of St. Augustine*, 42.
13. A nuanced discussion of this topic is found in Lorna Jowett, *Sex and the Slayer* (Middletown, CT: Wesleyan University Press, 2005). It is worth noting that, while Whedon deliberately pits a tiny blond with good fashion sense and a love for shopping against the powers of evil in order to challenge sexist assumptions, there are moments in his work that portray an unfortunate capitulation to sexism.

14. For example, Buffy takes off to Los Angeles after having to kill Angel to save the world; Willow flays a man alive and then tries to destroy the world after Tara is shot; and Angel goes dark and seeks revenge rather than working with his group to help those in need.

15. Both of the cited passages are from Stanley Cavell, "Thinking of Emerson," in Stanley Cavell, *Emerson's Transcendental Etudes*, ed. David Justin Hodge (1981; repr., Stanford: Stanford University Press, 2003), 16. The phrase "more-than-tragic emotion of thankfulness" is borrowed by Cavell from Newton Arvin.

16. Ibid., 17–18.
17. Ibid., 19.
18. Ibid.

BIBLIOGRAPHY

Augustine. *Augustine: Political Writings*. Edited and translated by E. M. Atkins and R. J. Dodaro. Cambridge: Cambridge University Press, 2001.

———. *City of God*. Translated by Henry Bettenson. London: Penguin Books, 2003.

———. *Confessions*. Translated by Gary Wills. New York: Penguin Books, 2008.

Cavell, Stanley. *The Claim of Reason*. Oxford: Oxford University Press, 1979.

———. "Thinking of Emerson." 1981. In *Emerson's Transcendental Etudes*, edited by David Justin Hodge, 10–19. Reprint, Stanford: Stanford University Press, 2003.

Deane, Herbert. *The Political and Social Ideas of St. Augustine*. New York: Columbia University Press, 1963.

Dodaro, Robert. "Augustine's Secular City." In *Augustine and His Critics: Essays in Honor of Gerald Bonner*, edited by Robert Dodaro and George Lawless, 231–259. London: Routledge, 2000.

Jowett, Lorna. *Sex and the Slayer*. Middletown, CT: Wesleyan University Press, 2005.

To Assemble or to Shrug?
Power, Responsibility and Sacrifice in Marvel's The Avengers

Russell W. Dalton

Many film critics were quick to peg *The Avengers* as a well-made summer blockbuster that was high in entertainment value but had little in the way of a message.[1] On closer viewing, however, the film serves as the latest story in Joss Whedon's oeuvre to explore recurring themes in his work related to how extraordinary people should use and conceive of power.

In recent decades the theme of power and its proper use in living out one's vocation has become an issue of vital importance to religious scholars and practitioners alike. This essay will explore issues related to power — including the violence that often accompanies it, the privileges due to those who have power, and power's responsible use and abuse — by comparing and contrasting Whedon's approach to power in *The Avengers* with those found in the fictional work of two diverse dialogue partners, Marvel Comics legend Stan Lee and novelist and philosopher Ayn Rand. Lee, who is not an adherent of any formal religious community, was the original cocreator and writer of the source material for the film, *The Avengers* comic book, and his stories take a distinct approach to the proper use of power. Ayn Rand was, like Whedon, an outspoken atheist. Her work was initially spurned by people of faith but it has more recently received a great deal of attention in the United States among Christians who embrace her political and economic philosophy. For this reason, she is a relevant interlocutor for Whedon as we seek to understand the significance of the political and philosophical views expressed in his work.

How can the heroic fantasy stories of atheists such as Whedon and other nonreligious writers help religious thinkers reflect on issues of power and vocation? This essay argues that the *Avengers* film reflects an approach to power and vocation that in many ways both resonates with the approaches taken by many religious leaders and raises points of concern. As is the case in Whedon's previous films and television series, *The Avengers* implicitly criticizes the use of power for selfish and narcissistic purposes. The film presents positive examples of the responsible use of power, which in Whedon's work is demonstrated by using one's power to help others in need, ensuring life and liberty for the masses, and by being willing to sacrifice oneself. At the same time, as in Whedon's previous work, the heroes in *The Avengers* earn personal freedom from those institutions that seek to monitor and control them.

Stan Lee, Ayn Rand and Joss Whedon

Stan Lee was the primary writer, coplotter, and cocreator of Marvel Comics' most famous heroes and, as the company's editor and chief, was the driving force behind the resurgence of superhero comics in the 1960s. Whedon has said that he started reading comic books when he was about twelve years old and acknowledges that the Marvel Comics he read in his childhood are among several influences on his thought and work.[2] He served celebrated stints as the writer of Marvel's *Astonishing X-Men* and *The Runaways* and in 2007 wrote a special tribute to Lee in the comic book *Stan Lee Meets ... Spider-Man*.

Critics lauded Whedon's work in *The Avengers* for managing the difficult task of balancing so many characters while staying true to each of them and for the way Whedon used humor to acknowledge the more fantastical elements of the story while at the same time treating the subject matter seriously.[3] As readers of Marvel Comics are aware, Whedon was simply following the approach that Lee and artist Jack Kirby used nearly fifty years earlier in the first two Avengers comic books from 1963. Like Lee and Kirby, Whedon had the team argue and even fight with each other before becoming a team. Also in a manner similar to Lee and Kirby, Whedon used the characters' diverse personalities as strengths of the story and the team rather than imposing conformity onto them. And while Lee and Whedon both took the subject matter quite seriously on many levels, they both used witty dialogue to poke fun at the ridiculous aspects of the situations.

The similarities between Whedon and Lee go beyond these external plotting and stylistic devices. In their stories and interviews, Lee and Whedon both champion diversity, inclusion, and the individual's right to make his or her own choices. While neither creator is a part of an established community of faith, both have created admirable characters who are religious and both embrace values such as compassion and the possibility of redemption, which are important to many contemporary religious thinkers. Both Lee and Whedon suggest that those with special power or privilege should not understand it as power to wield over others. Instead, power carries with it the burden and responsibility of service and compassion to others.

Perhaps the most striking parallels between the two creators' work are found in the early stories of their most famous creations, Lee's Spider-Man and Whedon's Buffy the Vampire Slayer. Peter Parker, alias Spider-Man, began as an outsider at Midtown High School who never asked for his power and often saw it as a burden rather than a blessing. He faced all the problems of an unpopular teenager while at the same time secretly keeping his high school and community safe, often making corny wisecracks as he fought off villains. The first season of *Buffy the Vampire Slayer* presents Buffy's life as practically parallel to Peter Parker's. Buffy starts off as an outsider at Sunnydale High School and sees her powers as a burden. She has family problems, is unpopular with her classmates, and makes corny wisecracks while fighting evil. As the series progresses, Buffy's friend Willow takes on the aspect of Peter who is the brilliant bookish student, while her friend Xander fills the role of Peter as the nerd who is mocked by the other high school girls. The characters in *Buffy the Vampire Slayer*, especially Xander, also make frequent direct references to Marvel superheroes and comic books.[4] Much of Whedon's work has been devoted to exploring the proper and improper use of extraordinary power, and Lee's work serves as a likely influence upon Whedon's perspective on that theme.

Ayn Rand was born in Russia in 1905 and during her childhood saw her homeland transition into the Communist Soviet Union. In 1925, she moved to the United States and developed a system of belief that she called *Objectivism*. Her writings reflect her ardent opposition to the Communism and collectivism that she saw in the Soviet Union and her support of unregulated, laissez-fair capitalism.

Among Rand's beliefs, found in both her novels and her nonfiction work such as *The Virtue of Selfishness: A New Concept of Egoism*, were that people should act in their own rational self-interest and not for the sake of others.[5] She wrote, "Man — every man — is an end in himself, not the means to the ends of others. He must exist for his own sake, neither sacrificing himself to others nor sacrificing others to himself. The pursuit of his own *rational* self-interest and his own happiness is the highest moral purpose of his life."[6] Rand found the concept of altruism abhorrent and was opposed to self-sacrifice for the sake of another person or for the communal good.[7] She wrote, "Altruism holds that man has no right to exist for his own sake, that service to others is the only moral justification of his existence, and that self-sacrifice is the highest moral duty."[8] Rand believed that altruism was counterproductive to the life and liberty of the individual.

Like Whedon, Rand was an outspoken atheist. In her books and national television appearances, she spoke openly and frankly against religions such as Christianity and Judaism that taught selflessness and personal sacrifice as positive virtues. For these reasons, Christians generally shunned Rand's work during her lifetime. In recent years, however, her work has received renewed attention and even admiration from some conservative Christians in the United States due to her staunch defense of laissez-fair capitalism and other beliefs that fall in line with conservative economic theories. This phenomenon has led to renewed efforts by conservative and progressive Christian scholars alike to delineate differences between Christianity and Objectivism.[9]

Rand did not write stories of costumed superheroes like the Avengers, but she intentionally presented the heroes of her novels as superior to the common person.[10] Unlike Lee's comic book stories, however, in Rand's novels living for oneself and asserting one's independence are lifted up as the highest virtues. The heroes of Rand's most popular novel, *Atlas Shrugged*, are a case in point. The novel's title is an allusion to the mythical character Atlas who must hold the universe on his shoulders, forever bearing the burden of its weight. In the novel, Rand presents a few elite champions of industry as having to bear the weight of the economy on their shoulders. The novel presents a scenario in which these industrialists, in effect, shrug. They sabotage the companies they lead and go on strike in protest of government regulations on their industries, ultimately causing the economy of the whole nation to collapse.[11] These elite "Atlases" of industry would rather destroy their companies and show the rest of the population how much they are needed than give their companies over to other managers or workers, whom they see as looters.

When these titans of industry retreat to a secret mountain headquarters, they must repeat the oath, "I swear by my life ... and my love of it ... that I will never live for the sake of another man ... nor ask another man ... to live ... for mine," before being allowed entry.[12] Later, a government official tortures one of these alleged titans, the novel's hero John Galt, and says to him, "We want you to rule! ... We order you to give orders! ... We demand that you dictate! ... We order you to save us!"[13] Galt does not give in. He will not live for the sake of others and will not live under their rules and restrictions. He and the other titans of industry only return to society when the government gives in to his demands and he is allowed to work for his own benefit and not that of others.

Some Rand supporters and libertarian groups hailed Whedon's television series *Firefly* and follow-up film *Serenity*, in which Captain Malcolm Reynolds and his renegade crew struggled for freedom and independence from the oppressive authoritarian government known as The Alliance. The Randian website *The Atlasphere Magazine* gave Whedon's television series *Firefly* a very positive review,[14] and the Libertarian Futurist Society awarded Whedon's film *Serenity* a special Prometheus Award. Whedon fans who are also Rand fans or libertarians were dismayed, however, by some comments Whedon made in 2012. First came what some characterize as Whedon's "anticapitalist rant" at the 2012 San Diego Comic-Con.[15] This was followed by a satirical video Whedon made in the days leading up to the 2012 U.S. presidential election in which he disingenuously supported Mitt Romney because, according to Whedon, he would bring on the "zombie apocalypse." In the video, Whedon makes a brief, disparaging reference to people who read Ayn Rand books, warning viewers to stay away from them.[16]

As an interesting side note, Lee actually had an early indirect encounter with Rand's philosophy of Objectivism, though it is quite possible that he was not aware of it. Lee's original coplotter and artist on *The Amazing Spider-Man* was Steve Ditko. One of the more mysterious and shocking events in the history of comic books occurred when Ditko abruptly quit working for Marvel after completing *The Amazing Spider-Man* #38 (August 1966). While Ditko has not publicly detailed his reasons for leaving Marvel, some suggest that it largely had to do with his growing devotion to the work of Rand and the philosophy of Objectivism at the time.[17] Ditko drew pages in which Peter Parker increasingly shows disdain for the supporting characters in the comic book and increasingly acts in his own self-interest. When Lee received the pages, however, he seems to have scripted thought balloons in ways that softened those sentiments.[18] This is perhaps because Lee had established early on that Peter Parker's altruism, his willingness to put his life on the line for the sake of others, was a key to his character.[19]

As shall be seen, Whedon's perspective on power and its proper use shares much in common with Lee's. While Whedon's stories contain several points of resonance with Rand's perspective on power and freedom, there are several significant points of distinction between their works as well.

Power and the Use of Physical Violence

One of the most basic questions regarding the responsible use of power is whether or not power entitles one to use it to inflict physical violence upon others. Does the power and strength of the bully on the playground, for example, entitle him or her to use that power to inflict physical harm upon others? Heroic fiction tends to tell stories that follow what theologians such as Walter Wink have referred to as "the myth of redemptive violence" in which conflicts are resolved and communities are saved through acts of physical violence.[20] In contrast, many of the world's religions teach a way of peace and not of violence, and religious leaders of the past century such as Mahatma Gandhi and Martin Luther King, Jr., taught and practiced nonviolent resistance as the way to pursue social change. *The Avengers* itself is a violent film, containing much more physical violence than a person would expect to see in normal, everyday life. In the film, superheroes use their special skills at doling out physical force and violence to resolve the problems of individuals and the community at large. What, then, does the film imply about power and violence?

Rand wrote that in her ideal political system, laissez-fair capitalism, no one should gain from initiating physical force against others[21]; but her novels seem to present a murkier view of an individual's use of violence. The heroes of her novels have a proclivity for blowing up buildings when they feel that their work or contributions are being undercompensated or overregulated by others. The use of violence by an individual to achieve certain ends is illustrated most graphically in a disturbing episode in Rand's novel *The Fountainhead*. The novel's hero, Howard Roark, meets Dominique, the beautiful daughter of a business rival. He looks at her with a gaze of ownership over her, but her response to him is cool. Later in the story, Roark violently rapes her. She fights back and screams in pain, but he persists in raping her in a way that leaves painful bruising. Rand writes, "He did it as an act of scorn. Not as love, but as defilement."[22] The rape was the act of "a master taking shameful, contemptuous possession" of a slave.[23] According to the story, this violent act is treated as a positive, virtuous, and admirable act on the part of the hero. It is what needed to be done. Through the rape, Roark asserts his power and mastery over Dominique and she acknowledges that being raped was just what she needed, and, by the novel's end, she marries him.

Stan Lee expressed his own discomfort with the violence in his superhero stories in a 1968 radio interview in which he debated a critic of comic books.[24] He also acknowledged that social ills could not be defeated by acts of violence the way problems are solved in superhero stories. In one of his 1968 "Stan's Soapbox" columns, he wrote, "Let's lay it on the line. Bigotry and racism are among the deadliest social ills plaguing the world today. But, unlike a team of costumed super villains, they can't be halted with a punch in the snoot, or a zap from a ray gun. The only way to destroy them is to expose them — to reveal them for the insidious evils they really are."[25]

Whedon's television series and films are quite violent. Like Lee, Whedon has acknowledged his own discomfort with the redemptive violence at work in his stories. In the *Angel* episode "Conviction" (5.1), an evil soldier tells Angel that he, the soldier, will win because he has the most powerful thing in the world, namely "conviction." Angel responds, "There is one thing more powerful than conviction. Just one. Mercy." Unfortunately, the point may be somewhat lost on viewers when, a few seconds later, Angel kills the soldier in a very violent manner. In his commentary track on the scene, Whedon acknowledges as much and says of the violence, "It's something that, for hero fiction, I think, works beautifully, to be as tough as that. In real life, uh, let's just say I believe it belongs in fiction."

Indeed, at the end of *The Avengers*, Iron Man uses a nuclear missile to kill countless enemy soldiers, and the story is constructed in such a way that this extreme act of physical violence is the only evident resolution to the conflict. In an interview with *Entertainment Weekly*, Whedon and the cast of *The Avengers* were asked about the differences between fighting problems in a superhero story versus fighting problems in the real world.

> EW: Superhero movies are all about escapism. But why don't we get the same catharsis from seeing powerful figures fight off real-world troubles?
> WHEDON: Hulk smash poverty?
> CHRIS HEMSWORTH (THOR): It doesn't really work that way.
> MARK RUFFALO (HULK): It's hard to smash your way to a positive outcome.
> WHEDON: The threats are so outrageous, they aren't really scary. And that's the point. We tell these stories in which there's a problem we can solve with our superhero fists because the bigger problems can't be. Those take time and millions of people and lots of dedication, and can't be solved in the space of a movie. What's really out there is a whole lot scarier than that alien army.[26]

Whedon, then, constructs stories, myths of a sort, in which violence solves the problem. While Whedon himself acknowledges that real world problems cannot be solved through the use of physical violence, he makes a personal distinction between the use of violence in the real world and the fantasy violence used in hero fiction.

Heroes: Power, Responsibility and Self-Sacrifice

The Avengers is the latest of Whedon's stories that commends to viewers the virtues of responsibility to community and self-sacrifice for the sake of others. In this way, Whedon's heroes are quite distinct from those of Rand and quite in step with those of Lee.

If Rand's heroes, such as those in *Atlas Shrugged*, live by "the virtues of selfishness," Lee's heroes have repeatedly demonstrated a virtue of responsibility to the larger community and selfless sacrifice for the sake of others. Likewise, while Rand's heroes pledge to live for themselves and fight to be free from responsibility to the wider community, Lee's heroes learn that their power and privilege come with an attendant responsibility to help others.

The very first Spider-Man story ends with perhaps the most well-known words that Lee ever wrote, "With great power there must also come ... great responsibility."[27] For Spider-Man, as well as other of Lee's heroes such as the Thing, Iron Man, Thor, the Hulk, and the X-Men, carrying out this responsibility is very often not in their own self-interest but rather experienced as a great burden that they must bear.

Many of Whedon's stories have followed this same motif. In a first season episode of *Buffy the Vampire Slayer*, "Never Kill a Boy on the First Date" (1.5), Buffy yearns for a normal life but realizes she cannot date and socialize like other teenagers. Instead, because of the power that has been given to her, she must carry the often heavy burden of responsibility that she accepts. Likewise, in the *Angel* episode "Hero," Doyle makes the ultimate sacrifice for the sake of others. Also, at the beginning of *Angel*, Cordelia Chase is a self-centered person who only desires to live a life of wealth, glamour, and fame. By season three of the series, however, she makes the choice to give up that life and instead live a hard and decidedly unglamorous life of a partial demon so that she can use her supernatural powers to help those in need.

In the film *The Avengers*, Whedon's interest in the themes of responsibility to others, self-sacrifice, and using power for the greater good instead of for selfish purposes is most clearly seen in the story arc he gives to the character of Tony Stark. Whedon inherited Stark's personality from the previous Iron Man films and makes effective use of the diva persona created by the previous screenwriters and actor Robert Downey, Jr., to make his point.

The change in Stark's character from the beginning of the film to the end can be seen in Stark's attitude toward Stark Tower. In the beginning of the film, Pepper Potts asks Stark to look at Stark Tower in downtown Manhattan, Stark's monument to his ego that has just been lit up with a new power source. As the building powers up, the last thing to light up is the word "STARK" in big, bold letters high atop the building for the entire world to see. "How does it look?" Pepper asks. Stark replies, "Like Christmas, only more ... me."

At this point, Tony Stark/Iron Man has clearly established his wealth and power and could be seen as being well on his way to becoming a Randian hero. John Galt, Rand's hero from *Atlas Shrugged*, used a dollar sign as his symbol, and Rand herself often wore a large gold broach with a dollar sign. As she had requested, when she died in 1982 a six-foot floral arrangement in the shape of a dollar sign was placed near her casket.

As is often the case in Marvel comic books, it is Steve Rogers/Captain America (Chris Evans) who challenges Stark on his approach to life. He tells Stark that being a hero is all about personal sacrifice. Stark boasts to Cap that, even without his Iron Man armor, he is a "genius, billionaire, playboy, philanthropist." Cap responds, "I know guys with none of that worth ten of you. I've seen the footage. The only thing you really fight for is yourself. You aren't the guy to make the sacrifice play, to lay down on a wire and let the other guy crawl over you." He adds, "You should stop pretending to be a hero." Stark tries to be dismissive, but Cap has clearly given him food for thought.

Later in the film, Stark is thinking aloud as he is trying to figure out Loki's (Tom Hiddleston) next move. He notes that Loki is "a full-tilt diva" and would want to tower over everyone with a big building with his name up in the sky for everyone to see. Stark has an epiphany, and it stops him short. He recognizes that he and Loki are not that different, and he knows that Loki is naturally going to choose Stark Tower as the base of his operations. The Avengers do indeed find Loki standing atop the Stark Tower as if it were some kind of throne for Loki as he looks down over the city. At the film's climax, Stark does make the sacrifice play. He is willing to die to save others. By the end of the film, we see that Stark is a changed man and is changing the tower's name. In his DVD commentary on the film, Whedon notes that it was by design that the shot of the tower, with only the "A" in "STARK" remaining, is the final shot of the film before the credits. Those familiar with Avengers history will presume that the building's name is being changed from the Stark Tower to the Avengers Tower. Stark no longer needs his name up in lights. He is no longer using his power and privilege to build a monument to his ego but instead to build headquarters where he can work with others for the sake of others.

Whedon has stated that, to his mind, this theme of community is the overriding message of *The Avengers*. It is the story of a group of diverse, troubled people, those Loki calls "lost creatures," who bond together when needed. Colonel Nick Fury (Samuel L. Jackson), the director of S.H.I.E.L.D., says, "There was an idea ... called the Avengers Initiative. The idea was to bring together a group of remarkable people to see if they could become something more. To see if they could work together when we needed them to, to fight the battles that we never could.... Well, it's an old-fashioned notion." In the DVD commentary on the scene, Whedon says, "If there is a single line in the movie that explains what the idea behind this movie is, it's that."[28] In an interview for *Entertainment Weekly*, Whedon explains, "It's about the idea — which is very old-fashioned — of community, of people working for each other. That's gone away. *The Avengers*, for me, is about bringing that back."[29]

Rather than Rand's rugged, self-sufficient individual living by the ethics of selfishness, Whedon's *Avengers* celebrates personal sacrifice and community. Even extraordinary people find meaning when working together in community for a cause greater than themselves. Whedon's heroes understand that with their power comes the responsibility to help others.

Villains: Elitism, Self-Interest and the Abuse of Power

In Whedon's work, one of the acts that signals that characters have become villains is when they feel that their power means that they are superior to other people and that they are therefore entitled to special moral license. In *Buffy the Vampire Slayer*, for example, when Faith tells Buffy that they "are better" than the people who need their help, and therefore she does not need to take responsibility for accidentally killing a man, it signals to Buffy and to the audience that she has become a villain ("Consequences," 3.15). Whedon says that the final season of the series was all about power, and in that season Buffy herself struggles with the issue. In "Conversations with Dead People," she says, "Sometimes I feel — this is awful — I feel like I'm better than them. Superior." She recognizes it as a wrong feeling, but for the rest of the series she struggles with whether she should be entitled to make decisions or whether those decisions should be left up to a democratic vote of the normal, non-powered people around her.[30]

In *The Avengers*, this motif plays itself out in the character of Loki (Tom Hiddleston), who perhaps sees himself as a god who is better than the humans of earth. Early in the film Loki refers to humankind as "ants" that could be crushed beneath his boot. Later, his brother Thor tries to convince him that this attitude of superiority is not the proper one to have, even for a ruler. In their conversation on a mountaintop, Loki reveals his contempt for the human masses.

> LOKI: The humans slaughter each other in droves, while you idly fret. I mean to rule them, and why should I not?
> THOR: You think yourself above them.
> LOKI: Well, yes.
> THOR: Then you miss the truth of ruling, brother. A throne would suit you ill.

According to the noble Thor, then, to think of oneself as above others and to hold them in contempt are sure signs that one is not qualified to rule them.

Along with this attitude of superiority, Whedon's villains tend to try to control others and take away their freedom. In a scene set in Stuttgart, Germany, Whedon has Loki go so far as to suggest that people actually *want* to be subjugated. Loki says to the crowd, "Kneel before me. I said, kneel! Is not this simpler? Is not this your natural state? It's the unspoken truth of humanity, that you crave subjugation." As if to prove Loki wrong, an older man stands in defiance. When Loki then shoots a ray from his scepter to kill the man, Captain America jumps in the way and blocks the blast with his shield. Loki screams, "Kneel!" but Captain America replies, "Not today!"

In his DVD commentary on the scene, Whedon acknowledges the tension inherent in having heroic, superpowered characters criticizing the elitism of villains. Superheroes are, after all, almost by definition people who are superior to the average person and made to be admirable by giving them noble and heroic motives and actions. Whedon says, "What [Cap] is saying to Loki is, 'No, you're not better than other people; you're not larger than life.' But he's a super soldier. He's a superhero. This is a movie about people who are larger than life. And for him to be the man of the people, you have to ... you gotta walk that line, too.'"[31]

Still, Loki's bravado and arrogance serves as a sure sign that his ultimate downfall and humiliation are near. When the Hulk finally confronts Loki, everything else seems to stop as Loki screams, "Enough! You are, all of you, beneath me! I am a god, you dull creature! And I will not be bullied by a —." At that point the Hulk grabs Loki by the legs and unceremoniously slams him to the ground repeatedly, leaving him in a heap like a limp rag doll. As the Hulk walks away, he dismissively says his only words of the film, "Puny god!" The scene is very violent but also very funny. Loki has become a comical, farcical parody of despots everywhere in his belief that he is better than others and entitled to rule over them.

In *The Avengers*, even those without super powers or special skills are portrayed as admirable when they resist limits being placed on their freedom. The older man in Stuttgart stands rather than kneels to Loki's control. The New York City policemen at first refuse to accept Captain America's authority until he proves it to them in battle. In the middle of the end credits of *The Avengers*, the alien known only as the Other tells his leader Thanos, "Humans, they are unruly, and therefore cannot be ruled." Seeking freedom and resisting external authority is highlighted as an important virtue.

Many of the villains of Marvel Comics that Lee created with the help of his artists, would-be rulers such as Doctor Doom, Maximus the Mad, and Kang the Conqueror, felt that their superiority entitled them to rule over the mindless masses and became frustrated with those who resisted them and would not merely acquiesce to their demands. Having been raised in a Jewish home, Lee would have been familiar with the Hebrew Bible proverb, "Pride goeth before destruction, and a haughty spirit before a fall" (Prov. 16:18); and in the case of these villains, it is often their arrogance, their supreme confidence that they are better, more intelligent, or more powerful than the heroes that leads to their downfall.

In Whedon's work, and in *The Avengers* in particular, the villains actually share some similar perspectives on power and the status and privilege it provides to them with the heroes of Rand's novels. Rand has long been charged with being an elitist. Many see Rand's novels as making the point that extraordinary people such as Howard Roark in *The Fountainhead* and John Galt and the other titans of industry in *Atlas Shrugged* must embrace their superiority and separate themselves from the less intelligent and talented masses who are their inferiors.[32] Economist Ludwig von Mises wrote a letter to Rand on January 23, 1958, praising *Atlas Shrugged*. In the letter, he says, "You have the courage to tell the masses what no politician told them: you are inferior and all the improvements in your conditions which you simply take for granted you owe to the effort of men who are better than you."[33] Her critics have also noted an attitude of contempt for others, especially those who could be seen as inferiors, in her work.[34] Meanwhile, some of her supporters have rejected that reading of her work and defend her from the charge of being an elitist.[35] In *The Avengers*, the villain Loki is an elitist who sees himself as superior to other humans. In this way he serves as a caricature of the type of elitist that Rand is accused of lifting up as heroes in her novels. As noted above, Loki feels that his superiority to the human masses entitles him to rule over them. While Loki feels his power entitles him to rule over the world, Rand's heroes feel that their superiority to the masses entitles them to rule over industries that depend upon their expertise. Still, Loki's efforts to rob people of their freedom and the heroes' struggle to resist those efforts are images that are more in line with Rand's primary themes.

Villainous Institutions: Power and Freedom from the Community's Authority

If there is one aspect of Whedon's work that most resonates with the thought of Rand, it is the prominent theme of freedom from the authority of government institutions and agencies. In Rand's nonfiction work and novels, people like Howard Roark in *The Fountainhead* and John Galt in *Atlas Shrugged* and others with extraordinary talents and skills that are beneficial to society should not be burdened with excessive supervision and regulation from government institutions. If they feel they are carrying too much of society's burden, Rand's novels suggest that they should take the initiative and shrug it off.

For those who have watched any of Whedon's television series, it does not take long to recognize his discomfort with institutional authority. Beyond individual villains such as Loki, Whedon's oeuvre contains more ambiguous and insidious corporate villains in the form of companies and government entities that try to assert control over individuals and limit their freedom. In *Buffy the Vampire Slayer*, Sunnydale High School, the Watchers Council, and the Initiative are all institutions that are trying to do good but become Buffy's enemies when they try to assert too much control over her and other people.

In "Anne," hell itself is able to work only when people become compliant drones and do not fight back. Likewise, the Wolfram & Hart law firm in *Angel*, the Alliance in *Firefly* and *Serenity*, and the Rossum Corporation in *Dollhouse* all in their own ways try to control people and take away their freedom.

In Whedon's work, the heroes establish their heroism, at least in part, by resisting these institutions' efforts to control them. A turning point in *Buffy*, for example, comes in "Checkpoint" (5.12), when Buffy makes it clear to the council that she is the one with the power and that they are impotent to assert control over her. By claiming her power and privilege, she robs them of their power to oversee her and her work. The antiauthoritarian streak that runs throughout Whedon's work is perhaps most famously expressed by Malcolm Reynolds who states his intent to resist the Alliance in the film *Serenity* by saying, "I aim to misbehave."

Whedon advances this subversive theme in *The Avengers* as well. Even Fury's government agency S.H.I.E.L.D. cannot be trusted. When the Avengers discover that S.H.I.E.L.D. has been secretly trying to weaponize the cosmic cube known as the Tesseract, they refuse to submit passively to Fury's commands.[36]

While Fury comes to change his mind about trying to control the Avengers, the World Security Council does not. At a crucial moment, the council decides to send a nuclear missile into Manhattan to kill the alien invaders and, collaterally, the many civilians living there. Fury refuses the council's order to launch the missile and tries to thwart their plans. For Whedon, Fury's independence is an admirable quality. Fury resists the council's authority and instead follows his own conscience.

Later, after the Avengers have saved the world, Fury tells the council that he is no longer overseeing their activities or keeping tabs on their whereabouts. Fury says that they have "earned a leave of absence." He argues, in effect, that because of their extraordinary power they should be free from institutional control and regulation. Though the Avengers assembled to defeat Loki and the alien hoard, by the end of the film they shrug off the supervision and regulation that the World Security Council wants to impose upon them. When they go their separate ways the music, camera angles, and facial expressions of the characters all suggest that this is a very happy and commendable turn of events.

It is in this way that the values inherent in Whedon's stories, which are so distinct from those found in Rand's work in many ways, parallel her work. In *Atlas Shrugged*, the titans of industry resist control by the rest of society and only agree to help society and not to sabotage their own companies when society agrees to give them the freedom to act on their own terms. While granting such freedom seems to be moral, people of faith have often struggled with the competing virtues of submitting to government control and lifting up the rights of individuals. Christians, for example, have long struggled to understand the precise meaning of Jesus's statement that people should "Give ... to the emperor the things that are the emperor's, and to God the things that are God's" (Matthew 22:21).

According to Colonel Fury, the Avengers were formed "to fight the battles that we never could." Like most superhero stories, *The Avengers* is set up in such a way that there are threats that normal people are unable to face. Therefore, special people must come in from outside of the community in order to save it. There is no guarantee, however, that these heroes will come back. When S.H.I.E.L.D. agent Maria Hill (Cobie Smulders) asks Fury what will happen if there is another crisis, Fury simply says, "They'll come back ... because we'll need them to." In *The Avengers*, then, heroes are given freedom to do as they wish. Their extraordinary abilities and society's dependence on them earn them freedom from society's control and regulation, and at the end of the film they proudly take advantage of that fact. They will, we hope, save us out of their own good graces when they recognize how dependent we are on them.

According to philosopher John Shelton Lawrence and New Testament scholar Robert Jewett, these motifs are common in American hero fiction. In their book, *The Myth of the American Superhero*, they examine the role of heroes (not just costumed superheroes) in hundreds of American novels and films. Based on their analysis, they describe what they refer to as the *American monomyth* as follows: "A community in a harmonious paradise is threatened by evil; normal institutions fail to contend with this threat; a selfless superhero emerges to renounce temptations and carry out the redemptive task; aided by fate, his decisive victory restores the community to its paradisiacal condition; the superhero then recedes into obscurity."[37]

Lawrence and Jewett also describe the hero as a loner who is not allowed to be a part of a community and often rides off into the sunset at the end of the story.[38] The authors explain that a danger of this monomyth is that it reinforces the status quo for the community. Instead of calling the institutions of society to change and find long-term solutions to meet similar threats in the future, the story suggests that society is powerless to protect itself and must just wait for an individual or small group with extraordinary power of some kind to come from outside the community and save the day out of their own good will.[39]

Alan Moore took the title for his 1986 landmark comic book series *The Watchmen* from the question "Who watches the watchmen?," famously posed by the Roman writer Juvenal who was concerned that no one was overseeing those in authority in Rome. Whedon's film begs the question, "Who watches the Avengers?" For Whedon, it appears that they should be free from any supervision, save their own good consciences.

Conclusion

Joss Whedon's *Avengers* is the latest work in his oeuvre to provide viewers with a nuanced view of power, its proper use, and the privileges that come with it. For people of faith, the images of power in *The Avengers* may present a mixed bag. Some themes seem to resonate quite well with the thinking of many religious scholars and practitioners, while others raise important questions. While Whedon expresses misgivings on the point, in *The Avengers* physical violence, albeit fantasy violence, is used to save and redeem people and communities. In addition, however, the storyline suggests that extraordinary power comes with the responsibility to help the wider community and insure its freedom. Self-sacrifice is seen as a heroic virtue. Those with extraordinary power or gifts should not feel that they are superior to other people and should not use their power for their own self-interest or to limit the freedom of others. Large and powerful organizations such as government institutions are not to be trusted, and people should resist these institutions' efforts to control them. Because they have exhibited so many heroic virtues, Whedon leads his audience to trust that his heroes will assemble and save the day when they are needed. Still, these heroes have no formal relationship or responsibility to the community, and the community has made no provision to save itself. The community, therefore, is left with some uncertainty. If another crisis comes, will these Avengers assemble and take upon themselves the responsibility of saving the community, or will they instead look after their own self-interests and simply shrug?

NOTES

1. For example, Tom Long says, "Look, we're talking about a movie in which a group of hyperbuff people in tight, shiny costumes fight off monsters from outer space. Nobody's pretending great drama is going on here." Tom Long, "Marvelous," *Detroit News*, May 4, 2012. Also, Richard Corliss says, "The movie guarantees fast-paced fun without forcing anyone to think about what it all means, which is nothing." Richard Corliss, "*Marvel's The Avengers*: A Superhero Roundup That's Almost Super," *Time Magazine*, April 25, 2012, http://entertainment.time.com/2012/04/25/marvels-the-avengers-a-superhero-roundup-thats-almost-super/.

2. *Joss Whedon: Conversations*, ed. David Lavery and Cynthia Burkhead (Jackson: University Press of Mississippi, 2011), xiii; Laura Miller, "The Man Behind the Slayer," in *Conversations*, 76.

3. Christy Lemire, "Review: Have a Blast with *Avengers*," *Daily Tribune*, April 24, 2012,

http://www.dailytribune.com/article/20120424/ENTERTAINMENT05/120429812/review-have-a-blast-with—145-avengers-146.

4. Examples in both *Angel* and *Buffy* abound, although most of the relevant episodes were written by others. To cite just two penned by Whedon, however, in "The Freshman," Xander says, "Then where's the gang? Avengers Assemble. Let's get it going"; and in "The Body" (5.16), he says, "The Avengers got to get with the assembly." The influence of Marvel on Whedon is evident in many other ways throughout these series, of course.

5. Ayn Rand, *The Virtue of Selfishness: A New Concept of Egoism* (New York: The New American Library, 1964).

6. Ayn Rand, "Introducing Objectivism," in *The Voice of Reason: Essays in Objectivist Thought* (New York: Penguin Books, 1990), 4.

7. Ibid.

8. Ibid., 4–5.

9. Jim Eckman, "Ayn Rand and Christianity," *Issues in Perspective*, June 18, 2011, http://graceuniversity.edu/iip/2011/06/18-1/; Steven Prothero, "My Take: Christianity and Ayn Rand's Philosophy are 2 Distinct Religions," CNN Belief Blog, August 15, 2012, http://religion.blogs.cnn.com/2012/08/15/my-take-christianity-and-ayn-rands-philosophy-are-2-distinct-religions/.

10. Ayn Rand, *Letters of Ayn Rand*, ed. Michael S. Berliner (New York: Plume, 1997), 669.

11. Ayn Rand, *Atlas Shrugged* (1957; repr., New York: Dutton, 2005), 455.

12. Ibid., 732.

13. Ibid., 1143. Ellipses in original.

14. Monica White, "The Ascendance of *Firefly*," *Atlasphere Magazine*, August 18, 2004, http://www.theatlasphere.com/columns/040819_white_firely.php.

15. Geoffrey Allan Plauché, "Joss Whedon Goes on Anti-Capitalist Rant at Comic-Con," Film, News, Science Fiction, Statism on Prometheus Unbound, July 15, 2012, http://prometheus-unbound.org/2012/07/15/news-joss-whedon-goes-on-anti-capitalist-rant-at-comic-con/.

16. "Whedon On Romney," YouTube video, 2:13, posted by WhedonOnRomney, October 28, 2012, http://www.youtube.com/watch?v=6TiXUF9xbTo.

17. Ditko's commitment to Objectivism and the ways in which it influenced his work in comic books is detailed in Blake Bell, *Strange and Stranger: The World of Steve Ditko* (Seattle: Fantagraphics Books, 2008).

18. See, for example, *Amazing Spider-Man* #31 (December 1965), 8–11, 13; *Amazing Spider-Man* #33 (February 1966), 17–18; *Amazing Spider-Man* #36 (May 1966), 6; *Amazing Spider-Man* #37 (June 1966), 5; and *Amazing Spider-Man* #38 (August 1966), 11.

19. For a further discussion of this phenomenon, see Russell W. Dalton, *Marvelous Myths* (St. Louis: Chalice Press, 2011), 52–55.

20. Walter Wink, *The Powers That Be: Theology for the New Millennium* (New York: Galilee Doubleday, 1998), 42.

21. Rand, "Introducing Objectivism," 4.

22. Ayn Rand, *The Fountainhead* (Indianapolis: Bobbs-Merrill, 1943), 230.

23. Ibid.

24. Steven Tice, "Face-to-Face with Wertham's Partner!" in *The Stan Lee Universe*, ed. Danny Fingeroth and Roy Thomas (Raleigh, NC: TwoMorrows, 2011), 57–70.

25. Stan Lee, *Stan's Soapbox: The Collection* (New York: Marvel, 2008), 16, 18.

26. Anthony Breznican, "Hero Worship," *Entertainment Weekly*, May 4, 2012, 42.

27. *Amazing Fantasy* #15 (1963), 11.

28. Joss Whedon, "Commentary," *The Avengers*, directed by Joss Whedon (Burbank, CA: Buena Vista Home Entertainment, 2012), DVD.

29. Breznican, 42.

30. See also "Empty Places" (*Buffy* 7.19) and the elitist words and actions of the Beast Master in the *Angel* episode "Inside Out."

31. Whedon, "Commentary."

32. For recent discussions of this theme, see Vladimir Shlapentokh, "How is elitist Ayn

Rand a tea party hero? The contradiction should concern America," *Christian Science Monitor*, Oct. 14, 2010; Jonathan Chait, "War on the Weak," *Newsweek*, April 18, 2011, 6–7.

33. Ludwig von Mises and Murray Rothbard, "Mises and Rothbard Letters to Ayn Rand," *Journal of Libertarian Studies* 21, no. 4 (Winter 2007), 11.

34. Michael O'Donnell wrote a review of two biographies of Ayn Rand. See Michael O'Donnell, "A Life of Contempt," *Washington Monthly* 41, nos.11–12 (November 2009), 58. See also Whittaker Chambers's famously harsh review in 1957 of *Atlas Shrugged*. Whittaker Chambers, "Big Sister Is Watching You," *National Review* 42, no. 21 (November 5, 1990), 120–122.

35. David Kelley, "Myth: Ayn Rand Was an Elitist," *Atlas Society*, December 19, 2011, http://www.atlassociety.org/atlas-shrugged/ayn-rand-elitist.

36. In a similar way, the secret government agency the Initiative tried to weaponize demons in the fourth season of *Buffy the Vampire Slayer*.

37. John Shelton Lawrence and Robert Jewett, *The Myth of the American Superhero* (Grand Rapids: Eerdmans, 2002), 6.

38. Ibid., 7.

39. Ibid., 14.

BIBLIOGRAPHY

Bell, Blake. *Strange and Stranger: The World of Steve Ditko*. Seattle: Fantagraphics Books, 2008.

Breznican, Anthony. "Hero Worship." *Entertainment Weekly*, May 4, 2012, 34–42.

Chait, Jonathan. "War on the Weak: How the GOP Came to View the Poor as Parasites — and the Rich as our Rightful Rulers." *Newsweek*, Apr 18, 2011.

Chambers, Whittaker. "Big Sister Is Watching You." *National Review* 42, no. 21 (November 5, 1990): 120–122.

Corliss, Richard. "Marvel's The Avengers: A Superhero Roundup That's Almost Super." *Time Magazine*, April 25, 2012. http://entertainment.time.com/2012/04/25/marvels-the-avengers-a-superhero-roundup-thats-almost-super/.

Dalton, Russell W. *Marvelous Myths*. St. Louis: Chalice Press, 2011.

Eckman, Jim. "Ayn Rand and Christianity." *Issues in Perspective*, June 18, 2011. http://graceuniversity.edu/iip/2011/06/18–1/.

Kelley, David. "Myth: Ayn Rand Was an Elitist." *Atlas Society*, December 19, 2011. http://www.atlassociety.org/atlas-shrugged/ayn-rand-elitist.

Lavery, David, and Cynthia Burkhead, eds. *Joss Whedon: Conversations*. Jackson: University Press of Mississippi, 2011.

Lawrence, John Shelton, and Robert Jewett. *The Myth of the American Superhero*. Grand Rapids: Eerdmans, 2002.

Lee, Stan. *Stan's Soapbox: The Collection*. New York: Marvel, 2008.

Lemire, Christy. "Review: Have a Blast with *Avengers*." *Daily Tribune*, April 24, 2012. http://www.dailytribune.com/article/20120424/ENTERTAINMENT05/120429812/review-have-a-blast-with—145-avengers-146.

Long, Tom. "Marvelous." *Detroit News*, May 4, 2012.

Miller, Laura. "The Man Behind the Slayer." In *Joss Whedon: Conversations*, edited by David Lavery and Cynthia Burkhead, 71–79. Jackson: University Press of Mississippi, 2011.

O'Donnell, Michael. "A Life of Contempt." *Washington Monthly* 41, nos. 11–12 (November 2009): 58–59.

Plauché, Geoffrey Allan. "Joss Whedon Goes on Anti-Capitalist Rant at Comic-Con." Film, News, Science Fiction, Statism on Prometheus Unbound. July 15, 2012. http://prometheus-unbound.org/2012/07/15/news-joss-whedon-goes-on-anti-capitalist-rant-at-comic-con/.

Prothero, Steven. "My Take: Christianity and Ayn Rand's Philosophy are 2 Distinct Religions." CNN Belief Blog. August 15, 2012. http://religion.blogs.cnn.com/2012/08/15/my-take-christianity-and-ayn-rands-philosophy-are-2-distinct-religions/.

Rand, Ayn. *Atlas Shrugged*. 1957. Reprint, New York: Dutton, 2005.
_____. *The Fountainhead*. Indianapolis: The Bobbs-Merrill Company Incorporated, 1943.
_____. "Introducing Objectivism." In *The Voice of Reason: Essays in Objectivist Thought*, edited by Leonard Peikoff, 3–5. New York: Penguin Books, 1990.
_____. *Letters of Ayn Rand*. Edited by Michael S. Berliner. New York: Plume, 1997.
_____. *The Virtue of Selfishness: A New Concept of Egoism*. New York: The New American Library, 1964.
Shlapentokh, Vladimir. "How is Elitist Ayn Rand a Tea Party Hero? The Contradiction Should Concern America." *Christian Science Monitor*, October 14, 2010.
Tice, Steven. "Face-to-Face with Wertham's Partner!" In *The Stan Lee Universe*, edited by Danny Fingeroth and Roy Thomas, 57–70. Raleigh: TwoMorrows, 2011.
von Mises, Ludwig, and Murray Rothbard. "Mises and Rothbard Letters to Ayn Rand," *Journal of Libertarian Studies* 21, no. 4 (Winter 2007): 11–16.
Whedon, Joss. "Commentary." *Marvel's The Avengers*. Directed by Joss Whedon. Burbank, CA: Buena Vista Home Entertainment, 2012. DVD.
_____. "Whedon on Romney." YouTube video, 2:13. Posted by WhedonOnRomney, October 28, 2012. http://www.youtube.com/watch?v=6TiXUF9xbTo.
White, Monica. "The Ascendance of *Firefly*." *Atlasphere Magazine*, August 18, 2004. http://www.theatlasphere.com/columns/040819_white_firely.php.
Wink, Walter. *The Powers That Be: Theology for the New Millennium*. New York: Galilee Doubleday, 1998.

National Treasures
Joss Whedon's Assembling of Exceptional Avengers
JOHN C. MCDOWELL

Entertaining Difference? Whedon's The Avengers *and Late Modern Religion*

According to Paolo Freire, "people are manipulated by ... [a]series of myths."[1] This statement comes in the context of Freire's book on education and the implication of his argument is that reflections on education need to be considerably more demanding than any simple concern with pedagogical techniques and practices and skills of learning would be. Popular culture has often reflected currents and shifts in the zeitgeist and the supporting mythologies, and in this science fiction and fantasy genres are often in the vanguard. As Kevin Wetmore argues, "science fiction has served as a distancing form, allowing analysis of and commentary on contemporary issues under the guise of the distant future or a fantasy world."[2] In fact, "the Hollywood film and television industries" have not only cashed in on "some of the most recognizable American pop culture symbols," argue Richard Gray and Betty Kaklamanidou, but have "turned them ... into modern day myths (according to the Barthesian definition which views myth as discourse).... Indeed, popular culture is a domain that ... produces multilayered narratives that contain and spread ideological and political messages to a wide audience."[3] Consequently, in a move not unlike that of Freire, cultural theorists recognize that so-called popular culture cannot be contained by being reduced to simple "entertainment," but claim that its discursive relation to deeper senses of identity is to be understood and tested. In a fashion inspired by Joseph Campbell, John Shelton Lawrence and Robert Jewett explain that a very specific monomyth has in fact religiously directed the American imagination since Puritan settling in North America, and which is detectable in much popular culture, especially in superhero fantasies. This generative stream exhibits "problematic tendencies of American culture" such as the stress on the individualized agent or vigilante with intense moral certainty (without self-reflexivity), the postcivic antidemocratic politics, the depiction of solution-by-violence, and the simplistic us–them dichotomy of "good" and "evil."[4] In its turn, moreover, it not only displays or expresses a political vision but also serves to significantly nourish and reinforce these tendencies by making it a "natural" part of the fabric directing the readers' imaginations of nation and of the individual's place within it.

The American national experiment, unlike that of the "old world," is now determined by the immigration of *different* peoples, and therein a different kind of us–them/good–evil binarism has politically developed than an ethnically charged one. Joss Whedon's multiethnic *Firefly* exemplifies these conditions by displaying without comment ethnic and spiritual diversity. Similarly, his *Buffy the Vampire Slayer* references not only the Romantic countermodernity of the Gothic but also a sexual fluidity through Willow (lesbian) and Angel (nonhuman because undead) echoing the shifting values and pluriform social performance of late "liquid" modernity (à la Bauman). Both series appear to further express the irrepressibility of the spiritual and the magical in cosmopolitan and religiously plural societies. *The Avengers* seems to strike a related ethnic cord with its gathering of such an array of vastly different persons into "the Avengers Initiative." In 1975 Chris Claremont revamped the mutant X-Men into something more ethnically diverse and nationally global, and this radicalized the superhero team-ups. The origins of the idea came from the success of DC's reworking of its earlier experiment with the Justice Society of America into the Justice League of America in 1960 and Marvel's subsequent *Fantastic Four* (November 1961). What is significant about the JLA, however, is that it contained several "aliens" (the Amazonian Wonder Woman, the Atlantean sovereign Aquaman, the Kryptonian Superman, and later J'onn J'onzz/Martian Manhunter) who had, for all intents and purposes, become naturalized *American* heroes. In this regard, it is intriguing, and suggestive, that Whedon has changed the original line-up of September 1963 in order to include the thawed-out Captain America and a reimagined Black Widow, replacing Wasp and Ant-Man. Even Mark Millar's and Bryan Hitch's *The Ultimates* of 2002, whose line-up is similar to Whedon's, retains these characters.

It is particularly through Cap, as he is more succinctly known, that Whedon, himself a self-proclaimed atheist, offers one of his few and distinctly underdeveloped references to religion. There is a thin recognition of religious plurality through including both Thor and Steve Rogers alongside the absence of mentions of religious matters among the other (more secular?) characters.

In other words, if religion is not invisible or discredited by broad critical swipes, it is hardly visible either. It is noticeable that Whedon does not make much of the reductionistic potential involved in the religious imagery attributable to the design of Thor, or at least not directly. This is a character developed by Marvel Comics at a time when much science-fiction and fantasy literature was suggesting that the gods were simply primordial extraterrestrial beings mistakenly taken as deities. As Kenneth Branagh's film *Thor* (2011) indicates, the Asgaardian "gods" are superbeings from another realm who have "slipped into myth and legend." The type of godness that Marvel's Thor characterizes is certainly quite different, then, from that of the ancient Nordic tales. Yet there is something also quite non–Feuerbachian at the same time about Marvel's depiction: the power of these gods is protective rather than inversely detracting and negating. Loki is not an exception to this since his conflictual colonialist drive, revealed in attempted genocide against Jotunheim in Branagh's movie, is born specifically of the angst of a very human identity crisis and as a psychologically reactive move to take control of his destiny in response to his discovery of his true lineage. In a humorous reference, Whedon's Cap claims that "there is only one God, ma'am, and I'm pretty sure he doesn't dress like that." This theological reference may be particularly significant by virtue of the fact that it is offered by a character who hails from a now temporally displaced and culturally remote society. Is this, then, a reference to a form of Christian nostalgia or even to Captain America as a religious anachronism? Agent Phil Coulson's (Clark Gregg) earlier comment on the continuing contemporary relevance of Cap's patriotic attire might find a parallel here: "people might need a little old fashioned." Moreover, not only does the narrative not display any explicit contestation to Cap's claim, it is interesting that the theological statement is made by someone whose super abilities are the product of the *scientifically* developed superserum research. In this regard, Cap actually embodies a refusal to understand scientific progress as inversely related to religious commitment.

The Politics of National Pleasure

Something more politically problematic emerges for critical consideration at this point, however. Whedon's slender nod to religion occurs in the context of a piece that does not challenge American nationalism, and that is partly conceptually connected with the most nationally symbolic and patriotically associated of the characters. This deflects the kinds of tensions that religious commitment can generate for the consciousness of identity as national citizens. Of course, one might argue that Whedon's purpose was not to do this as his attentions are elsewhere. But I want to suggest that matters are more interesting for the religiously informed reader than simply looking for explicit religious references, commenting on their infrequency, and even paying attention to the director's intentions. Religious reflection consequently becomes more fruitful when it teams up with political and cultural analysis.

To put it at its starkest, the danger would be that *The Avengers* can suggest (either wittingly or not) a binding of religion to the national project, the commitment to the wellbeing of the state and the state's frequent violent relations to other states. In this way, it could imply and reinforce the ethos of, in Robert Bellah's terms, national "civil religion" that bonds a civic and multi-ethnic state, and that makes for minimalist unity of a population increasingly ethnically, culturally, and religiously fragmented.[5] In order to sustain such a critical reading much work needs to be done in analyzing the political significance of Whedon's movie.

The film's scenes in India and Russia are utilized in order to provide a sense of the global, but the new breed of hero (the Russian spy Black Widow, and the Norse god Thor) is then drawn back to the United States in order to do heroic business. The sense here is less that of Claremont's X-Men and more that of DC Comics' post–1950 redevelopment of Kal-El. The socially minded crusader for justice from the late 1930s became the immigrant who is integrated *into* the nation, emerging as both one of the people and as a national idea referred to as "truth, justice, and the American way." That connection between Superman, the world, and the American way is politically telling, as Jeph Loeb and Tom Morris imply when suggesting that the Kryptonian orphan is "an ongoing example of ... [what] the genuinely *human* way should look like."[6] However, given the deep connections made between this character and the nation-state, this universalizing consequently reflects the long-standing mythology of national exceptionalism which is proclaimed in George W. Bush's early 2003 State of the Union Address: "The liberty we prize is not America's gift to the world, it is God's gift to humanity."[7] As with the so-called Golden Age of comic books, right up through the 1960s, this mythos portrays the United States as a righteous and ideologically unique nation, possessing a messianic mission on behalf of the global good. That is largely why Superman is a political conservative who deals only with surface crime and not with the corrupting system. Similarly, while in the 2008 film *Iron Man* Tony Stark declares his lack of comfort with the "system" of weapons manufacturing and trade that brings death, he in no way moves against the system of political governance that puts stock in the power of its arsenal, or the system of international relations that requires expensively equipped military complexes. It is not insignificant, then, that it is Tony Stark who leads the pro-registration group in Marvel's 2006–2007 comic book event series *Civil War*.

The images in Whedon's superhero movie certainly do not receive the kind of explicitly nationalized treatment that directly co-opts the heroes into the national project in the way that *Civil War* comes to, or as explored in the revisionist politics of the *Watchmen*'s in the way Dr. Manhattan and the Comedian were by Richard Nixon during the Vietnam War. In many ways that fact is deserving of comment in relation to Whedon's *intentions*. Even Whedon's Captain America is more understated than a more jingoistic director could have constructed. Yet, the potential for a globalized politics is circumvented, and the heroes' involvement with what appears to be a largely American shaped S.H.I.E.L.D. venture reinforces the conditions conducive to the so-called myth of American exceptionalism, the project rhetorically launched by John Winthrop's famous 1630 sermon. S.H.I.E.L.D. (originally Supreme Headquarters, International Espionage, Law-enforcement Division) is, after all, supposed to be a powerful international organization responsible for *global* security — introduced in the comics in August 1965 — which answers only to the United Nations. Yet this is not suggested in Whedon's piece. Not only do those working on the S.H.I.E.L.D. helicarrier who speak in the movie display an American accent, but the main figure of the council directing Nick Fury's group is likewise American. Even the former KGB agent and defector to the United States, Natasha Romanov/Black Widow, comes complete with an American accent. The only other member of the council to address the director, and does so very much in a subordinate role to the American councilman, is English. But the underlying suggestion here is not so much one of global cooperation but one of a British government aligned with U.S. foreign policy in the Middle East. While Whedon's narrative does contest the governance of those in power, with S.H.I.E.L.D.'s ordering of the Avengers to avert a nuclear strike on Manhattan, the movie does not contest America's leadership as such but only the motives and wisdom of judgment of those particular persons in power. After all, the comic books of the 1970s with which Whedon himself was familiar develop their morally unambiguous forms of vigilantism against a backdrop of disillusionment with the Vietnam War and Watergate, and slip into the early 1980s with Ronald Reagan's appeal to the myth of the Wild West and American moral and political supremacy. One could make a case from *The Avengers* for a conservative politics of small government and the altruistic actions of well-placed individuals, but not for a global politics that challenges the myth of America as beacon to the world (there is too little reference to the world to sustain much sensible democratic reflection here).

Moreover, Whedon's film falls into the trap of portraying a plot mechanism required by the Manichaean undertones within the mythos of exceptionalism: that the threat is from the "other," the wholly and irreconcilable alien. While not tending to trade in explicitly dehumanizing insults, much superhero literature is pervaded and even framed by this broad sensibility of the utterly irredeemable other, particularly that which predates the 1970s. As Stan Lee once admitted, "the battle between a hero and a villain (which is what virtually all our stories get down to) is basically a conflict between a good guy and a bad guy, or between good and evil."[8] Of course, one could argue that the ethnic connection between Loki and Thor mitigates that vulgar ideology somewhat, since they are both alien Asgaardians. And yet, Loki is revealed to not be a child of Odin at all, having been stolen by Odin from the Frost Giants of Jotunheim with a view to someday enabling an alliance between these two realms. In this sense, his menace is an echo of older fears of illegitimacy (Shakespeare's Edmund in *King Lear* is a good example) and of a form of familial disruption (with the sins of the fathers rebounding on them), along with otherness. Whedon does make much of this origin story, which is more fully and Shakespearianly explored by Branagh, and he softens its potential Manichaean blow through Thor's attempts to make familial connection with his half-brother.

But the use of the colonializing alien race the Chitauri remains significant. In a moment of post–9/11 angst and catharsis, and echoing the *Transformers* movie franchise, Whedon's New York suffers an act of terrorism sustained by an imperialist threat, only to be saved (not without sustaining heavy property damage, of course) by the morally uncomplicated and selflessly motivated superhero squad. The heroes are presented towards the end of his movie not with the kind of public fear that forces Batman into the shadows as a vigilante; or the government to move to control the superpowered as in *Smallville* and Bryan Singer's two X-Men movies (2000 and 2003); or the attempt to publicly curtail the heroes' activities in Alan Moore's *Watchmen* (with its Keene Act of 1977) and Pixar's *The Incredibles* (dir. Brad Bird, 2004). Instead, they are icons of a publically celebrated *militia* organization. Unlike in Frank Miller's Batman series and Marvel Comics' *Civil War*, for instance, there is no ambiguity regarding the heroes' relation to civil society or public debate concerning civil rights, vigilante action, extreme violence, and so on. The mood of *The Avengers* is instead akin to Lucas's *Star Wars* of 1977, even if the latter did begin to substantively deconstruct that sensibility in and through the appearance of each new movie in the saga. The heroes never face the kinds of tragic dilemmas that complicate moral existence or are caught by the enforcement of the governance of others who themselves are more self-interested. In evident contrast to this, the comic books' Tony Stark is designed in morally ambiguous terms, for example, as self-destructively compulsive, hedonistic and narcissistic. According to Tony Spanakos, "Stark's conception of the beautiful and the good are too superficial and material and he is too much a slave to his passions."[9] As a result of these character flaws he struggles particularly with alcoholism and this occasionally leads to tragic incidents. This imperfect armored hero often has to repair the very conditions he has consciously or unintentionally created. In many ways it is his intransigent and uncompromising enforcing of the government's registration of all costumed heroes that makes for the tragic conditions of Marvel's superhero civil war. Moreover, he even attempts to manipulate a war with Namor's Atlantis in order to unite the heroes, and tragically uses the Green Goblin to do so. Whedon's movie suggests little of this Stark, even if he does have him announce to Agent Coulson that he "does not play well with others." Equally, the writer-director's instinct-driven Hulk eventually becomes domesticated and harnessed to the defensive task at hand. The frightening unleashing of raw aggression so violently turned initially and momentarily on Thor and Black Widow gives way to a character who stands in the outward facing circle of the hero initiative, a "circling of the wagons" moment as they heroically face a seemingly overwhelming enemy bent simply on human life's annihilation. There is in the narrative no sense of the destructively rampaging angry beast who in the comic books and the two recent big screen outings (*Hulk* [dir. Ang Lee, 2003] and *The Incredible Hulk* [dir. Louis Leterrier, 2008]) is intensely suspicious of General Thaddeus Ross and the American military complex[10]; or whose rampage leads to the very formation of the Avengers in the first place in Marvel's Avengers origins story; or who has to be banished from planet Earth by Stark and Reed Richards after devastating Las Vegas in a more recent comics storyline.

At its best, Whedon's *Avengers* offers characters who, put most starkly, appear to be stripped of recognizable human psychology at key points. The movie's earlier portrayal of conflict among the group has considerable potential for offsetting that concern, but this is insufficiently pressed, and when placed under threat their differences dissipate and they all pull together as one — as visually stated in the moment of their defensive circling. The team, and presumably then their mutual trust and friendship, forms by default in a moment of facing a mutual threat. This is a process reflecting Marc Copper's observation very soon after 9/11: "Domestically, the attacks produced a spontaneous outpouring of mutual solidarity and community compassion.... Twenty years of Reaganite individualism appeared to melt overnight."[11] Consequently, Jewett and Lawrence's claim about one of the key features of what they call the *American monomyth* characterizes Whedon's work with *The Avengers*: "In the exercise of redemptive power, purity of intention suffices. Heroes are either static, innately possessing all the wisdom they need, or they learn all they require from a single incident."[12]

At worst, something different emerges. The initiative is largely saved by virtue of Fury's visual discourse — the display of bloodied Captain America trading cards that were on (or rather, for effect, Fury after the fact placed on)

Coulson's dead body. The connection between the union of the group (albeit here it is only Stark and Rogers who are present) and the display of Americanness — the cards celebrating the patriotically *American* costumed and entitled hero — is suggestive. Coulson's death not only makes poignant the notion that he died for something, but indicates the intensive wickedness of the deadly perpetrators of the hostility whose action preemptively strikes against the city. This latter idea is particularly crucial in the development and maintenance of wartime nationalism. So Bernard Brandon Scott argues that in a Manichaean scheme "conflict is resolved by having a purified savior destroy the enemy. Our villains must be morally evil so that we may be morally pure and our violence justified."[13] Therefore, even if the covering by one's flag should give us a certain protection from the chill of the winter of national crisis, it should not obscure our view of what has been going on underneath the covers others wear.

It is little wonder, then, that the contrast is so evidently drawn between the self-sacrificiality of "earth's mightiest heroes," on the one hand, and the evidently and morally simplistically self-serving Loki and the imperialist Chitauri, on the other. This echoes the strand of American exceptionalism iterated by Harvard professor Irving Babbitt, for instance, when he naïvely exaggerates about national benevolence in 1924, missing the power-interests it so profitably serves and the interests it does not: "We are willing to admit that all other nations are self-seeking, but as for ourselves, we hold that we act only on the most disinterested motives."[14] Not only that, but an old tradition among popular cultural artifacts identified the villain by his aesthetic otherness as well, and this was a caricaturing step particularly visible in certain portrayals of ethnic minorities. Ridley Scott's monster in *Alien* (1979) and Tolkien's orcs, goblins, Uruk-Hai, and even Gollum are all good examples of this tendency, in contrast to the identifiably human-like design of the hobbits, elves, and dwarves. In *The Avengers* the Chitauri are a race provided by the "Titanian Eternal" Thanos (whose name itself is an ominous play on the Greek *thanatos*, or death) bent on a brutal colonial project of enacting cosmic hygiene against disorder and free will. Brian Ott claims that "the path to [morally questionable] torture begins long before even the capture of 'enemy combatants.' It begins with the naming of the Other, for if one does not see an enemy as human, then one does not feel compelled to treat 'it' humanely."[15] Purposely or not, then, Whedon colludes with an ideology of a threatening *racial* other, an other that is itself given no complicating psychological backstory. Not only is this psychologically lazy but it potentially politically valedicts a Manichaean sensibility that colors the current politicocultural fear of the racially stereotyped Middle Eastern Muslim other.

However, there is something particularly interesting that emerges for further critical reflection at this point. Whedon fascinatingly does not utilize the themes, characterizations, or symbols from Marvel's controversial *Civil War* and yet this series offers a potentially rich set of materials for politically complicating the psychology of the "national consciousness." It is this series that Roz Kaveney argues "is the closest Marvel has ever come to writing political satire and protest."[16] One character in particular demands reflection — Captain America.

To Cap It All Off...: Whedon Captains a Team without a Super Challenge

Jewett and Lawrence identify Cap as a particularly good exemplar and expression of the American superiority complex and the "contradictory form of civil religion" whose mission occurs through "violent crusading."[17] They briefly offer a case study of his origin (March 1941) in which patriot Steve Rogers's superpowers were a product of the military industrial complex. In the conflict with the Axis powers that was looming, Cap's stories offered a way for comic-book-reading children to patriotically cheer on the coming American war effort. Accordingly, Joe Simon and Jack Kirby's Nazi-bashing flag-draped hero sold almost a million copies per issue. What relevance does the character have today, however? Whedon's Rogers makes such a self-critical suggestion to Coulson when he asks, "Aren't the stars and stripes a little old-fashioned?" The agent's response exhibits the unifying relevancy of the new patriotism. This entails, then, a quite particular and uncomplicated reading of the character in *The Avengers*, and the political impact of this is pronounced. Jewett and Lawrence, for instance, use Cap for their title in order to express the very shape of the mythological complex that accounts for the crusading politics they critique. The *Captain America* comic books' "crudeness," they comment, along with the "broad mythic stream that flows through superheroic comics," amounts "to a kind of mythic induction into the cultural values of America."[18]

Yet Jewett and Lawrence's linking of Cap and the American politicians and soldiers in the war against terror is actually distinctly misleading. It may work for the supersoldier's earliest depictions, but works particularly poorly in relation to his later character development in which he is more aligned with those who understand America as a developing and politically ambiguous *project*. Whatever his reasons for continuing to wear the stars and stripes, Rogers's flag certainly does not drape over his eyes so as to obscure his perception of the messy realities of the political life of his nation or to secure his identity as uncritical patriot. As early as 1970, Stan Lee admitted that Captain

America is "beginning to have second thoughts.... He realizes he can't really side with the establishment 100 percent."[19] He is closer to the good patriot who carries "on a lover's quarrel with their country."[20] As with many of the time, after the Watergate scandal of 1974, the comics depict Cap in conflict with his government. In *Captain America* #169 (January 1974), the Committee to Regain America's Principles frames Cap for murdering the Tumbler. Rogers becomes so disillusioned with his nation, learning that the Secret Empire has been led by none other than the president himself, that he even lays aside his stars and stripes costume in December 1974 and dons the garb of the superhero Nomad for a period (four comic book issues, until April 1975), the "man without a country," instead. By 1980 the national Populist Party seeks Cap to run for the presidency, but his refusal to accept the challenge is the fruit of the realism of his dedication to American values that would be mitigated by the realities of public office. Rogers was even challenged for the role of Captain America in Oct 1986 by the Super-Patriot and resigned from his position in August 1987 (briefly returning for issue 335 in November), being rebooted by Jeph Loeb and Rob Liefeld in November 1996 and further rebooted by Ed Brubaker in January 2005. With his character development, the prominent moral certainty and muscular self-assertiveness of the nation is continually questioned and is frequently portrayed as imperialistically self-interested.

From this complication of the most patriotic of the mainstream popular superhero characters it makes sense that he is the one to be particularly reimagined after 9/11. According to Terry Kading, "The superhero comic, in response to 9/11, provides a distinct medium from which to reflect on and explore the fears, insecurities, and varied individual reactions generated by the attacks."[21] *Civil War*, resulting from a massive catastrophe at Samford and the consequent suppression of certain civil liberties, significantly makes this character who is most heroically associated with the nation the focus of political engagement against the current political regime and the forms of nationalism that are invoked to maintain its power. In *Civil War* the doubt about the U.S. government comes to the fore when the Superhuman Registration Act requires heroes to register their identities with the federal authorities. Cap helps form an underground rebellion in response to what he conceives to be an unconstitutional act, an invasion of privacy for those heroes requiring secret identities for the protection of their loved ones, an erosion of the civil liberties, and an undemocratic step on the way to an abusive totalitarian political system with the heroes functioning as government agents. In consequence, he comes face to face with his former friends (led by Stark) in brutal (and eventually, seemingly, fatal) conflict.

Nevertheless, even here with the deeper political complexity of the *Civil*

War series and of its use of the character of Captain America, it remains only partially interrogative. It can question forms of unquestioning patriotism, the blind faith that is put in governments that legitimates them in such a way that they become considerably less contingent, fragile, and morally responsible than they might otherwise be on proper critical reflection. However, it does not contest or complicate the very sense of commitment to national particularity, to the disciplining of self-identifying spatiality and temporality, and to the narrated myth of the nation-state as something more than contingent body for broad forms of managing the conditions for social, cultural and political life.

Conclusion

According to Gray and Kaklamanidou, "If we consider mainstream films to be a form of escapism, which offer a mixture of education and entertainment, superhero films of the new millennium lean greatly toward the latter characteristic."[22] This, according to several commentators, tends to be the case during periods of trauma as the need for consolation and escape become the psychological order of the day. This might account for the recent success of the superhero movie. After all, in Joe Johnston's *Captain America: The First Avenger* (2011) Rogers's time in the 1940s ends as he redirects a plane bound destructively for New York by the terrorist cult Hydra led by the Red Skull.

For its part, *The Avengers* is largely a visually impressive, quickly paced but narratively and psychologically thin superhero "shoot-'em-up." At its worst, it remains unable to challenge and transform increasingly dominant and "official" forms of patriotism. It is in danger of slipping into simplistic and cathartic forms of characterization of self and the other, ideologically shrink-wrapped in the civil religion with a flag. It would seem that in its conscious mood of moral nostalgia it has utterly ignored the moral ambiguity of character and the necessary hermeneutic of suspicion learned from histories of corrupt and corrupting forms of governance, and the political potential for hero myths with the "righteous us" versus "evil them" type ethos. The movie's psychologically unambiguous superhero universe and its Manichaean streak ride roughshod over reasoned skepticism — all the while aided by the emotion-regulating score of Alan Silvestri — and the film utilizes a form of violence that is too clean and noncatastrophic in what appears to be a morally clear-cut war. The climax, moreover, is an anemic happy ending. In many respects Whedon's *Avengers* harks back in mood to an earlier period of comic book lore, with its crude representation of the good–wicked, hero–villain binaries and with flat characterizations of the psychology of the main protagonists.

Long gone are the more complex and tragic clashes of different ideologies in the likes of, for instance, *Civil War*, *Watchmen*, and Bryan Singer's *X-Men* and *X2*, and even more broadly the cultural artifact of the *Battlestar Galactica* reboot. To say this is not to use extratextually other materials from which to critique Whedon's superhero movie, but rather to indicate the ways in which identifying complex motivations and identity determinations can be handled in complex ways. The questions, then, are why Whedon's work here takes the specific form that it does, what it is that directs his directorial selections, and what the religiopolitical implications of these are. The answers may not be what most fans of the talented Whedon expect or hope to hear.

Acknowledgment

My thanks to my son Archie McDowell, who guided my reading of Marvel's *Avengers*.

Notes

1. Paolo Freire, *Pedagogy of the Oppressed*, trans. Myra Bergman (London: Penguin Books, 1996), 128.
2. Kevin J. Wetmore, Jr., *The Empire Triumphant: Race, Religion and Rebellion in the "Star Wars" Films* (Jefferson, NC: McFarland, 2005), 5ff.
3. Richard J. Gray II and Betty Kaklamanidou, introduction to *The 21st Century Superhero: Essays on Gender, Genre and Globalization in Film*, ed. Richard J. Gray II and Betty Kaklamanidou (Jefferson, NC: McFarland, 2011), 5.
4. Robert Jewett and John Shelton Lawrence, *Captain America and the Crusade against Evil: The Dilemma of Zealous Nationalism* (Grand Rapids: Eerdmans, 2003), 27.
5. Robert Bellah, "Civil Religion in America," *Daedalus* 96, no. 1 (1967): 1–21.
6. Jeph Loeb and Tom Morris, "Heroes and Superheroes," in *Superheroes and Philosophy: Truth, Justice, and the Socratic Way*, ed. Tom Morris and Matt Morris (Chicago and La Salle: Open Court, 2005), 18.
7. George W. Bush, "President Delivers State of the Union," accessed June 30, 2005, www.whitehouse.gov/news/releases/2003/01/20030128-19.html.
8. Stan Lee, *Son of Origins of Marvel Comics* (New York: Simon & Schuster, 1975), 165.
9. Tony Spanakos, "Tony Stark, Philosopher King of the Future?" in *Iron Man and Philosophy: Facing the Stark Reality*, ed. Mark D. White (Hoboken: Wiley, 2010), 135ff.
10. This point is argued by Anthony Peter Spanakos, "Exceptional Recognition: The U.S. Global Dilemma in *The Incredible Hulk, Iron Man*, and *Avatar*," in *21st Century Superhero*, 15–28.
11. Marc Cooper, "A Year Later: What the Right and Left Haven't Learned," in *The Iraq War: History, Documents, Opinions*, ed. Micah L. Sifry and Christopher Cerf (New York: Touchstone, 2003), 225.
12. Jewett and Lawrence, *Captain America*, 42.
13. Bernard Brandon Scott, *Hollywood Dreams and Biblical Stories* (Minneapolis: Fortress, 1994), 53.
14. Cited in Claes G. Ryn, *America the Virtuous* (New Brunswick: Transaction, 2003), 129.
15. Brian L. Ott, "(Re)Framing Fear: Equipment for Living in a Post-9/11 World," in *Cylons in America: Critical Studies in "Battlestar Galactica,"* ed. Tiffany Potter and C. W. Marshall (New York and London: Continuum, 2008), 17.

16. Roz Kaveney, *Superheroes! Capes and Crusaders in Comics and Films* (London and New York: I. B. Taurus, 2008), 185.
17. Jewett and Lawrence, *Captain America*, xiii.
18. Ibid., 28.
19. *Stan Lee: Conversations*, ed. Jeff McLaughlin (Jackson: University Press of Mississippi, 2007), 22.
20. William Sloane Coffin, Jr., cited in Geiko Müller-Fahrenholz, *America's Battle for God: A European Christian Looks at Civil Religion* (Grand Rapids: Eerdmans, 2007), viii.
21. Terry Kading, "Drawn into 9/11, but Where Have All the Superheroes Gone?" in *Comics as Philosophy*, ed. Jeff McLaughlin (Jackson: University Press of Mississippi, 2005), 219.
22. Gray and Kaklamanidou, 3.

Bibliography

Bellah, Robert. "Civil Religion in America." *Daedalus* 96, no. 1 (1967): 1–21.
Bush, George W. "President Delivers State of the Union." Accessed June 30, 2005. www.whitehouse.gov/news/releases/2003/01/20030128-19.html.
Cooper, Marc. "A Year Later: What the Right and Left Haven't Learned." In *The Iraq War: History, Documents, Opinions*, edited by Micah L. Sifry and Christopher Cerf, 225–228. New York: Touchstone, 2003.
Freire, Paolo. *Pedagogy of the Oppressed*. Translated by Myra Bergman. London: Penguin Books, 1996.
Gray, Richard J., II, and Betty Kaklamanidou. Introduction to *The 21st Century Superhero: Essays on Gender, Genre and Globalization in Film*, edited by Richard J. Gray II and Betty Kaklamanidou, 1–13. Jefferson, NC: McFarland, 2011.
Jewett, Robert, and John Shelton Lawrence. *Captain America and the Crusade Against Evil: The Dilemma of Zealous Nationalism*. Grand Rapids: Eerdmans, 2003.
Kading, Terry. "Drawn into 9/11, But Where Have All the Superheroes Gone?" In *Comics as Philosophy*, edited by Jeff McLaughlin, 207–227. Jackson: University Press of Mississippi, 2005.
Kaveney, Roz. *Superheroes! Capes and Crusaders in Comics and Films*. London and New York: I. B. Taurus, 2008.
Lee, Stan. *Son of Origins of Marvel Comics*. New York: Simon & Schuster, 1975.
_____. *Stan Lee: Conversations*. Edited by Jeff McLaughlin. Jackson: University Press of Mississippi, 2007.
Loeb, Jeph, and Tom Morris. "Heroes and Superheroes." In *Superheroes and Philosophy: Truth, Justice, and the Socratic Way*, edited by Tom Morris and Matt Morris, 11–20. Chicago and La Salle: Open Court, 2005.
Müller-Fahrenholz, Geiko. *America's Battle for God: A European Christian Looks at Civil Religion*. Grand Rapids: Eerdmans, 2007.
Ott, Brian L. "(Re)Framing Fear: Equipment for Living in a Post-9/11 World." In *Cylons in America: Critical Studies in "Battlestar Galactica,"* edited by Tiffany Potter and C. W. Marshall, 13–26. New York and London: Continuum, 2008.
Ryn, Claes G. *America the Virtuous*. New Brunswick: Transaction, 2003.
Scott, Bernard Brandon. *Hollywood Dreams and Biblical Stories*. Minneapolis: Fortress, 1994.
Spanakos, Anthony Peter. "Exceptional Recognition: The U.S. Global Dilemma in *The Incredible Hulk, Iron Man,* and *Avatar*." In *The 21st Century Superhero: Essays on Gender, Genre and Globalization in Film*, edited by Richard J. Gray II and Betty Kaklamanidou, 15–28. Jefferson, NC: McFarland, 2011.
Spanakos, Tony. "Tony Stark, Philosopher King of the Future?" In *Iron Man and Philosophy: Facing the Stark Reality*, edited by Mark D. White, 129–143. Hoboken: Wiley, 2010.
Wetmore, Kevin J., Jr. *The Empire Triumphant: Race, Religion, and Rebellion in the "Star Wars" Films*. Jefferson, NC: McFarland, 2005.

As It Ever Was ... So Shall It Never Be

Penal Substitutionary Atonement Theory and Violence in The Cabin in the Woods

J. Ryan Parker

In the spring of 2012, moviegoers had the option of seeing two films that had as their central theme the sacrifice of youth. In *The Hunger Games* (dir. Gary Ross), based on Suzanne Collins's blockbuster trilogy, a postapocalyptic United States has been refashioned into the nation of Panem and is now composed of thirteen districts surrounding the capital. At some point in time, the districts revolted and were promptly crushed. As punishment for their hubris, every year the districts must select two "tributes" between the ages of twelve and eighteen to fight in a battle to the death known as the "Hunger Games." The heroine of the series, Katniss Everdeen, takes her sister's place in the games and, over the course of the novels, becomes a symbol of resistance for the oppressed and of power for those who would overthrow the capital. That Collins's series and the film based on its first installment touched a collective cultural nerve is without a doubt. As of this writing, there are over fifty million print and digital copies of the trilogy in circulation and the film adaptation of the first novel raked in over $683.9 million worldwide. The DVD was released on August 18, 2012, and, to date, has earned over $115 million.[1] Yet due to their violent nature, the novels and film drew criticism from viewers and commentators who decried its images of violence against and between children, reviving the ongoing debate about the negative effects of violent images in pop culture.

Three weeks after *The Hunger Games*'s theatrical release, Joss Whedon released the metahorror film *The Cabin in the Woods*.[2] Though directed by long-time collaborator Drew Goddard, Whedon cowrote and produced it, leaving his signature witty style on the production. With a contemporary setting, the film presents a scenario similar to that of *The Hunger Games*. Countries around the world must sacrifice a select number of young people (preteens to college students) every year in order to appease "the ancient ones," also referred to as "old gods." Should the faithful fail in their duty, the old gods will rise up and rain down utter destruction on all of existence. Like the titular games in Collins's series, the sacrifices in *Cabin in the Woods* are part of a tightly orchestrated scenario designed to bring about the participants' deaths. Unlike Collins's characters, Whedon and Goddard's are not aware of their participation in the ritual. This ignorance, according to the engineers of the sacrifice, gives these sacrificial lambs the illusion of free will. They may be in a controlled environment, but they still choose how they will act, rebel, and, ultimately, be punished. As a horror film, Whedon's work is much more violent and gruesome than the cinematic adaptation of its teen-lit counterpart.

In *Cabin in the Woods*, Whedon, a self-professed atheist, offers up potentially his most atheistic work to date. Where god(s) and religion played key roles in his previous television series and films, *Cabin in the Woods* advocates the complete destruction of a particular and popular Christian theology. While not putting Whedon's atheism completely aside, I want to suggest that, rather than simply advocating deicide (after all, as we will see, the gods are very much alive at the end of the film), Whedon and Goddard promote the destruction of one of the most popular versions of Christian soteriology (or doctrine of salvation), the penal substitutionary theory of atonement, even if they do not explicitly refer to it as such. Very much like the sacrificial system in Whedon and Goddard's film, penal substitutionary atonement argues that Jesus died on the cross as a substitute for sinners and to satisfy both the wrath and righteousness of God. At the conclusion of the film, two of the main characters, sacrificial offerings in the system, make a choice that brings about the end of this practice that has been victimizing their kind for centuries. As one of the characters says, "It's time to give someone else a chance." Or, to put it another way, it's time to find a better atonement. In the process, these characters, like Katniss in *The Hunger Games*, expose the violence in which this pseudoreligious practice has been rooted.

In the rest of this essay, I will discuss the parallels between the sacrificial system in *The Cabin in the Woods* and the penal substitutionary atonement theory (hereafter PSA). I will also show the ways in which both theologians and Whedon and Goddard critique PSA. Of course, since violence plays a key role in PSA and because Whedon and Goddard's film is also a commentary on what is frequently the most violent film genre, I will close this essay with a reflection on the problems inherent in deconstructing a violent religious practice with a violent work of filmmaking. I conclude by arguing (and I recognize that this is up for debate) that for all its wit, wisdom, and self-awareness, *The Cabin in the Woods* is ultimately overshadowed by its own violence, which, in the end, prevents it from being a more effective critical voice against both the horrific in pop culture and in our own religious experiences.

Setting the Scene

The Cabin in the Woods opens on a banal conversation between two engineers, Sitterson (Richard Jenkins) and Hadley (Bradley Whitford), discussing their plans for the weekend. After the opening credits, we meet five friends who are gathering to go away to the titular destination for the weekend. These friends cover the spectrum of pop-culture/horror film archetypes: good-looking Jules (Anna Hutchinson), athletic Curt (Chris Hemsworth), brainy Holden (Jesse Williams), geeky stoner Marty (Fran Kranz), and "virgin" Dana (Kristen Connolly). Little do they know that all is not as it seems, although a constantly stoned Marty has his suspicions. In fact, the friends are part of a tightly controlled sacrificial rite that Sitterson and Hadley help coordinate. Similar rituals simultaneously take place around the world and constitute a collective offering to the old gods, colossal beings that will destroy the world unless the engineers appease their anger on a yearly basis.

Although the filmmakers leave out many details about the sacrificial rite (its origins and development, for example), it is important to present as clear a description of it as possible for purposes of this discussion. Sitterson and Hadley head up a group of engineers who select and subtly guide the doomed offerings through the ritual. Through an intricate network of surveillance cameras, bugs, drugs, chemicals, and rigged environments, the offerings will all, ideally, face a gruesome death. While the offerings face overwhelming odds, they do have an element of freedom, a key theme in much of Whedon's work. Though four of them will definitely die (we later learn that the virgin's death is optional so long as it is last and she suffers), the way in which they do hinges on their choices and interactions with each other. In this version of the rite, the basement of the cabin in the woods contains numerous artifacts of a terrifying past, any of which will trigger a series of events leading to their death. Here, the five friends unknowingly choose death by zombies, but not just any zombies: a "zombie redneck torture family," the Buckners.

Though the offerings trigger the zombie attack, things do not go according to Sitterson, Hadley, and the Director's (Sigourney Weaver) plans. While Jules dies in expected fashion, Curt, Holden, Marty, and Dana's survival skills test the limits of the engineered destruction. Curt and Holden soon meet their fate as one escape attempt after another fails. Marty and Dana return to the cabin and, following his hunch that outside forces are at work against them, delve further below the cabin in both an attempt to escape and to expose the forces that have been tormenting them. They quickly learn that the cabin is one of many stages on which such violent scenarios take place. As Marty and Dana move through the behind-the-scenes depths, they uncover a multitude of nightmarish creatures that run the horror gamut from the classic (werewolf) to the contemporary (torture porn villains).[3]

Marty and Dana eventually encounter the director of the rite, who fills them in on their unfortunate selection as the most recent offerings in a long line of sacrifices to appease the old gods. During their conversation, the earth begins to tremble as the old gods grow restless over the ritual's delayed ending. Again, since the virgin can survive, Dana can either kill Marty or resist and bring about the destruction of all humanity. After a surprise werewolf attack, during which a zombie kills the Director, Marty and Dana collapse against a wall, light a joint, and console one another as the world collapses around them.

Theological Parallels

The reality of the old gods and the sacrificial rite in *The Cabin in the Woods* make the film a likely target for religious discussion, even though the generic bloodbath explosion in the third act of the film threatens to derail any attempt to take the film seriously. However, flowing blood is central to the film (a point of contention to which I will return later), just as the blood of Jesus is a controversial element in Christian theology and, more specifically, whether and how it has salvific or atoning power. For knowledgeable and attentive viewers, the parallels between PSA, one of the most popular atonement theories in Christian theology, and the engineered sacrifices in *The Cabin in the Woods* are readily apparent. After briefly defining this theory, I will discuss those parallels and then move on to highlight some theological critiques of PSA before finally focusing on the ways in which the film criticizes this understanding of the relationship between god(s) and humanity.

While calling for a new theory of atonement in his book *Triune Atonement: Christ's Healing for Sinners, Victims, and the Whole Creation*, minister and theologian Andrew Sung Park provides a concise history of atonement theories. He starts by naming the tension at the heart of the process: "On the one hand, some theologians want to avoid mentioning the blood of Jesus for the redemption of humanity because the cross of Jesus has been used for abusing others and for promoting violence in the world. On the other, to millions of people, the cross of Jesus holds deep meaning for grace and salvation."[4] As Tony Jones shows in his book, *A Better Atonement: Beyond the Depraved Doc-*

trine of Original Sin, entire sects of the Christian church even disagree on the event(s) that necessitate salvation in the first place. Jones writes, "I discovered that whole branches of the Christian family tree — most notably, the Orthodox Church — have never embraced Original Sin. I have come to reject the notion of Original Sin. I consider it neither biblically, philosophically, nor scientifically tenable."[5] Given this tension, it is not surprising to see that there is not (nor has there ever been) a universally accepted theory of atonement or salvation among the diverse body of the Christian church. Park writes, "There are several major theories explaining the effect of Jesus' blood. They draw on certain aspects of the Scripture, partially explaining the biblical metaphors of soteriology, the doctrine of salvation.... [Traditional] atonement theories [include] the ransom, Christus Victor, satisfaction, moral influence, penal substitution, last scapegoat, and narrative Christus Victor theories."[6] In different ways, both Park and Jones are searching for a better atonement, one that would faithfully integrate God's self, relationship to creation, and fallible humanity.[7] Yet as PSA is one of the most popular atonement theories across numerous Christian denominations, we still must better understand its arguments and shortcomings.

Two important Christian figures are responsible for PSA as we know it today, Anselm (1033–1109) and John Calvin (1509–1564), and, as Park and Jones show, the two utilized other atonement theories in their development of it. Park summarizes the penal substitution theory:

> Before our reconciliation with God through Christ, we were God's enemies [as a result of Original Sin], deserving God's wrath, vengeance, and eternal death. A perfectly just God could not love our iniquities. God's love, however, urged God to receive us into God's favor. That action of God's love was the atonement of Christ. Through his obedience, Christ accomplished his atonement for us. His obedience was his voluntary subjection to God's will. He was condemned to death as an evildoer. His suffering was real and awful because he assumed our infirmities. He struggled with condemnation and death. The punishment Christ took upon himself includes the agony of his soul through which he completed the substitution of our spiritual and physical punishment.[8]

For nearly all Christians, whether they support or oppose PSA, this aspect of God's wrath and vengeance is the linchpin of this theory. While the belief that Jesus willingly took the place of guilty sinners might be seen as a testament to his self-sacrificial love for humanity, the reality of an angry, vengeful God who demands blood sacrifice to appease that anger is far more troubling. Therefore, many Christians and theologians object to Calvin's assertions that "Christ's blood expiates our sins and propitiates God's anger.... Concretely, Jesus' blood acts as 'the laver to purge our defilements.'"[9] In this theological worldview, God might be bound by justice, but God is also angry.

At first glance, it is odd that such a seemingly barbaric notion of salvation would still appeal to so many Christians in the twenty-first century. However, Jones points out that most Western Christians were raised on PSA because it made sense both theologically and culturally and that an adequate understanding of PSA is impossible without recognition of the cultures from which and into which it moves. Jones elaborates on the theme of justice in PSA and ultimately concludes that PSA appeals to many Western Christians because "our lives are governed by laws that attempt to instantiate justice. Consequently, PSA also lends itself to metaphors, allegories, and parables that appeal to us."[10] While both Park and Jones accept that PSA is and has been a meaningful interpretation for many Christians and that it does have its strengths, they are both aware that it is deeply problematic. I will return to these critiques after an analysis of the theological parallels in *The Cabin in the Woods*.

Though differences exist, the sacrificial rite in *The Cabin in the Woods* embodies three key elements of PSA: a broken relationship between god(s) and humanity, an offended and angry divinity, and a blood sacrifice that appeases that anger and satisfies the god(s)' desire for justice. First, in terms of the ruptured relationship between humans and the divine, the film gives more hints than definitive explanations. If various Christian explanations exist for the separation between God and humanity, there is no clear "original sin" or similar instigator of fallenness in *The Cabin in the Woods*. All we know is that the offerings "transgress." When Hadley and Sitterson clear up the free will/deterministic tensions for Truman (Brian White), they argue, "[If] they don't transgress, they can't be punished." While it remains unclear what constitutes transgression, several signs point to illicit sexual behavior as seen in the numerous references to Jules as "the whore." Early in the film, Jules also refers to the affair that Dana had with one of her professors. When Mordecai/The Harbinger (Tim De Zarn) contacts the engineers to let them know of the offerings' successful passage to the cabin, he tells them to "cleanse them, cleanse the world of their ignorance and sin." Therefore, the system seems to be tied to some predetermined accepted modes of behavior that the offerings (and possibly, by extension, the rest of humanity) have violated.

Second, like the PSA version of God, the ancient ones in *The Cabin in the Woods* are angry. While there is no clear description of who these gods are or an in-depth presentation of their relationship to humanity, it is clear that they are pissed off. But at what, we also have no clear indication. Nor do we have an understanding of what they demand from humanity. Justice? Righteousness? That the gods are angry is evident in human conversations about and reactions to them. Throughout the process of designing the offerings' deaths, Sitterson and Hadley are visibly anxious and afraid of the system falling apart. When Truman confronts them for taking pleasure in Jules and

Curt's tryst, the engineers ask him, "You think we're the only ones watching? You got to keep the customers happy." After Jules's death, Sitterson prays, while holding some sort of token, "This we offer in humility and fear for the blessed peace of your eternal slumber. As it ever was." Hadley repeats, "As it ever was." Later in the film, as Dana and Marty uncover the network beneath the cabin, the Director warns them, "You've seen horrible things ... an army of nightmare creatures. But they are nothing compared to what came before ... what lies below. It's our task to placate the ancient ones. As it's yours to be offered up to them." For whatever reason, the ancient ones are angry, and they will only be appeased by blood.

Third, like the angry, vengeful God of PSA, the old gods demand blood sacrifice to appease this anger. As in PSA, the sacrifices in the film must be human, and blood must flow. In the sizable inner sanctum wherein Marty and Dana eventually meet the Director, this blood flows through images of each of the sacrifices that have been carved into the wall. Apparently, these are channels that lead down to the residence of the old gods who either consume or bathe in the blood. Like the Christian church, the engineers have a liturgy around which they build the rite, as evidenced by Sitterson and Hadley's prayer after Jules's death. A participant in the rite, Mordecai/The Harbinger is perhaps the most fervent believer in the process and employs some of the most liturgical dialogue in his conversation with the engineers.

A key difference between the rite in *The Cabin in the Woods* and PSA is certainly the number of deaths required to appease angry gods. The former is an ongoing sacrifice, whereas the latter only required one death, that of Jesus. Yet, like the yearly sacrifice over which Sitterson and Hadley preside, every time Christians celebrate or commemorate the crucifixion it is a reinvigoration, or reenactment, of that violent death. Differences aside, both PSA and the sacrificial system in *The Cabin in the Woods* beg an ultimate question: regardless of what the sin actually was, is it a sufficient defense of or explanation for the ongoing death and destruction that follow as punishment? As such, both PSA and the film demand criticism.

Theological Critiques

Along with their succinct histories of atonement theory and explanation of PSA, Park and Jones offer essential criticisms of it as well. First, for Jones, a shortcoming of PSA is a problem for all atonement theories: "Every theory of the atonement is ... human and ... bound to a context."[11] He continues, "God cannot be bound by a law, a moral code, a universal sense of justice, or a 'deep magic from the dawn of time.' God could have forgiven us of our sin however God wanted to — with or without the execution of his son."[12] Park is equally bothered by some of PSA's assertions. While it seems that Park struggles to find strengths of PSA, he has no difficulty laying out its shortcomings. His concerns include

- a highly literal interpretation of scriptural passages
- a promotion of violence in the name of salvation
- an implication that the forgiveness of God, which is the essential teaching of Jesus, becomes overshadowed or ignored
- an assumption that our portion of punishment should be transferred to Jesus, which is itself an unjust act
- a lack of human involvement in Jesus's redemptive drama[13]

This last point is a key problem for Park regarding almost all popular atonement theories. Each one fails to address human freedom and responsibility beyond original sin or simply accepting the gift of God's salvation in Jesus Christ, however it may be understood. Atonement becomes either a cosmic battle between God and the devil or else merely a case where Jesus dies to pay a ransom to God, death, or the devil.

This theme of human freedom is a foundational element in much of Whedon's work, and fans and scholars have reflected on it at length. In his article "Free Will in a Deterministic Whedonverse," Thomas Flamson argues that freedom is a fundamental question in *Buffy the Vampire Slayer*, *Angel*, and *Firefly* and that, at their core, these series ask if we can ever truly be or need to be free.[14] Flamson even provocatively claims that in Whedon's worlds, "the greatest threats to freedom are the gods."[15] Few of Whedon's works make this point as clearly and strongly as *The Cabin in the Woods*. Again, I am arguing here that Whedon and Goddard's film can be viewed, theologically, as a denunciation of PSA. Through characters that question the ritual or see through the veil, *The Cabin in the Woods* critiques the ritualistic killing that drives the plot forward. There are three avenues through which the filmmakers do this: the organization's voice of reason, the not-so-subtly named Truman; Sitterson and Hadley, the engineers that orchestrate much of the torture; and the ever-stoned offering, Marty.

As the newest member of the organization, Truman struggles to make sense of it all, particularly the engineers' enjoyment of the brutal killings. As the engineers begin to set the stage for the offerings' torture, Truman and Lin (Amy Acker) watch the proceedings on a video screen. He expresses dismay, "Monsters, magic, gods," to which Lin responds, "You get used to it." Truman's question lingers, "Should you?" Throughout the film, he is clearly disturbed by the deaths of the five friends and disgusted by his coworkers' enthusiasm over them. As I mentioned earlier, Truman confronts Hadley and Sitterson over their enjoyment of Jules's near-naked lovemaking with Curt.

Second, and most surprisingly, Sitterson and Hadley are also avenues through which the filmmakers critique the system. There seem to be two types of believers in the film: those who take the old gods seriously and those who recognize that so much of the ritual is just business and even an occasion for a friendly wager (the two lead a gambling pool over how the offerings will trigger their own deaths). Sitterson and Hadley represent the latter, while Mordecai/The Harbinger represents the former, and the two engineers even make fun of him when he calls to report on the offerings' procession to the cabin. When the Japanese rite fails (the engineers had trapped a group of nine-year-old girls in a classroom with a demon spirit), Sitterson screams, "How hard is it to kill nine year olds?!" Shortly thereafter, Hadley complains that they will all soon be singing, "What a friend we have in Shinto." While Sitterson and Hadley enjoy the proceedings and consistently lighten the mood, they eventually take their job seriously when the chips are down, as evidenced by both their prayer over the first sacrifice and the panic that ensues when the tunnel almost fails to collapse in time to prevent Curt, Holden, and Dana's escape and when Marty returns after they thought he had already died.

Speaking of Marty, he is the third and most critical voice of both the rite and the broader culture that promotes it. It is clear that Marty is the character with whom Whedon (and Whedonites) most closely identifies. From the start, Marty suspects that there is more to their existence than meets the eye. On the way to the cabin, Jules complains about not being able to pinpoint their route or location on her GPS and Marty responds, "That's the whole point. Get off the grid, right? No cell phone reception, no traffic cameras. Go someplace for one goddamned weekend where they can't global position my ass." The single friend among two (potential) couples, Marty spends time alone at the cabin. Throughout the night he hears voices, one of which tells him to go outside for a walk, where, we know, he will be attacked. Marty yells at the voices, "What do you want? You think I'm a puppet huh? Think I'm a puppet gonna' do a little fuckin' puppet dance? I'm the boss of my own brain, so give it up.... I'm gonna' go for a walk." Here we see not only his perceptiveness but also his inability to resist those voices, due, in part, to engineered marijuana. Of course, this scene is one of Whedon and Goddard's many humorous jabs at horror films' tendency to send a victim exactly where he or she should not go.

Throughout the film, Marty constantly pushes back against the system. When the five friends uncover the artifacts that would trigger their demise, he pleads with them to leave the basement. When Dana begins to read from Patience Buckner's journal (the device that seals their fate), Marty begs her to stop reading. As she begins the Latin incantation that will cause the zombie family to rise, Marty screams, "I am drawing a line in the fucking sand! Do not read the Latin!" Later, he tells his few surviving friends, "You're not seeing what you don't want to see." By the end of the film, Dana is his only friend who, as Marty promised Jules at the beginning of the film, comes to see things his way.

As the film progresses, Marty realizes that things are terrifyingly worse than he could have ever imagined. When he and Dana enter the bowels of the stage upon which their sacrifices take place, they uncover a treasure trove of nightmarish and horror-film-inspired creatures, but it is not until they encounter the Director that they realize just how dire their situation is. The Director tells Marty and Dana (and by extension the audience) about the reality of the ancient ones, the old gods that demand the sacrifice of youth to appease their anger or else will rain down destruction on all of humanity. Facing a sacrificial standoff, the Director tells Marty, "You can die with them, or you can die for them." Marty sarcastically responds, "Gosh, they're both so enticing."

After an ensuing werewolf and zombie attack, Marty and Dana are left alone. Dana tells Marty, "You were right. Humanity. It's time to give someone else a chance." By refusing to succumb to the sacrificial system, Dana and Marty make a truly sacrificial decision, dying with the world instead of for it. In doing so, they implicitly ask a host of important questions. If the gods once "ruled the earth," why does this ritual continue? What kind of gods demands such a sacrifice? What type of believers are they who so readily give it? By raising such questions, Marty and Dana make a truly atheistic choice and assert that the death of all of existence is surely better than the perpetuation of a belief system that so willingly pays such a high theological price on a yearly basis the world over. In this way, Marty's and Dana's deaths are similar to the death of Jesus, who hung on a cross between two criminals and exposed the brutality of the system that hung him there in the first place. In the process, Jesus (and Marty and Dana) stand on the side of all victims of injustice and violence mediated by both the secular state and the sacred church.[16]

Critics of religion (or more specifically Christianity) often cite its inherent violence in texts, theologies, and practices as a hindrance to its ability to speak effectively to our lived experiences, which are themselves frequently marred by violence. As I have shown thus far, *The Cabin in the Woods* (in)directly addresses one of the most notorious examples of religious violence, PSA, one that is increasingly shunned by many Christians as well. At the same time, as many commentators have pointed out, Whedon and Goddard's film is also a work of intentional criticism aimed at the horror genre and our pop cultural fascination with and enjoyment of it. The tension that arises, therefore, results from a cinematic critique of religious violence that is itself brutally violent. If, as Marty and Dana's actions suggest, it is time to find, so to speak, a better atonement, then perhaps it is also time to find a better critique.

Critiquing the Violent Critique

Earlier in this essay, I mentioned that while Goddard directed *The Cabin in the Woods*, viewers can still detect Whedon's influence on the production. Along with his signature wit, the film articulates common themes in his oeuvre including human freedom, feminism, violence, the power of community to confront evil forces, and the list goes on. Suffice it to say that it is no coincidence that "geek" Marty and "virgin" Dana are the last two friends left standing to decide the fate of the world. In their introduction to *The Psychology of Joss Whedon*, editors Joy Davidson and Leah Wilson comment on Whedon's body of work, which, they argue, "forces us to peer into the remotest corners of our own morally capricious, emotively turbulent world."[17] Yet this is a demand Whedon places on an audience that is all too willing to comply: "We like confronting our darkness, even if, in doing so, we think we're still just having fun." Davidson and Wilson add, "The Whedonverse reveals our human condition in its most glorious and depraved variations, capturing our collective consciousness with unyielding pathos and rollicking humor."[18] As we have seen, *The Cabin in the Woods* certainly lives up to this assessment of Whedon's work, and audiences' compliance with it signals a flaw in the system.

Whedon and Goddard's metahorror film is an intentional commentary on the genre in the vein of the *Scream* series that first thrilled and entertained audiences in the summer of 1996. Numerous critics and commentators have written at length about this subgenre and Whedon and Goddard's approach to it. Writing for Pop Matters, Cynthia Fuchs gets to the heart of the film's meta nature, highlighting the tensions that develop between knowledge and anxiety. She writes, "You want the kid(s) to survive but also you don't, because the pleasure to be derived from this exercise is both voyeuristic and visceral.... As all such events and cinematography are foreseeable, the kick is in the foreseeing."[19] Fuchs argues that this is not the first horror film to operate in this way, but the directness with which Whedon and Goddard do so sets the film apart from its peers. Fuchs writes that the film rewards viewers "not only for taking pleasure in the gore but also for taking pleasure in your own smartness in taking that pleasure.... You don't pay to pay in any broader sense, that is, you don't feel remorse or consternation after watching *The Cabin in the Woods*. It doesn't make you rethink your assumptions or ponder how you take pleasure. It lets you feel smart. Again."[20] In an article posted at themOvieblog.com, one writer further clarifies this knowing relationship between these two filmmakers and their audiences: "What's remarkable about *The Cabin in the Woods* is that it's not actually that violent. In fact, Goddard seems to tease us about it. During a brutal sequence where the first victim is beheaded, the camera cuts to black for a second.... It seems almost like Goddard's direction is teasing us: did you really want to see that? And, if you did: what does that say about you?"[21]

As these critics show, Whedon and Goddard's attempt to confront religiously sanctioned violence is hamstrung by a pleasure-inducing aesthetic. The filmmakers offer an interesting viewing experience: not only do we watch the horrific events at the cabin in the woods, but we watch other people watch as well. As such, Sitterson and Hadley become stand-ins for us audience members and, in the process, provide comic relief that unsettles the horror and complicates our engagement with it. Again, when Truman confronts the two for taking pleasure in a private moment between Jules and Curt, Hadley butts in, "We're not the only ones watching," and Sitterson adds, "We gotta' keep the customers satisfied. You understand what's at stake here?" This time, we know they are also talking about the fans in the seats and not just the gods underground. Later in the film, when it appears that the ritual has been a success, Sitterson, Hadley, and Lin toast each other with bottles of beer. They watch Dana being tortured by the most intimidating zombie member of the Buckner family. Hadley observes, "It's so strange. I'm — we're actually rooting for this girl.... She's got so much heart ... think of all the pain ... and — tequila is my lady! My lady! Come on in guys!" Members from the other departments spill in and a party begins. As the employees mingle, images of Dana's torture continue to play on the big screen. Like us, the engineers take pleasure in the filmed brutalization of the five friends, but it is a short-lived pleasure that does not hold their attention as Dana's victimization just becomes background noise and visuals for their party.

While Sitterson and Hadley provide avenues through which to comment on the horror genre and audiences' enjoyment of it, Whedon and Goddard's comic aesthetic might undercut this sober commentary. This all echoes Stephen Prince's analysis of aestheticized cinematic violence in which he argues, "To compel viewers to watch, filmmakers routinely embed violence within an audiovisual design that provides aesthetic pleasure. Screen violence is made attractive, whether by dressing it up in special effects or by embedding it in scenarios of righteous (i.e., morally justified) aggression."[22] Here, Whedon and Goddard employ a spoonful of humor to help the gruesome violence go down. Of course, the degree to which Whedon and Goddard's humorous aesthetic problematizes the film's commentary on religious violence is a subjective issue open for debate. It is certainly a key avenue for criticism of the film itself. Whedon and Goddard's film is a welcome contribution to the genre, and Whedonites and numerous critics certainly enjoyed it. One wonders, however, whether or not the film's "effects outrun its causes," to borrow Frank Burch Brown's question of kitsch.[23] Some critics, like A. O. Scott of the New York Times, were less convinced than fans of the film. Scott compares *The Cabin in the Woods* to *Scream*, which "proved that it was possible to be spoofy and scary at the same time, to activate the cognitive and sensory circuits that produce both laughter and fear." On the other hand, Scott claims that Whedon and Goddard's film "bungles that relatively straightforward trick, partly because it wants to do a lot more than provide a dose of shrieks and giggles. There is a scholarly, nerdy, completist sensibility at work here that is impressive until it becomes exhausting."[24]

Writing for movieline.com, Jen Yamato was one of the few critics to even reference the religious themes in the film. She writes, "Themes of faith and religion hinted at throughout the film give way to a disappointingly uninspired new mythology and an ending that is, perhaps, pointedly meaningless in many ways and more than a little nihilistic." At the same time, Yamato argues that Whedon and Goddard's "ultimate smartypants, knowing, deconstructed, playfully reverential horror movie" is an attempt to "close the lid shut on the genre as it stands." While this might be an admirable attempt, it ultimately begs the question, "But then where do we go next?"[25]

Both fans and detractors of *The Cabin in the Woods* inevitably react differently to Whedon and Goddard's knowing treatment of horror and violence. While it might work on a number of levels, it does betray some of Whedon's real-world concerns. In a May 2007 article for the fan site, Whedonesque.com, Whedon comments on a video of the fatal beating and stoning of seventeen-year-old Dua Khalil and CNN's decision to air some of that video. In it, he bemoans the violent treatment of women in many parts of the world and writes:

> How did more than half the people in the world [women] come out incorrectly? I have spent a good part of my life trying to do that math, and I'm no closer to a viable equation. And I have yet to find a culture that doesn't buy into it. Women's inferiority — in fact, their malevolence — is as ingrained in American popular culture as it is anywhere they're sporting burkhas. I find it in movies, I hear it in the jokes of colleagues, I see it plastered on billboards, and not just the ones for horror movies. Women are weak. Women are manipulative. Women are somehow morally unfinished.... And the logical extension of this line of thinking is that women are, at the very least, expendable.[26]

The title of Whedon's article, "Let's Watch a Girl Get Beaten to Death," could have been an alternate title for *The Cabin in the Woods*. Ironically, Whedon fails to note the religious motivations behind Khalil's stoning, a similar theme that would eventually, as we have seen, motivate the characters in *The Cabin in the Woods*. Whedon clearly believes that a change needs to take place in both the real and reel worlds, but we as audience members find ourselves in an unfortunate situation vis-à-vis the film's violence. Whedon's send up of religious violence (like PSA) is simultaneously an all-too-willing participant in the ongoing dehumanization and abuse of women that he and so many other filmmakers bemoan.

As witty and self-aware as Whedon and Goddard's film is, *The Cabin in the Woods* still revels in the very violence and gore that appeases both the old gods and the viewers in theaters around the world. The tropes of the horror genre have been encoded in our own collective consciousness (whether we know it or not), much like more traditional religious myths. While it might be an academic effort to further expose the rules of the horror genre game (and especially how religion, gender, mythology, and so forth coalesce), *The Cabin in the Woods* still gives us everything we want even as it tells us that we are wrong for wanting it. In many ways, Whedon and Goddard seem to have painted themselves into a corner reminiscent of Mel Gibson's *The Passion of the Christ* (2004) (a far different cinematic approach to PSA) and audiences' reactions to it, a phenomenon that also highlights the puzzling relationship between violent films and religious viewers. The same audience that frequently decries cinematic violence, conservative Evangelical Protestants, helped make one of the bloodiest films ever committed to celluloid one of the biggest box office successes of all time. One would imagine that conservative Christians would run away from a film described as "the bloodiest, goriest, flesh-rippingest film your church-going grandma will ever want to see."[27] Yet studies reveal that Evangelical Christians are just as likely to watch popular entertainment and are just as attracted to violent productions as their nonreligious counterparts (compared to their more liberal or nonreligious counterparts, it's a third more).[28]

Like *The Hunger Games* that released shortly before it, *The Cabin in the Woods* is yet another example of our cultural obsession with violent ritual sacrifice, even as both films have (female) characters who defy that obsession within the film narratives themselves. Like Katniss Everdeen, Marty and Dana are the focal points of the filmmakers' denouncement of violence against youth. Unfortunately, their efforts are overshadowed by the aestheticized violence of the Hunger Games or the purged system in which they fight to survive. Yamato's assessment of Whedon and Goddard's intentions is spot on and her concluding question seems to beg for more creativity. Yamato's lingering question of "what next" points to one of Prince's suggestions to filmmakers working with violent content: "A critique of violence may be best pursued on screen in its absence, that is, by not showing—at least not in graphic detail—the very phenomenon that a film would address. Otherwise, filmmakers risk that their moral efforts be undone by established characteristics of the medium in which they would work."[29] In light of Prince's reflections and frustrations with the excessive violence in *The Cabin in the Woods*, new questions begin to take shape. Can filmmakers produce nonviolent horror films? Are we in need of a new film genre, or will filmmakers like Whedon and Goddard attempt to reinvent a popular film genre now that they have shut the lid on well-worn versions of it?

Of course, all of this also demands a new way of being in the world, one that even Christian filmgoers might need to embrace: a rejection of violence in all of its forms or at least a louder call for films that are as creative in their approach to reconciliation, for example, as they are to destruction. Unfortunately, we do not have to look too closely to see how *The Cabin in the Woods* parallels our own real world experiences. We are sacrificing way more than five youths to appease a host of gods on a daily basis. Who are they, these sacrificial lambs and the gods to which we sacrifice them? How do we sacrifice them and for what? Why do so many people cling to a theology built around an angry, blood-thirsty god? These are a few tough questions, the answers to which, like the film's scenes of sacrificial rites the world over, will be different both between and within different cultures. And still, two questions linger. When, like the nerd and the virgin in *The Cabin in the Woods*, will we stand up and say enough is enough, and how will filmmakers respond?

Acknowledgment

I would like to thank my coeditor Anthony R. Mills for the conversations and suggestions that helped shape and clarify this essay.

Notes

1. See "Scholastic Announces Updated U.S. Figures for Suzanne Collins's Bestselling The Hunger Games Trilogy," Scholastic, accessed December 17, 2012, http://mediaroom.scholastic.com/press-release/scholastic-announces-updated-us-figures-suzanne-collinss-bestselling-hunger-games-tril; "The Hunger Games," The Numbers, accessed January 25, 2013, http://www.the-numbers.com/movie/Hunger-Games-The.

2. Metahorror is a subset of the horror genre and includes films that are highly self-referential and consciously expose the cinematic conventions that filmmakers use to terrify audiences. The origin of this subgenre lies in Wes Craven's 1996 film *Scream*. There are countless visual and audible allusions to other horror films throughout *Cabin in the Woods*.

3. Splatter or gore films are subgenres of horror films that deliberately focuses on graphic portrayals of violence. Through the use of detailed special effects, these films tend to explicitly focus on the prolonged, theatrical mutilation of the human body. The combination of graphic

violence and sexually suggestive imagery in some films has, more recently, been labeled *torture porn*. While some violent horror films, like George Romero's zombie films, function as social commentary, torture porn often embraces violence for violence's sake, showcasing filmmakers' abilities to envision increasingly gruesome torture scenarios and deaths.
   4. Andrew Sung Park, *Triune Atonement: Christ's Healing for Sinners, Victims, and the Whole Creation* (Louisville: Westminster John Knox Press, 2009), x.
   5. Tony Jones, *A Better Atonement: Beyond the Depraved Doctrine of Original Sin* (Minneapolis: The JoPa Group, 2012), Kindle edition, location 42–44.
   6. Park, *Triune Atonement*, xi.
   7. Though countless theologians have written extensive volumes on atonement theories and salvation, I turn to more recent works from Parks and Jones because they both offer concise summaries of these various theories, the histories of their development, and the ways in which they shape each other, all while searching for and developing a more holistic theory themselves. While elements of satisfaction and last scapegoat theories of atonement are present in *The Cabin in the Woods*, I will limit my discussion here to PSA.
   8. Park, *Triune Atonement*, 23.
   9. Ibid., 24.
   10. Jones, *A Better Atonement*, location 400.
   11. Ibid., location 375.
   12. Ibid., location 623–624.
   13. Park, *Triune Atonement*, 25–26.
   14. Thomas Flamson, "Free Will in a Deterministic Whedonverse," in *The Psychology of Joss Whedon: An Unauthorized Exploration of "Buffy," "Angel," and "Firefly,"* ed. Joy Davidson and Leah Wilson (Dallas: BenBella, 2007), 35.
   15. Ibid., 42.
   16. See Walter Brueggemann, *The Prophetic Imagination*, 2nd edition (Minneapolis: Augsburg Fortress, 2001), 81–100. At the same time, other theologians and philosophers like Rene Girard and Slavoj Žižek, for example, argue that the death of Jesus is an indictment of violent sacrificial practices altogether rather than simply an example of one.
   17. Joy Davidson and Leah Wilson, introduction to *The Psychology of Joss Whedon*, 1.
   18. Ibid., 2.
   19. Cynthia Fuchs, "*The Cabin in the Woods*: You've Been Here Before," PopMatters.com, April 13, 2012, http://www.popmatters.com/pm/review/157199-the-cabin-in-the-woods-youve-been-here-before.
   20. Ibid.
   21. Darren, "Does *Cabin in the Woods* Out-'Hunger Games' *The Hunger Games*?" The m0vieblog, April 19, 2012, http://them0vieblog.com/2012/04/19/does-cabin-in-the-woods-out-hunger-games-the-hunger-games.
   22. Stephen Prince, *Screening Violence* (Piscataway: Rutgers University Press, 2000), Kindle edition, location 408–410.
   23. Frank Burch Brown, *Good Taste, Bad Taste, and Christian Taste: Aesthetics in Religious Life* (New York: Oxford University Press, 2000), 146.
   24. A. O. Scott, "Taking a Chain Saw to Horror Movie Clichés: *The Cabin in the Woods*, by Drew Goddard and Joss Whedon," *The New York Times*, April 12, 2012, http://movies.nytimes.com/2012/04/13/movies/the-cabin-in-the-woods-by-drew-goddard-and-joss-whedon.html?partner=rss&emc=rss.
   25. Jen Yamato, "SXSW: Meta-Horror *Cabin in the Woods* Dismembers, Deconstructs the Genre," movieline.com, March 10, 2012, http://movieline.com/2012/03/10/sxsw-meta-horror-cabin-in-the-woods-dismembers-deconstructs-the-genre-spoilers-redacted.
   26. Joss Whedon, "Let's Watch a Girl Get Beaten to Death," Whedonesque.com, May 20, 2007, http://blog.whedonesque.com/post/20676987522/lets-watch-a-girl-get-beaten-to-death.
   27. Charles Laurence, "After The Passion, Hollywood Asks: What about the sequel?" *The Telegraph*, March 20, 2004, http://www.telegraph.co.uk/news/worldnews/northamerica/usa/1457429/After-The-Passion-Hollywood-asks-what-about-the-sequel.html.

28. Sharon Waxman, "Hollywood's Newfound Passion for Christ," *International Herald Tribune*, July 20, 2005, http://www.iht.com/articles/2005/07/19/business/christians.php?page=1.
29. Prince, *Screening Violence*, location, 414–416.

Bibliography

Brown, Frank Burch. *Good Taste, Bad Taste, and Christian Taste: Aesthetics in Religious Life*. New York: Oxford University Press, 2000.
Brueggemann, Walter. *The Prophetic Imagination*, 2nd edition. Minneapolis: Augsburg Fortress, 2001.
Darren, "Does *Cabin in the Woods* Out-'Hunger Games' *The Hunger Games*?" them0vieblog.com. April 19, 2012. http://them0vieblog.com/2012/04/19/does-cabin-in-the-woods-out-hunger-games-the-hunger-games.
Davidson, Joy, and Leah Wilson. Introduction to *The Psychology of Joss Whedon: An Unauthorized Exploration of "Buffy," "Angel," and "Firefly,"* edited by Joy Davidson and Leah Wilson, 1–6. Dallas: BenBella, 2007.
Flamson, Thomas. "Free Will in a Deterministic Whedonverse." In *The Psychology of Joss Whedon: An Unauthorized Exploration of "Buffy," "Angel," and "Firefly,"* edited by Joy Davidson and Leah Wilson, 35–50. Dallas: BenBella, 2007.
Fuchs, Cynthia. "*The Cabin in the Woods*: You've Been Here Before." PopMatters.com, April 13, 2012. Accessed December 17, 2012. http://www.popmatters.com/pm/review/157199-the-cabin-in-the-woods-youve-been-here-before.
"The Hunger Games." The Numbers. Accessed December 17, 2012. http://www.the-numbers.com/movie/Hunger-Games-The.
Jones, Tony. *A Better Atonement: Beyond the Depraved Doctrine of Original Sin*. Minneapolis: The JoPa Group, 2012. Kindle edition.
Laurence, Charles. "After The Passion, Hollywood Asks: What About the Sequel?" *The Telegraph*, March 20, 2004. http://www.telegraph.co.uk/news/worldnews/northamerica/usa/1457429/After-The-Passion-Hollywood-asks-what-about-the-sequel.html.
Orr, Christopher. "*The Cabin in the Woods* Disembowels the Slasher Film." The Atlantic, April 13, 2012. Accessed December 17, 2012, http://www.theatlantic.com/entertainment/archive/2012/04/the-cabin-in-the-woods-disembowels-the-slasher-film/255810.
Park, Andrew Sung. *Triune Atonement: Christ's Healing for Sinners, Victims, and the Whole Creation*. Louisville: Westminster John Knox Press, 2009.
Prince, Stephen. *Screening Violence*. Piscataway: Rutgers University Press, 2000. Kindle edition.
"Scholastic Announces Updated U.S. Figures for Suzanne Collins's Bestselling The Hunger Games Trilogy." Scholastic. July 19, 2012. http://mediaroom.scholastic.com/press-release/scholastic-announces-updated-us-figures-suzanne-collinss-bestselling-hunger-games-tril.
Scott, A. O. "Taking a Chain Saw to Horror Movie Clichés: *The Cabin in the Woods*, by Drew Goddard and Joss Whedon." *The New York Times*, April 12, 2012. Accessed December 17, 2012. http://movies.nytimes.com/2012/04/13/movies/the-cabin-in-the-woods-by-drew-goddard-and-joss-whedon.html?partner=rss&emc=rss.
Waxman, Sharon. "Hollywood's Newfound Passion for Christ." *International Herald Tribune*, July 20, 2005. Accessed January 25, 2013. http://www.iht.com/articles/2005/07/19/business/christians.php?page=1.
Whedon, Joss. "Let's Watch a Girl Get Beaten to Death." Whedonesque.com, May 20, 2007. Accessed December 17, 2012. http://blog.whedonesque.com/post/20676987522/lets-watch-a-girl-get-beaten-to-death.
Yamato, Jen. "SXSW: Meta-Horror *Cabin in the Woods* Dismembers, Deconstructs the Genre." movieline.com, March 10, 2012. Accessed December 17, 2012. http://movieline.com/2012/03/10/sxsw-meta-horror-cabin-in-the-woods-dismembers-deconstructs-the-genre-spoilers-redacted.

"I'm sorry I ... ended the world"
Eschatology, Nihilism and Hope
in The Cabin in the Woods
W. Scott Poole

"You think you know the story," reads the tagline promo for the critically acclaimed 2012 film *The Cabin in the Woods*, produced and cowritten by Joss Whedon. This wholly original take on the horror genre came as a pleasant surprise to many jaded horror fans. Not only did this new classic, directed by longtime Whedon collaborator Drew Goddard, show us that we didn't really know the story, it analyzed our need for the kinds of stories that horror films tell.

The Cabin in the Woods ends with the destruction of the human race. Its final moments, written entirely by Whedon, display a strange mixture of Whedon's atheism and H. P. Lovecraft's nihilism, a paean to the possibilities of human community. This odd amalgam has a potentially fruitful connection to the work of two late–twentieth-century Christian theologians, Dorothee Soelle and Jürgen Moltmann. Both have also attempted a reimagination of eschatology, one that ties it to the ethics of community and attempts to address the absurdist fatalism that Whedon's body of work often suggests.[1]

This essay seeks to explore Whedon's joyful nihilism and how it naturally intertwines with his narratives of the apocalypse. Rather than simply reading his apocalyptic ponderings in relation to simplistic end-times fundamentalism, it suggests that Whedon's work can be read fruitfully alongside, and against, some of the most sophisticated theological work of the contemporary Christian tradition. Whedon has made creative use of the fantastic to explore the same fields of meaning as some of Christianity's most important recent thinkers. His vision, though often dark and disturbing, offers a thoughtful response to the human condition and suggests the possibility of human community even without the comforts of eschatological hope. Indeed, Whedon's nihilism is not a rejection of meaning or a celebration of moral anarchy, as is often associated with the idea of nihilism. Rather, Whedon follows Sartre, who defined it as the belief that although human life may have no intrinsic value, meaning still must be shaped and created.[2]

Whedon's interest, indeed his artistic obsession, with the theme of the apocalypse has a long history. Beginning with the first season of *Buffy the Vampire Slayer*, Whedon explored the notion of what could be called the *preventable apocalypse*. "If the apocalypse comes, beep me," a pre–cell-phone era, teenaged Buffy quipped back in 1997. The cult hit's narrative arcs tended to center on a major villain (the Big Bad) who attempted a global genocide. Indeed, this conceit played such an important role in the series that Whedon and his writers began to parody it. "It's the apocalypse," solemnly declares Buffy's mentor Giles in season five. "Again?!," cry out Buffy and her friends in unison.

Whedon's 2009 television series *Dollhouse* explored similar ideas in a very different context. In the unaired episode "Epitaph One," Whedon and his writers imagined a technological apocalypse triggered by the malfeasance of an underground military–corporate collective. Much as in *Buffy*, the apocalypse of *Dollhouse* never allowed the narrative of social chaos to overwhelm the thematic importance of human connection and friendship. But Whedon made full use of the idea that humanity lacked the moral maturity to use new technology and that the aftermath of social breakdown would be anarchic, violent, and terrifying.

The Cabin in the Woods takes the idea of apocalypse further than Whedon has ever gone before, drawing the curtain on humanity in an explosive roar of human extinction reminiscent of horror maestro H. P. Lovecraft. An early twentieth-century New England author, Lovecraft wrote for pulps such as *Weird Tales* in the 1920s, brewing a horrifying cocktail of interdimensional monsters and cosmic terror. Lovecraft has exercised enormous influence over the horror genre with his blend of creeping terror and elements of science fiction and an insistence that the human race means little in relation to an indifferent universe. Lovecraft imagined a cosmos full of beings, "Great Old Ones," who had once inhabited the human world and would at some point reclaim it. His vision of cosmic horror included the notion that these beings would simply destroy the human race, not from malice but from sheer indifference.[3]

In fact, despite Lovecraft's ability to describe slimy, reptilian, physically horrifying ancient powers, his real interest lay in creating a nihilistic universe where human beings' sense of insignificance in relation to the cosmos drives them to madness. Tim Airaksinen describes Lovecraft's stories as "texts that preach their own gods in a universe where no god can find his niche."[4] The vast and empty space at the heart of existence, an arctic void of nothingness, constitutes the real horror.

Lovecraft haunts much of Whedon's work. In fact, Drew Goddard has said that he and Whedon discussed having a specific reference to the Lovecraftian god Cthulhu as one of the giant evil gods of *Cabin in the Woods*.[5] The mythology behind *Buffy* suggests that humanity came late to the game with regard to life on earth, born into a world dominated by demons not so different from Lovecraft's elder gods. The first vampires are, in fact, born of similarly described "great old ones." *Cabin* also features "dark old ones," the giant evil gods who must be placated by sacrifices of the young, endlessly repeated.

In *Buffy*, the dark ones waiting beneath the earth are defeated, without fail, through a combination of courage and sacrifice. In *Cabin*, however, the ancient evil does rise and humanity comes to a cataclysmic end. This conclusion surprised some who, while used to Whedon's apocalyptic fixations, also expected to see from him the averted apocalypse of *Buffy*, which also appeared regularly in the *Buffy* spinoff *Angel*. Whedon himself has noted this difference in *Cabin*, describing the end of the film as "an apocalypse that's straight up ... an apocalypse with no extras."[6]

This ending suggests an element of Whedon's thought often hinted at in his narratives and in interviews but seldom fully explored. Here, enemies can sometimes see themes better than friends. Conservative religious critics attacked the ending of *Cabin* as nihilistic, based on a hatred of humanity they denominated as a hatred of God's creation. A reviewer for the highly conservative *National Catholic Register* (connected with the equally conservative Eternal Word Television Network), described *The Cabin in the Woods* as "literally antihuman." Suggesting that the film "cynically invites you to enjoy the destruction of people," the reviewer argued that Whedon's atheism played a significant role in his dim view of human existence.[7]

Anyone with much knowledge of the themes of Whedon's work knows that drawing the curtain on humanity with a bit of misanthropic spite is actually nothing new for the writer/director/producer. His oeuvre has always tended to display very strong nihilistic tendencies, often hidden behind whipsmart dialogue and sudden, and sometimes unexpected, moments of whimsical sweetness.

Nihilism and a conception of the absurd turn up in unexpected places in Whedon's corpus. *Firefly*, the short-lived cult favorite science fiction series, seems the most optimistic example of his television work, with no apocalypse in sight. And yet its hero Mal, the captain of the firefly-class starship Serenity, exudes bitterness over everything from politics to religious faith to love. In the deeply philosophical episode "Objects in Space," River Tam displays the ability to see behind the other characters' words into their deepest thoughts and even the root feelings that lie beneath their thoughts. Through her eyes we see Mal looking at Inara, the woman he loves and who may be leaving the ship and his life forever, and thinking, "none of it means a damn thing." Television and film critic Emily Nussbaum describes the character of Mal as "a man of action frozen by his conviction that nothing matters." Whedon describes his hero as "a man who looks into the void and sees nothing but the void."[8] In other words, a hero that Camus and Sartre might have imagined.

Whedon's nihilistic tendencies are tied to a view of human experience that conjoins the irony of suffering with the need for compassion. In this way his work departs from Lovecraftian nihilism, which makes an analysis of it in relation to specific kinds of theological reflection meaningful. Like some modern Christian theological reflection, he has attempted to reimagine the mythos surrounding eschatology. For example, the ending of *Buffy* season six, in many ways so similar and yet so different from the conclusion of *The Cabin in the Woods*, gives us an early sign of how dark Whedon could go and the strange glimmer of love and compassion for human suffering that could outline that darkness.

Both seasons six and seven of *Buffy* are frequently held up as examples of Whedon's willingness to rework conventional television conceits by endangering his characters and thus complicating fan affection for the show. Season six proved especially troubling, and especially moving, along these lines. The Big Bad of the season turned out to be one of the show's heroes, Buffy's powerful Wiccan friend Willow. Utterly stricken with grief after the death of her beloved partner Tara, Willow becomes a conduit for incredibly powerful dark energies that threaten to destroy her, her friends, and the world.

Willow is ultimately driven to attempt this monstrous act because the powerful magics she has summoned allow her a penetrating insight into the absurdity of human existence. "I'm connected to everything," she says after getting juiced with a blast of mystical energy, "I can feel ... everyone." But Willow's ability to see into the heart of human existence opens to her unimaginable horrors that drive her to attempt magical mass murder: "Oh my God ... the emotion ... the pain," she wails, "it's just too much. I have to stop this. I have to make it go away.... Poor bastards ... your suffering has to end" ("Grave").

It's here that Whedon's understanding of human suffering most resonates with the concerns of Moltmann and Soelle and also where we see them in sharp relief. Both theologians share Whedon's interest in tying the suffering of humanity and the world to conceptions of the apocalypse. Both have attempted to rework the New Testament conceptions of eschatology in ways that would make these ancient narratives into sites of reflection about compassion and social ethics.

Joss Whedon has never given any indication that he has studied Christian theology beyond noting "that the Christian mythos has a powerful fascination for me."[9] Moreover, and perhaps obviously, there's no reason to believe that he has the slightest awareness of the work of Moltmann and Soelle. And yet, many of his ideas about the nature of history, particularly the end of history and its ethical possibilities, resonate with their deeply theological conceptions. Reading them alongside one another reveals the depths of each and shows how Whedon differs fairly radically from Lovecraftian conceptions of nihilism. At the same time, what we could call Whedon's "*a*theology" points to some of the limits of the Christian theological tradition, even the work of interpreters of that tradition like Soelle and Moltmann who have attempted to go beyond dogma to map fundamental aspects of the human experience.

Whedon has made his atheism clear in numerous interviews, though he has nuanced this position by defining it as a literal a-theism, a rejection of the claims of theism, rather than an antithetical attitude toward the sacred or even toward religious practice. Although he once described himself as "a hardline, angry atheist" he also has a special fascination and desire to explore what he calls "the concept of devotion." Whedon has acknowledged that the "mythical structures" of a variety of religious traditions continue to resonate with most people and sees his own work as, in part, creating narratives that creatively borrow from those structures and put them to new purposes.[10]

Whedon has further outlined his own philosophical position as a nihilism rooted in a deeply felt sense of the absurd. In this, some of his religious critics have it right. He has described this position in basically existentialist terms, speaking of a point in his life when he discovered what he calls "the joy, terror and misery" that comes from the "ecstasy of a meaningless existence." Camus's *Myth of Sisyphus* and Sartre's *Nausea* are central texts in the formation of his belief system.[11]

These ideas appear throughout his work. Indeed, in *Angel*, Whedon sought to turn his vampire with a soul into Albert Camus's "saint without God" from the 1947 novel *The Plague*. Angel seeks redemption from his vampiric past, but it's not redemption that comes from the heavens. The Powers that Be, as the closest things to divine beings in the Buffyverse are called, seem uncaring, uncertain, and mostly uninvolved in human affairs. This leaves Angel with the option of noble action in a universe where it may make little difference to the outcome of the cosmic struggle and may or may not result in his own redemption. "I want to help because people shouldn't suffer as they do," Angel explains in "Epiphany." "Because if there is no bigger meaning, then the smallest act of kindness is the greatest thing in the world."

These do not seem like the roots from which a rich set of fantasy universes might grow. But, in truth, it's this nihilistic sense of the universe that gives

Whedon's work its depth and meaning. Although *The Cabin in the Woods* can be read in part as an unveiling of a richly textured Lovecraftian mythology of world history, it also hides ultimate meaning. Who are these giant evil gods and why do they demand the sacrifice they do? Doesn't their existence obviate any human system of meaning? In fact, the existence of the shadow organization that seeks to preserve the human race seems like a metaphor for a failed effort to extricate or embody meaning. Designed like a 1950s fallout shelter with pre–Apple tech of knobs, buttons, and flashing lights, the work of the unnamed organization that tries to keep the sacrifice to the dark gods going seems to suggest obsolescence and a failure at holding back the tides of nonmeaning.

The universe of Joss Whedon, packed with all manner of gods and demons, speaks ironically as a testament to the vacuity of existence; its essential emptiness. In this, Whedon's nihilism of the fantastic follows political and cultural theorist Fredric Jameson's notion that because of the postmodern condition, "the place of the fantastic" becomes "a marked absence at the heart of the secular world."[12] In other words, in a universe that seems vacuumed of human-centered meaning (it's unclear what other kind of meaning we could grasp or that would matter if we could grasp it), images of transcendence (e.g., gods and devils) become question marks and empty signifiers. Fantasy characters become symbols of emptiness little more than the brightly colored and heavily symbolic figures of a medieval miracle play. In this view, the realm of fantasy serves as the harshest of reminders that such things are not real, that events may be random, and that the universe might not care to answer our existential questions.

Clearly Whedon's worldview has little place for the claims of Christian theology. Indeed, his work has made this more than plain. Though references to Christian systems of meaning play no role in *Cabin*, *Buffy* kept up a running critique of traditional religion, connecting it to evil vampire cults, bloody underground rituals, and, in the final season, the ultimate incarnation of evil empowering a misogynistic preacher. Wendy Love Anderson has argued that "what is striking about the Buffyverse's conception of religion is how regularly and frequently it is demonized.... [Religious] activity ... signals the presence of demons or other forces of evil."[13]

However, Whedon's fascination with and repulsion by the Christian apocalyptic combined with his absurdist philosophy allows for an interesting comparison with Moltmann and Soelle, who have themselves questioned the viability of certain contemporary notions of eschatology. Both thinkers hope to rediscover certain elements of the Christian message that gel with modernity's concerns. Indeed, at least one strand of twentieth century theology can be described as an ongoing effort to come to grips with the aggressive claims of modernity, the expansion of scientific knowledge, and the undeniable historical relativity of Christianity's scriptures and its traditions. European Protestantism, forced to confront both the demands and horrors of modernity after two world wars, has attempted to reframe and reimagine its most sacred traditions.

The works of Karl Barth and Rudolph Bultmann, though radically different in their orientation and conclusions, both sought to map the geography of what Barth called "the world of the Bible" in response to both post–Enlightenment liberalism and twentieth-century fundamentalisms. Much of what they and many other European theologians produced came to be loosely categorized with the label *neoorthodoxy* for its efforts to come to grips with the challenge of modernity while also shaping a Christian message that offered a piquant critique of many aspects of post–Enlightenment experience.[14]

Moltmann's work emerged in the post–World War II era, heavily influenced by the neoorthodox interest in thinking about the Christian revelation as historical while also criticizing its unwillingness to engage in the actual trials of history. Early on, Moltmann sought to link a concern for social justice with an eschatological understanding of history and suggested that what he saw as openness to the future represented a basic Christian posture. In this he was deeply influenced by the ideas of Marxist philosopher Ernst Bloch who wrote of the "principle of hope" as integral to any politically meaningful conception of history. The seemingly desperate nature of human history had hidden possibilities tied to the ethics of community.[15]

Moltmann's first major work, *Theology of Hope*, expanded on these themes and created a conception of Christian eschatology that transformed simplistic ideas of the apocalypse from a story about the end of history into a narrative about a revolutionary openness to history. He argued against any conception of human history that saw it as a closed system, either in a secular and materialist sense or in a religiomythical sense that turned history into a simple narrative of God's revelation, a timeline of God's intervention in human affairs. Instead, insisted Moltmann, history could only be understood in relation to "the possibilities of good and evil." Christian proclamation, he argued, doesn't assume history as a dead letter, but as something awaiting a fundamental transformation.[16]

Moltmann's understanding of the role played by hope in human history did not blind him to the realities of suffering or to the nihilistic possibilities that the human experience of history awakens. In his second major work, *The Crucified God*, he explored the relationship between human suffering and history. Describing his own generation as "shattered and broken" by the events of the Second World War, he argued that the Christian church should adopt a prophetic stance of criticism toward society that grows out of a sense of the

Crucifixion as the basic experience of the divine in the world and at that particular moment in history: "A theology that would not speak to us in the sight of the one who was abandoned and crucified would have had nothing to say to us then."[17]

Moltmann also directly engaged the kind of pessimistic absurdism that would influence Whedon. In *Theology of Hope*, he contended that the bourgeois post–Christian West wore a mask of "smiling resignation." Moltmann diagnosed this sense of existential despair as a false realism, a "positivistic realism" that did not allow for the possibility of something new in history. In fact, Moltmann offered a powerful critique of modern pessimistic absurdism when he described it as an addiction to seeing the world as "a fixed body of facts" rather than a set of "processes" in which change could occur. Moltmann views the nihilist as a kind of fundamentalist of positivism, so certain of the fact that they are unable to allow for the possibility that history contains the powers of a future that belongs to God.[18]

Dorothee Soelle pursued her interests in social justice and the theological meaning of suffering in the context created by both Moltmann's "theology of hope" and the rise of the "death of God" theology of the 1960s. An activist against the Vietnam War and a staunch advocate for economic justice in and toward the developing world, Soelle carried out her theological work in constant conversation with the darkest aspects of human experience. For her, the concept of God needed rescuing from conceptions of the divine that made it an authoritarian presence on a throne that presided over a world of genocide and death squads. In her seminal work on this topic, *Suffering*, she defines traditional theological ideas about the meaning of human pain as a kind of "Christian sadism," the notion that God creates suffering and uses it to torture the godly and ungodly alike.[19]

Like Moltmann, Soelle argued for a Christian eschatology that emphasizes the idea of hope. Also like him, her work reimagined the idea of personal eschatology or life after death in such a way that it proved unrecognizable to Christians who believe in the notion of a literal heaven. Writing in her unfinished work of meditation on the meaning of death (begun as she herself lay dying), Soelle raised doubts about whether the Christian idea of eternal life really had to mean anything like personal immortality. Promises of reunion with the beloved dead in a heaven of bliss seemed to her a kind of blank check human beings yearned to write themselves, a denial of finitude.

In this way, Soelle actually made use of certain strands of the early Christian tradition that focused primarily on the resurrection of the body rather than the immortality of the soul. Moltmann has also described the resurrection as anything but an individual experience. Indeed, in his view the resurrection of Christ "was not a fortuitous miracle" but rather an announcement made by God that history contained the processes that would lead to the transformation of the cosmos. The death of the historical Jesus, Moltmann believes, points toward the eschatological future of the Christ and thus the redemption of the human world and of creation. In this way, he united the Christian conception of Jesus's resurrection with a promised future of peace and justice, a world and a history remade.[20]

In place of doctrines of personal immortality that seem to confirm Freud's critique of Christianity as an "immortality system," both Moltmann and Soelle imagine the possibility of a theology of death that removes the focus from the self and transforms the hatred of death into a protest against the unjust death of others. Christian concepts of compassion and social justice, Soelle argued, made the "immortality system" of Christian belief obsolete. The protest on the lips of Christians should not be against death as a physical fact but rather death embodied in the social structures that kill, maim, and torture. Human finitude, at least one's own personal finitude, becomes a question of little import.[21]

Soelle, following this line of thought, urged Christians to reject simplistic notions of bodily resurrection and argued that the idea really had nothing to do with individual salvation or the resuscitation of corpses. In her view, biblical faith encouraged believers to think about the resurrection of the dead as working for "the coming of ... God's justice."[22] The struggle against genocide, war, poverty, and inequality takes the place of hopes for otherworldly bliss. Moltmann makes a similar point in his work *The Spirit of Life*. The resurrection becomes something that believers in Jesus experience in the present. It is the "spirit of liberation and rebirth" that allows followers of Jesus to fight for social justice.[23]

Both Soelle and Moltmann viewed their work as an effort to fashion an eschatology that presented to believers and unbelievers alike a vision of history that holds inherent meaning. Moltmann believed, for example, that his emphasis on the suffering God, crucified along with humanity, offered an alternative to "the grimace of absurdity and nothingness" offered by nihilistic atheism. Although he sympathized with atheism's "protest" against the idea of a God presiding over a suffering world, he also worried that a rejection of the sorrowful God entailed a deep misunderstanding of the God of the Bible (a misunderstanding he freely admitted that much Christian theology had shared and propagated).[24]

The kind of "smiling resignation" that Moltmann critiqued seems perfectly expressed in Whedon's corpus, especially *Cabin in the Woods*. Whedon's work has sought to completely reinterpret Christian myths of the apocalypse in line with his own views about the future prospects of humanity and ethics in the face of annihilation. It's important to note that Whedon's notions of the apocalypse, at least of the type he reacted against, seems to be influenced by the transatlantic phenomenon of *premillennialism* (especially represented by certain Evangelical varieties expressed in the work of Hal Lindsey and in the popular *Left Behind* series). Growing out of the American and British Evangelical and Pentecostal movements, the notion of a sudden end of the world that includes fire and blood for the lost and ungodly has exercised an enormous influence over much of conservative Christianity in both the Western and the developing worlds.

Thus Whedon's critique grew out of a confrontation with a simplistic, though widely influential, concept of eschatology. His own apocalyptic imaginings completely reworked this schema. In *Buffy*, he took the idea of a "chosen one," a messianic conception common to patriarchal religious systems, and made the chosen Buffy Summers, "the one girl in all the world." At the end of the series, he radically restructured religious mythologies of anointed ones by imagining the special powers of the slayers distributed to all the girls of the world. Predetermined eschatologies are defeated, including those brought on by prophecies and religious cults. In season six, as noted above, it's the love of two friends for one another that averts the destruction of the world.

The Cabin in the Woods ignores the possibility of personal eschatology and offers a full-throated challenge to the idea of a collective eschatology. Community does not mean the salvation of the world but rather an expression of human empathy that takes place on the brink of destruction. The world comes to an end with dark gods rising and a highly uncomplimentary elegy for the human race. Marty, the moral heart of the film that makes the decision to let humanity be destroyed rather than killing his friend and perpetuating a cruel system of sacrifice, apologizes to Dana in the film's final moments: "I'm sorry I let you get attacked by a werewolf and ended the world," he says through a haze of the last joint smoked on earth. "Humanity," Dana says with a "pfft," "It's time to give someone else a chance." As the floor bulges and cracks and dark old ones rise to the earth to devour the world, Dana reaches out her hand and Marty grasps it. They hold for a long moment as love and friendship seal the moment. But this moment of human connection does not save the world or function as anything resembling a principle of hope.

Such an ending certainly separates Whedon's sense of the universe's possibilities definitively from the work of Soelle and Moltmann. Both theologians imagined a kind of inherent hopefulness about the structures of reality. Both imagined a God of hope who gifted the human race with a future rich with potentiality. Moltmann, more than Soelle, emphasizes the action of God for this hopeful future as Soelle puts more emphasis on the role of human beings becoming partners with God in alleviating the suffering of the world.[25]

Neither ultimately faced the extreme possibility suggested by *The Cabin in the Woods*: the idea that all struggles are essentially fruitless but that this very fact gives them value and meaning. Whedon and Goddard's reworking of the struggle against the apocalypse, a creative act that includes significantly reimagining elements of their own oeuvre, reveals something of the limits of Christian theology's usefulness in the investigation of the dark possibilities of the human future. The Lovecraftian dark gods of *The Cabin in the Woods* have a will as inexorable and blind to human concerns as ecological crisis, climate change, and all the other possible variables that could call time on the human race. Unlike Moltmann and Soelle, the narrative Whedon and Goddard spin does not imagine an inherent goodness to the cosmic will. Instead, the human race is going down.

But annihilation doesn't have to come with a howl of despair, however. Here, Whedon departs from both his Lovecraftian influences and the Christian narrative that would seek to deny, or perhaps simply cloak, nihilism with various theologies of hope. Unlike Lovecraft's characters who "have looked upon all the universe has to hold of horror" and been driven to frenzy and insanity, Whedon's share a joint at the end of the world, accept their fate, and seal their friendship with one another by holding hands.

"We want to believe that we'll be able to go on forever," Whedon has said, "that when we die there will be ice cream and cake and we'll play hooky every day."[26] Soelle and Moltmann's theological reimaginings of personal and collective eschatology are thoughtful efforts to present Christian eschatology in meaningful language. They both recognize that the images of an eternal heaven for eternal souls do nothing to answer the human dread of finitude or tell us much about how to live in this world. They also are aware that death does not mean ice cream and cake and playing hooky every day.

Yet both theologians also rely on conceptions of a "theology of hope" and a "kingdom of God" in which positing a brand of hopeful theism proves absolutely necessary. Their emphasis on the idea of hope, the possibility that history will unleash a cosmic transformation, depends utterly on the idea of God's intervention in history. In both cases, the resurrection of Christ functions as the *deus ex machina*, an eschatological event in history that points toward the kingdom of God as both present and breaking into historical experience.

Ultimately, both seem to be addressing the emptiness of the void with an intermixture of political action and a somewhat vague, but deeply held, messianic hope. "Messianism," writes Moltmann, "is made concrete through the production of real utopias." Here he borrows further from the work of Ernst Bloch, who believed that social action on behalf of democratic socialism both anticipated, and left unfulfilled, what he called "the leap into the wholly Other."[27]

The Cabin in the Woods tells a different story. Its imagery of shadow organizations that practice supreme cruelty in order to keep the human race going points to the structural cruelties and systemic injustices that Soelle and Moltmann rightfully protest against. But its vision of human connection at the end of the world offers something very different from what Moltmann calls "an openness to the future of God" or the idea that "the world is not yet finished."[28] *Cabin*'s eschatology proposes that human beings can build community without a principle of hope. They can face the void of history, and of their own personal histories, and still hold hands.

Whedon thus challenges Moltmann's view that the building of a human community must be built on a baptized version of Ernst Bloch's principle of hope. Moltmann argued for a future grounded in the resurrection in which even the death of the victims of history has been explained. Moltmann writes in *The Crucified God* that in the suffering of Jesus, connected to the eschaton in the resurrection, "even Auschwitz is taken up into the grief of the Father, the surrender of the Son and the power of the Spirit."[29] Although moving as a kind of theological poetry and grounded in an effort to reimagine theodicy, it's impossible to see what meaning such an idea provides for those who see in Auschwitz yet more proof of the nonexistence of the loving God Moltmann needs to intervene in history (or at the end of history) for such a statement to express meaning. And yet, Whedon's pessimism, while offering no metaphysical answers, offers the creation of community around a sense of meaninglessness. No small feat and yet one grounded in the willingness to face the harsh possibilities of human existence unflinchingly.

"You eventually get to a place where you realize you aren't the point," Whedon told the Harvard Humanist Chaplaincy in a 2009 speech. "You can get to a place," he added, "where you realize that when your time is up, the worms are hungry ... and kinda cute." This is an atheology of hope, a joyful nihilism that refuses to surrender to despair ... even if the weekend ends with giant evil gods rising.[30]

Notes

1. Goddard describes Whedon as being entirely responsible for the writing of the final scene in the *The Cabin in the Woods* director's commentary.

2. See Jean Paul Sartre, *Existentialism is a Humanism* (New Haven: Yale University Press, 2007); and *Joss Whedon: Conversations*, ed. David Lavery and Cynthia Burkhead (Jackson: University Press of Mississippi, 2011), 68.

3. S. T. Joshi, introduction to *The Annotated Lovecraft* (New York: Dell, 1997).

4. Timo Airaksinen, *The Philosophy of H. P. Lovecraft: The Route to Horror* (New York: Peter Lang, 1999), 215.

5. Marc Savlov, "The Scare Game: Drew Goddard and Joss Whedon on what went wrong with Horror and where to Go from Here," *Austin Chronicle,* March 12, 2012.

6. Joss Whedon and Drew Goddard, *The Cabin in the Woods: The Official Visual Companion* (New York: Titan Books, 2012), 41.
7. Matt Archbold, "I Think This Movie Hates People," *National Catholic Register*, April 15, 2012.
8. Whedon, *Conversations*, 69.
9. Whedon on message board "The Bronze"; quoted in Wendy Love Anderson, "Prophecy Girl and the Powers That Be: The Philosophy of Religion in the Buffyverse," in *Buffy the Vampire Slayer and Philosophy: Fear and Trembling in Sunnydale*, ed. by James B. South (Chicago: Open Court, 2003), 213.
10. Whedon, *Conversations*, 68–69.
11. David Baggett, "*Firefly* and Freedom," in *The Philosophy of Joss Whedon*, ed. Dean A. Kowalski and S. Evan Kreider (Lexington: University Press of Kentucky, 2011), 10, 11.
12. Fredric Jameson, *The Political Unconscious: Narrative as a Socially Symbolic Act* (Ithaca: Cornell University Press, 1981), 134–135.
13. Wendy Love Anderson, "Prophecy Girl," 214.
14. *Neoorthodox* may seem inappropriate to describe such radically different theologians as Barth and Bultmann. It's important to note, however, that both actually rejected the label and others used it to describe both them and a larger theological cohort. Moreover, many of their differences emerged out of different readings of Emil Brunner (who influenced both) and from different conclusions about the nature of the Christian *kerygma*. Both, however, understood their work as a rediscovery of *kerygma* in "the world of the Bible." In fact, Bernd Jaspert's introduction to *Karl Barth/Rudolph Bultmann: Letters, 1922–1961* (Edinburgh: T&T Clark, 1982), suggests that the two worked in tandem to answer similar questions posed by the twentieth century to Christian theology, although they reached very different conclusions (see pages x, xi).
15. Moltmann details his debt to Bloch in *Theology of Hope* (New York: Harper & Row, 1967), 16, 208. See also his chapter entitled "'Where There Is Hope, There Is Religion': Ernest Bloch," in Jürgen Moltmann, *History and the Triune God* (New York: Crossroads Press, 1992), 143–155.
16. Moltmann, *Theology of Hope*, 283.
17. Jürgen Moltmann, *The Crucified God* (San Francisco: HarperSanFrancisco, 1991), 1.
18. Moltmann, *Theology of Hope*, 23–25.
19. Dorothee Soelle, *Suffering* (Philadelphia: Fortress, 1975), 24, 25
20. Moltmann, *Crucified God*, 162–165.
21. Dorothee Soelle, *The Mystery of Death* (Minneapolis; Fortress, 2007), 30–40.
22. Ibid., 92.
23. Jürgen Moltmann, *The Spirit of Life: A Universal Affirmation* (Minneapolis: Fortress, 1993), 270 272.
24. Moltmann, *Crucified God*, 219, 226–227.
25. Soelle, *Suffering*, 150–152.
26. Joss Whedon, "Speech to Harvard Humanist Chaplaincy," accessed October 24, 2012, http://www.thenewhumanism.org/authors/video/articles/joss-whedon-cultural-humanis.
27. Moltmann, *History and the Triune God*, 149–151.
28. Moltmann, *Theology of Hope*, 338.
29. Moltmann, *Crucified God*, 278.
30. Whedon, "Speech."

Bibliography

Airaksinen, Timo. *The Philosophy of H. P. Lovecraft: The Route to Horror*. New York: Peter Lang, 1999.
Anderson, Wendy Love. "Prophecy Girl and the Powers That Be: The Philosophy of Religion

in the Buffyverse." In *Buffy the Vampire Slayer and Philosophy: Fear and Trembling in Sunnydale*, edited by James B. South, 212–226. Chicago: Open Court, 2003.
Archbold, Matt. "I Think this Movie Hates People." *National Catholic Register*, April 15, 2012.
Baggett, David. "*Firefly* and Freedom." In *The Philosophy of Joss Whedon*, edited by Dean A. Kowalski and S. Evan Kreider, 9–23. Lexington: University Press of Kentucky, 2011.
Jameson, Fredric. *The Political Unconsciousness: Narrative as Socially Symbolic Act*. Ithaca: Cornell University Press, 1981.
Jaspert, Bernd. Introduction to *Karl Barth/Rudolph Bultmann: Letters, 1922–1961*. Edinburgh: T&T Clark, 1982.
Joshi, S. T. *The Annotated Lovecraft*. New York: Dell, 1997.
Moltmann, Jürgen. *The Crucified God*. San Francisco: HarperSanFrancisco, 1991.
_____. *History and the Triune God*. New York: Crossroads, 1992.
_____. *The Spirit of Life: A Universal Affirmation*. Minneapolis: Fortress, 1993.
_____. *Theology of Hope*. New York: Harper & Row, 1967.
Sartre, Jean Paul. *Existentialism Is a Humanism*. New Haven: Yale University Press, 2007.
Savlov, Marc. "The Scare Game: Drew Goddard and Joss Whedon on What Went Wrong with Horror and Where to Go from Here." *Austin Chronicle*, March 12, 2012.
Soelle, Dorothee. *The Mystery of Death*. Minneapolis: Fortress, 2007.
_____. *Suffering*. Philadelphia: Fortress, 1975.
Whedon, Joss. *Joss Whedon: Conversations*, edited by Cynthia Burkhead and David Lavery. Jackson: University Press of Mississippi, 2011.
_____. "Speech to Harvard Humanist Chaplaincy." Accessed October 24, 2012. http://www.thenewhumanism.org/authors/video/articles/joss-whedon-cultural-humanis.
_____, and Drew Goddard. *The Cabin in the Woods: The Official Visual Companion*. New York: Titan Books, 2012.

About the Contributors

Hope K. **Bartel** is a freelance copyeditor, proofreader and artist. She holds a B.F.A. in studio arts with an emphasis in painting from Biola University, and membership in the Torrey Honors Institute. She sees her professional practice as informal research into the comprehensibility of variations of English language usage. Her visual practice focuses on studies of line, light and shadow in graphite and ink.

Timothy E. G. **Bartel** is a Ph.D. candidate in the Institute for Theology, Imagination, and the Arts at the University of Saint Andrews, where he specializes in American poetry and the writings of the Church Fathers. He holds an M.F.A. in poetry from Seattle Pacific University and his work has appeared in *Christianity and Literature, Saint Katherine Review, Relief,* and *The Other Journal.* His first book of poems, *The Martyr, the Grizzly, the Gold,* was published in 2012.

Julie **Clawson** is a writer and frequent speaker on the topics of faith, culture, and justice. She has a master's degree in intercultural studies and missions from Wheaton Graduate School and is studying theology at Seminary of the Southwest. She is the author of *Everyday Justice: The Global Impact of Our Daily Choices* (2009) and *"The Hunger Games" and the Gospel: Bread, Circuses, and the Kingdom of God* (2012).

Russell W. **Dalton** is an associate professor of Christian education at Brite Divinity School in Fort Worth, Texas. He holds advanced degrees from Union Presbyterian Seminary and Harvard Divinity School. He is the author of *Marvelous Myths: Marvel Superheroes and Everyday Faith* (2011) and *Faith Journey through Fantasy Lands: A Christian Dialogue with Harry Potter, Star Wars and The Lord of the Rings* (2003), along with other books, essays, and articles.

Desirée **de Jesus** is a Ph.D. student in the Mel Hoppenheim School of Cinema at Concordia University. For her M.A. thesis she placed the philosophical anthropology of Stanley Kubrick's films in dialogue with St. Augustine's theory of the will (King's College London, 2012). Her primary research interests are philosophy and film phenomenology, feminist film theory, transnational cinemas, theology, and ethnicity and race.

Susanne E. **Foster** is an associate professor of philosophy at Marquette University. Though her main research work is in environmental philosophy and virtue theory, she has a developing interest in philosophy of popular culture. She has coauthored three pieces on Whedon's work with James South, in *The Philosophy of Joss Whedon* (2011), *Homer Simpson Ponders Politics* (2013), and the present collection. Her next popular culture project focuses on the work of Terry Pratchett.

Dean A. **Kowalski** is an associate professor of philosophy at the University of Wisconsin–Waukesha, and serves as chair of the UW–Colleges philosophy department. He is the author of *Classic Questions and Contemporary Film* (2004) and *Moral Theory at the Movies* (2012). He is the editor of *The Philosophy of "The X-Files"* (2007), *Steven Spielberg and Philosophy* (2008), and *"The Big Bang Theory" and Philosophy* (2012); and the coeditor of *The Philosophy of Joss Whedon* (2011).

Valerie **Mayhew** is a graduate of New York City's prestigious drama division of the Juilliard School as well as an alumnus of Fuller Seminary in Pasadena, California, where she was a Brehm Scholar at the Brehm Center for Worship, Theology, and the Arts. As a television writer/producer, she worked on such shows as *The X-Files* and *Charmed*, among others. She is a cofounder of the Whole Artist Studio in Glendale, California.

John C. **McDowell** is the Morpeth Professor of Theology and Religious Studies at the University of Newcastle in Australia and was the Meldrum Lecturer in Theology at the University of Edinburgh. Educated at Aberdeen and Cambridge, he is the author of *The Gospel According to "Star Wars": Faith, Hope and the Force* (2007) and *Hope in Barth's Eschatology* (2000); the editor of *Philosophy and the Burden of Theological Honesty: A Donald MacKinnon Reader* (2011); and the coeditor of *Conversing with Barth* (2004).

Anthony R. **Mills** received a Ph.D. in theology and culture from Fuller Seminary. His dissertation was published in 2013 by Routledge as *American Theology, Superhero Comics, and Cinema: The Marvel of Stan Lee and the Revolution of a Genre*. He is also a contributor to poptheology.com and keeps a blog at transgressive spaces.blogspot.com.

John W. **Morehead** is a scholar working in the area of religion and popular culture. He has contributed to a number of journals and books, coedited and contributed to *The Undead and Theology* (2012), and writes for his blog TheoFantastique.com as well as Cinefantastique Online.

J. Ryan **Parker** is the creator, editor, and main contributor of Pop Theology (www.poptheology.com). He has a Ph.D. in religion and the arts from the Graduate Theological Union in Berkeley, California, with a focus on particularly the history of religious cinema and contemporary independent religious films. He is the author of *Cinema as Pulpit: Sherwood Pictures and the Church Film Movement*

(2012) and has contributed chapters to *Light Shining in a Dark Place: Discovering Theology through Film* (2012) and *The Undead and Theology* (2012).

J. Leavitt **Pearl** is completing a Ph.D. at Duquesne University in Pittsburgh, Pennsylvania. His primary research focuses upon the relationship between the "theological turn" of French phenomenology and medieval mystical theology, as well as the phenomenology of the body.

W. Scott **Poole** is an associate professor of history at the College of Charleston, where he teaches courses on the concept of Satan in the Western world and seminars on horror and popular culture. He wrote *Monsters in America: Our Historic Obsession with the Hideous and the Haunting* (2011), winner of the Popular Culture Association's 2011 John G. Cawelti award. He is writing a cultural biography of Maila Nurmi (better known as Vampira).

Jeremy R. **Ricketts** is an assistant professor of English at Bethel University in Tennessee, where he teaches American literature, writing, and humanities courses. He completed his doctorate in American studies at the University of New Mexico with a focus on religion and culture. His research interests include representations of religion, spirituality and irreligion; popular culture; memoir; and visual culture. He has published articles on such subjects as sacred space and Mormonism.

James B. **South** is an associate professor and chair of the Philosophy Department at Marquette University. He is the editor of the journal *Philosophy and Theology*. He edited *Buffy the Vampire Slayer and Philosophy* (2003) and co-edited *James Bond and Philosophy* (2006), *Buffy Goes Dark* (2009), and *"Mad Men" and Philosophy* (2010), and has written essays on movies, comic books, and popular music, and extensively in late medieval and renaissance philosophy.

Roslyn **Weaver** holds a Ph.D. in literature from the University of Wollongong in Australia. She is the author of *Apocalypse in Australian Fiction and Film: A Critical Study* (2011) and the coauthor of *Werewolves and Other Shapeshifters in Popular Culture: A Thematic Analysis of Recent Depictions* (2012), with Kimberley McMahon-Coleman. Her research and publishing interests include speculative fiction, religion, children's literature, and the medical humanities.

Jason Lawton **Winslade** holds a Ph.D. in performance studies from Northwestern University. He teaches courses on the works of Whedon at DePaul University as an adjunct member of the department of Writing, Rhetoric, and Discourse. He offers seminars on occultism and Paganism, comic books, and popular culture and he has published in various journals and anthologies, including *Slayage* and *Buffy in the Classroom: Essays on Teaching with the Vampire Slayer* (2010). He serves on the faculty of Phoenix Rising Academy.

Index

Anastasis (painting) 31, 33–34
Angel (TV series) 58, 102, 155, 159–163; conversion 13–27; ethics 116–118, 121*n*29, 217; self-sacrifice 172; violence 170–171
Aristotle 108–111, 113, 115–116

The Birth of a Nation (film) 86–87, 90, 92
Bogle, Donald 87
Buffy the Vampire Slayer (film) 47
Buffy the Vampire Slayer (TV series) 11–80, 155–64; apocalypse 67–80; conversion 11–27; and Greek Orthodoxy 28–38; and political theology 155–164; and sexism 163*n*13; sexuality 43–45; and the Virgin Mary 45–48; witchcraft 51–65

The Cabin in the Woods (film) 196–226; and atonement 199–210; and eschatology 213–226
Calvin, John 200
Campbell, Jospeh 187, 25*n*9
Camus, Albert 216–217
Captain America 172, 174–175, 184–185, 191–193
Cavell, Stanley 153–154, 162
Civil War (graphic novel) 186–189, 192
The Clansman (film) 87, 92
Clark, Lynn Schofield 71, 75
Crowley, Aleister 53, 57, 59

Deane, Herbert 157, 161
Descartes, René 141–144
Ditko, Steve 169
Dodaro, Robert 156
Dollhouse (TV series) 123–151, 155, 160, 177, 214; and phenomenology 123–139; and theological relationality 140–151

Eliade, Mircea 13, 19, 22
Emerson, Ralph Waldo 162
Erickson, Greg 62, 73, 78

Firefly (TV series) 83–122, 184, 203, 215–216; and Ayn Rand 168–169; ethics 102–111, 117–121; and political theology 152, 161, 163; racism 83–100

Gardner, Gerald 53, 59, 63*n*7
goddess 40–42, 52–55, 58
Goldenberg, Naomi R. 54–55, 58, 62
Goltz, Jennifer 90
Gray, Richard J., II 183, 193
Greene, Eric 88, 92–95

Heidegger, Martin 132
Hildegard of Bingen 42, 46
The Hunger Games (film) 196–197, 209

James, William 12–13, 15–16, 22, 24, 25*n*11
Jesus Christ 31–35, 38*n*13, 69–70, 199–200, 202–203, 221
Jewett, Robert 178, 183-4, 189, 191
Jones, Tony 199–202

Kaklamanidou, Betty 183, 193
Kant, Immanuel 102, 106–108, 110–111, 113, 115, 118, 137*n*9, 138*n*12
Kermode, Frank 71–72, 75
Kirby, Jack 166, 191
Koontz, K. Dale 24*n*4, 105, 110, 119*n*13
Kraemer, Christine Hoff 55, 57, 58

Lawrence, John Shelton 178, 183–184, 189, 191
Lee, Stan 165, 166–169, 171–172, 175, 188, 191–192

Lewis, C.S. 14, 72
Locke, John 142, 146, 151n8
Loeb, Jeph 186, 192
Lovecraft, H.P. 214–215
Lusted, David 85, 88

Marvel's The Avengers (film) 165–195; and American nationalism 185–191; and late modern religion 183–185; and power 165–166, 169–179
McAvan, Emily 70, 73
Merleau-Ponty, Maurice 130–131
Moltmann, Jürgen 143, 216–221, 223–224

Park, Andrew Sung 199–203
Pojman, Luis P. 113–114, 117

Rand, Ayn 165, 167–173, 175–177

St. Augustine 152–157, 161–163
St. John Chrysostom 31–35
St. Teresa of Avila 42, 44

Sartre, Jean-Paul 129, 214, 216, 217
Serenity (film) 102, 110–111, 177; and Ayn Rand 168–169; and political theology 153–155; racism 83, 88, 91–98
Soelle, Dorothee 216–218, 220–224
Spider-Man 167, 169, 172
Starhawk 53–54, 60–61
Stearns, Lee 52, 54, 64n12
Stevenson, Greg 75–76

Tolkien, J.R.R. 72, 190

Uncle Tom's Cabin (book) 86–87

the Virgin Mary 45–48
Volf, Miroslav 143, 146–147

Williams, Linda 85–86, 96

the X-Men 166, 172, 184, 186, 188, 194

Zynda, Lyle 90–91, 99n25

www.ingramcontent.com/pod-product-compliance
Lightning Source LLC
Chambersburg PA
CBHW020811230426
43666CB00007B/959